100 GREAT WESTINDIAN TEST CRICKETERS

100 GREAT WESTINDIAN TEST CRICKETERS

from Challenor to Richards

By Bridgette Lawrence with Reg Scarlett

HANSIB PUBLISHING

First published in Great Britain in 1988 by Hansib
Publishing Limited, Tower House, 139/149 Fonthill
Road, London N4 3HF. All rights reserved.

Typesetting and Design by Hansib Publishing
Limited.

Printed in England by Camelot Press,
Southampton.

Cover design by Kash Ali and Michelle Wilson.
Cover picture: Where it all began...
Photographer: Allan Aflak

ISBN 1 870518 65 9

Acknowledgements

In writing this book I have had great support and encouragement from many people.

In particular, I would like to thank Arif Ali for inviting me to write the book, and for his help and advice from its inception to its completion. I am indebted to Reg Scarlett, who spent many hours going through the profiles, for giving me a unique insight into the players, many of whom he has played with or against. I believe that the light he has thrown on various cricketers and incidents, exploding many myths that have gained factual credence, have enhanced the book considerably.

I would also like to extend my thanks and appreciation to *The Cricketer International* who kindly allowed me to borrow various reference books, and answered many of my more obscure questions or put me in contact with people who could. *50 Great Westindian Test Cricketers* by Henderson Dalrymple proved an invaluable reference point, as did *Caribbean Cricketers from the Pioneers to Packer* and *West Indians at the Wicket* both by Clayton Goodwin, and *The West Indies: Fifty Years of Test Cricket* by Tony Cozier. *The Benson & Hedges West Indies Cricket Annuals* were especially helpful, while many other publications, too numerous to mention, provided enlightening accounts of various events. *Wisden* proved an impeccable source for checking statistical information, as did *Cricket in the Sun* edited by Garfield Sobers and J.S. Barker and *The Complete Who's Who of Test Cricketers* by Christopher Martin-Jenkins. Thanks are also due to Arif Ali, Reg Scarlett, Ian Davies and Chris Florence who lent me books.

I have had tremendous support from the design and production team at Hansib Publishing, notably Kash Ali, who co-ordinated the project; the typesetters: Janice Moore, Paula Edgar, Drucilla Daley, Amina Hussein and Lesley Hallett who patiently unravelled my copy; the designers: Michelle Wilson and Jenny Pace; and the layout artists: Salvatore Zuccarello, Chris Hill, Kevin Saul, Joanna Reid, Calvin Adams, Shireen Bocas, Ming Chan, Dean Bebb and Trevor Lake. Also from my merry band of proof-readers: Nick Ames, Paul Batemen, Yvonne Chew, Julie Griffiths, Sheila Lawrence, Pauline Rozario, Frances Rout, Reg Scarlett and Sandra Winfield, without whom I would have been lost. I would like to reserve a special additional thank you for Sheila Lawrence, my Mother, who gave me my love of cricket and the inspiration to write about it, and to Pauline Rozario, whose friendship and words of wisdom have helped me complete the book.

I also have to thank Ken Kelly and Roger Mann for providing many of the splendid photographs that illustrate this book. They have both been enthusiastic and generous supporters of this project, and I would like to express my sincere appreciation to them for their help and guidance. Also, to all the other photographers who have contributed to this book, and to the BBC Hulton Picture Library and Photo Source.

Finally, thank you to all the cricketers that I interviewed for this book, for your time and geniality. Also to those whom, for various reasons, I have not been able to talk to, thank you for providing me with such wonderful material to write about. I hope that I have done you all justice.

Bridgette Lawrence

Members of the first touring Test party to England in 1928

(l-r) Snuffy Brown, Frank Martin, Ted Hoad, George Francis, Karl Nunes, Learie Constantine, Clifford Roach, Edward Bartlett, George Challenor, Herman Griffith, Small

Contents

Caribbean Cool

are pleased to be associated
with the publication of

100 Great Westindian Test Cricketers

Foreword

The publishers have commissioned this book to celebrate the Diamond Jubilee of Westindian Test cricket, and have launched it to coincide with the Pakistan tour of the Westindies and the Westindies tour of England in 1988. It gives an invaluable insight into our Test match history through the portrayal of 100 of the personalities that have played in Westindian colours during the period.

Through the eyes of the individuals concerned, Bridgette Lawrence re-lives some of the most exciting moments in Test cricket, from the earliest matches to the remarkable successes of the 1970s and 1980s, including Gary Sobers' world record 365 not out against Pakistan in 1958 and the roles of Joe Solomon and Wes Hall in the first ever tied Test, against Australia in 1960. She has brought many of our best-loved players to life with some fascinating insights into their lives away from the cricket field, and often updates us on what some of the more recently retired players are doing now.

Cricket is an integral part of life in the Westindies and, over the years, has brought the peoples of the Caribbean closer together as they celebrate our triumphs and rally during our traumas.

This book, I am sure, will give all followers of Westindian cricket many hours of happy reading, as well as providing an invaluable work of reference. In this the author has been helped greatly by Reg Scarlett, who has played with or against many of the featured cricketers, and who has been able to separate fact from fiction.

Altogether, this book is a fitting tribute to 60 glorious years of Westindian Test cricket, with Hansib Publishing once again at the forefront of sponsoring such a project.

Viv Richards
Captain of the Westindies
Antigua, 1988

Introduction

Over the years, Westindies' cricketers have brought pleasure to millions of people with a swashbuckling approach to the game which seems unique to the Caribbean. Their progress has been closely linked to the political and social development of the region as a whole and, in 60 years, they have climbed to the top of world cricket, having taken their first tentative steps at Lord's in 1928. The most obvious example of the parallel advances came with the appointment of Frank Worrell as captain for Westindies' tour of Australia in 1960-61. This was the first occasion that a black man had been chosen to lead the Westindies on a long-term basis, and coincided with the granting of independence to the region.

Using their sporting ability, Westindies' cricketers have broken down many racial barriers and, in the process, have been undisputed Test match champions for over a decade. Yet, in spite of all this, they have never compromised their scintillating style of play. Learie Constantine, one of the great figures of Westindian cricket, was at pains to combine the vitality of the Westindian style with the competitiveness of the Test match arena. In his book *Cricket and I,* he wrote: "Conditions are such in the West Indies that we shall never be able to play cricket in the style that it is played by so many Englishmen and now a few Australians and it is my firm belief that we can learn the atmosphere of Test cricket, get together as a side in order to pull our full weight and yet, as a side, preserve the naturalness and ease which distinguish our game."

It was that "naturalness and ease" which distinguished the great players who have graced the world's Test match venues over the past 60 years: from the acknowledged "father" of Westindian batting, George Challenor, through to the incomparable George Headley, the three "W"s, Rohan Kanhai, Clive Lloyd and Viv Richards. The majesty of Westindies' batsmen bears comparison only with the beauty of their fast bowlers, from the likes of Manny Martindale to Wes Hall and, later, Michael Holding. For good measure, the islands have also produced two of the finest cricketers the game has known: Lord Constantine, whose electrifying performances have ensured his immortality in cricketing history, and Sir Garfield Sobers, who is acknowledged as the game's greatest all-rounder.

The above mentioned players have risen to the heights of world recognition and international sporting fame, yet the youngsters who play cricket on the beaches and in the villages of the Caribbean today embody that same carefree approach we have come to associate with Westindies. Neville Cardus, perhaps, most aptly summed up the difference when, in the preface to Constantine's *Cricket and I,* he wrote: "When we see Constantine bat or bowl or field, we know he is not an English player, not an Australian player, not a South African player. We know that his cuts and drives, his whirling fast balls, his leapings and clutchings and dartings – we know they are the consequences of impulses born in the blood, a blood heated by the sun and influenced by an environment and way of life much more natural than ours; impulses not common to the psychology of the overcivilised places of the earth."

For the pleasure and joy Westindian cricket has brought to a world often absorbed by the less pleasant spectacles of life, long may they continue to thrive and prosper in the manner which has become their hallmark.

Bridgette Lawrence
London, 1988

NB: The 100 profiles and career records are current to the end of the 1987 English first-class season and, where appropriate, also include references to the 1987 World Cup.

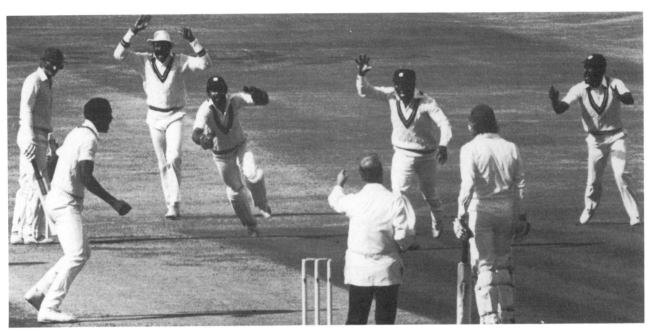

Howzat!

Ellis "Puss" Edgar Achong

"Puss" Achong was, it seems, responsible for the introduction of the expression "chinaman" into cricket terminology after his peculiar style of spin-bowling foiled England during Westindies visit in 1933. It appears that the phrase was first used when Achong had Walter Robins stumped for 55 in the second Test at Old Trafford. Many years later, Achong recalled: "It pitched perfectly and turned back nicely and when Robins saw it coming back at him, he opened his legs and the ball went through. On his way from the wicket, Robins turned to Learie (Constantine) and said: 'Fancy being out to a bloody Chinaman!' because it had been reported in the Press that I was the first person of Chinese origin to play Test cricket."

The slow left-armer made his debut against England in the second Test at Port-of-Spain in 1930, after he had bowled Trinidad to victory over the visitors, to register the only defeat of the touring team. In the Test Achong removed Patsy Hendren whose unbeaten double century shepherded England to victory, but the debutant spinner struggled to bridge the gap between inter-territorial competition and Test cricket

His cause was hampered further when he suffered a nasty injury fielding on the boundary in England's second innings, which kept him out of the rest of the series and probably ruled him out of the tour to Australia later that year.

Achong returned to the Test side for the trip to England in 1933 after bowling Trinidad to success over Guyana in the final of the 1932 inter-colonial tournament. He took 10 wickets for 147 in the match, including seven for 73 in the second innings, prompting a tribute in calypso: "Puss Achong was the bowling star, Ah we lick up Demerara".

The Trinidadian played in all three Tests in England and was the second leading wicket-taker with five victims. The superb Manny Martindale headed the bowling with 14 scalps from just three innings, illustrating the huge gulf between himself and the other bowlers. Achong bowled over 1,000 overs on the tour and, despite applying himself conscientiously, he was generally expensive with his 71 wickets costing 36.14 each.

In the pre-War years, however, spin bowling played a decidedly secondary role to the pace attack and, apart from a few isolated spells from Achong and Tommy Scott, slow bowling was not taken seriously.

Nonetheless, the Trinidadian bowled an immaculate line and length and was held in high esteem by both his opponents and team-mates, although his Test figures failed to reflect his notable success at regional level.

He married an English girl during Westindies' 1933 tour and lived in Lancashire for many years, taking over 1,000 wickets in league cricket, including all 10 in an innings for Burnley against Todmorden in 1945.

Achong returned to the Caribbean in 1952, where he became a Test umpire and heavily involved in the development of the game in Trinidad. He coached the island side and became a selector for Trinidad, as well as being consulted on the laying of turf wickets.

Career details

Born: *16 February 1904*
Died: *29 August 1986*
Role: *Left-arm off-spinner*
Clubs: *Trinidad, North of England Leagues*
First-class record: *[1929-35] 110 wickets (30.23) and 503 runs (14.37)*
Tests: *6*
Test debut: *v England 1930*
Test wickets: *8 (47.25)*
Test runs: *81 (8.10)*
Tour: *England 1933*

Franz Copeland "Gerry" Murray Alexander

The selection of the phlegmatic wicket-keeper "Gerry" Alexander for the 1957 trip to England caused some raised eyebrows in many quarters, especially as Rohan Kanhai, who used gloves, was in the party. Alexander appears to have clinched his place in a trial match, where he shared in a 134-run partnership with the young Wes Hall, who was also selected for the tour. The wicket-keeper's selection was doubtless helped by his familiarity with English conditions, as he had been a Cambridge University blue in 1952 and 1953 after graduating from Wolmer's Boys' School in Kingston.

Despite a disappointing time in England, Alexander was retained for the subsequent series against Pakistan in the Westindies, and was made captain after Frank Worrell had declined the job because of his studies. The Jamaican enjoyed a much happier series behind the stumps, seeming more comfortable keeping to the fast men on Caribbean wickets.

Alexander proved adept at leading the stronger team in the 1958 series, so it was a formality when he was asked to captain the side on the tour to India and Pakistan later that year, with Worrell still unavailable. Their potent batting line-up and devastating pace attack allowed Westindies to conquer India 3-0, and it was Alexander who stepped into the breach on the one occasion when the visitors looked vulnerable, as leg-spinner, Subhash Gupte, reduced them to 88 for six on the first day of the second Test at Kanpur. Gupte went on to collect nine wickets in the innings, but not before Alexander had steadied his side with a resolute 70, paving the way for their victory, and inspiring his side to their huge declared totals in the rest of the series. The captain also enjoyed more success behind the stumps, as he collected five catches at Calcutta and Madras.

Westindies were tamed on the Pakistan leg of the tour, however, losing by two games to one. Their pace attack was weakened, as they were without their main strike bowler, Roy Gilchrist, who had been sent home and were further undermined by indifferent umpiring.

Alexander retained the captaincy for the visit by England to the Caribbean in 1960 but, after Westindies lost the series as a result of their solitary defeat in the second Test at Port-of-Spain, the Jamaican was made the scapegoat. Even though he had just equalled the then world record of 23 dismissals in a series, Alexander must have felt his position was under threat, after Worrell had made an

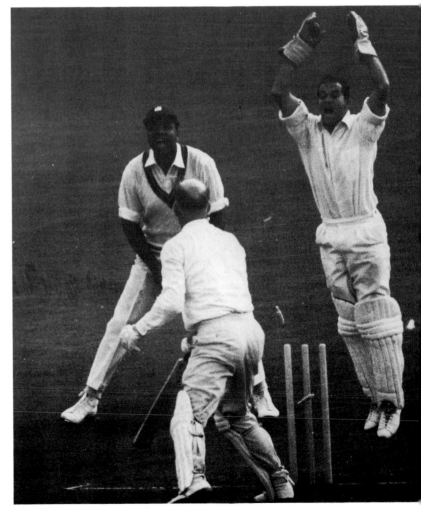

Gerry Alexander catches Tony Lo... the fifth Test at Oval in 1957. C... Walcott is at firs...

auspicious return by scoring 197 not out in the first match at Bridgetown.

When he was replaced by Worrell as skipper for the tour to Australia in 1960-61, Alexander could take comfort from the fact that his style of captaincy had allowed the people who would set the 1960s ablaze – Hall, Gary Sobers, Kanhai, Lance Gibbs, Conrad Hunte and Basil Butcher – to develop unhindered. He also deserves recognition for the way in which he evolved a corporate identity for a team which could have fallen easily into territorial disarray.

Ironically, after he was relieved of the captaincy, Alexander came into his own as a batsman, and was relied upon time and again to buttress the middle-order. He made 60 in the first tied Test against Australia, and caught Richie Benaud hooking a bouncer off Hall's memorable last over in that game. He scored 72 in the second match; 108 in the third, the solitary first-class century of his career; was unbeaten on 63 and 87 respectively in the fourth, a game in which he also made six dismissals; and top-scored with 73 in the fifth, to head the batting averages with 60.50.

In the end, the man whose initial selection had caused surprise, and, whose subsequent appointment as captain was seen, by many, as perpetuating the tradition of selecting a white man with an English university background for the job, finished his Test career on a high note and, eventually, would have made the team on merit.

Alexander played in 25 consecutive Tests as wicket-keeper, with only Clyde Walcott of previous Westindian 'keepers playing in more than 10. As captain in 18 of those Tests, Alexander laid the foundations of a new side from the successes in India and, as he grew more confident of his own abilities, he became an invaluable asset in Worrell's team.

As well as being a Cambridge cricket blue, Alexander was also a soccer blue and won an England cap and an F.A. Amateur Cup Winner's medal.

In later life, he moved to Guyana to pursue his career as a veterinary surgeon.

Career details

Born: *2 November 1928*
Role: *Wicket-keeper, right-hand batsman*
Clubs: *Jamaica, Cambridge University*
First-class record: *[1952-61] 217 catches and 39 stumpings, and 3,238 runs (29.17) including 1 century*
Tests: *25*
Test debut: *v England 1957*
Test catches: *85; Test stumpings: 5*
Test runs: *961 (30.03); HS: 108 v Australia, Sydney, 1961*
Tours: *England 1957; India and Pakistan 1958-59; Australia 1960-61.*

Denis St. Eval Atkinson

Denis Atkinson was a good all-rounder who had the misfortune to play most of his Test cricket in the company of the likes of the three 'W's, Jeff Stollmeyer, Allan Rae and Gerry Gomez. Batting in the lower order, Atkinson rarely had a chance to settle into an innings and, when the better-known players failed, lack of practise was invariably his downfall.

He made 45 on his debut against India in the first Test at New Delhi in 1948 but, his failure to make any other notable contribution and the inclusion of Frank Worrell as an all-rounder, meant that the Barbadian missed the triumphant tour to England in 1950.

When he returned to the Test fold for the tours of Australia and New Zealand in 1951-52, Atkinson again failed to establish his credentials and, once more, missed out on a successful series, this time against India in the Caribbean in 1953.

Atkinson seemed to be kept in reserve for stronger opposition, and played in four of the five Tests against the powerful MCC side which toured the Caribbean in 1954. He made a sound half century on his home ground in the second match at Bridgetown, and hit 74 and 53 not out in the fourth game at Port-of-Spain. In the final Test at Kingston, he made a gallant 40 in a vain attempt to prevent England from levelling the series.

Nonetheless, Atkinson's consistency in that series was rewarded with his appointment as vice-captain to Jeff Stollmeyer for the visit by Australia in 1955. But, after Stollmeyer was injured, Atkinson, a white insurance salesman, soon found himself the casualty of a volatile political situation, as he took over the reins of captaincy for three of the four Tests in which he took part, without having yet established himself as a player.

Against a backdrop of political and social change, there was intense pressure, especially in Jamaica, to have Atkinson removed. Eventually the furore diffused and Atkinson answered any remaining critics with one of the most memorable rearguard actions in Test history. He and wicket-keeper,

Clairmonte Depeiza, added a world record 347 for the seventh wicket, after Australia had compiled a first innings total of 668, and then reduced the home side to 146 for six, in the fourth Test at Bridgetown.

It is a feat often recalled by Bajans who witnessed the unlikely stand between their two local players, who joined forces on the third day and were not separated until the first over of the fifth. Atkinson, who went on to his highest Test score of 219, told *Wisden Cricket Monthly* many years later: "I remember when I was on 99, (Ian) Johnson put all the men on the off-side when Keith Miller was bowling. He had only one man at mid-on, and Miller said: 'Don't mind him. I'll give you a half-volley on the leg peg and let you get your hundred.' I said: 'You can't trick me', but when he bowled the next ball, true, it was a half-volley for me to get my hundred. My first and only hundred in Test cricket." After his sterling

Denis Atkinson is caught behind for four by Godfrey Evans, against England at Trent Bridge in 1957

16

performance with the bat, Atkinson took five wickets for 56 in Australia's second innings to secure a draw for his side, in a series in which the tourists were much the stronger team. This was the first occasion that a Westindies captain had made a hundred and taken five wickets in an innings in a Test.

Atkinson captained the successful touring team to New Zealand in 1956 where, after making a duck in the first Test at Dunedin, his attacking 85 in the second game at Christchurch buttressed a minor middle-order batting collapse; while his 60 in support of Everton Weekes, followed by five for 66 in New Zealand's second innings, in the third Test at Wellington, ushered the tourists to another comprehensive victory.

Atkinson, however, was summarily dismissed from the captaincy after losing the last match at Auckland, even though his medium pace claimed seven wickets for 53 in New Zealand's second innings. His victims included John Reid, whose first innings 84 was crucial in a low-scoring game in conditions which subsequently helped New Zealand to bowl out the visitors for 77. The decision to relieve Atkinson of the captaincy after winning the rubber in New Zealand 3-1, seemed particularly severe now that Stollmeyer had retired. The Barbadian was replaced by his compatriot, John Goddard, although the former was included in the side to England in 1957. Atkinson began brightly enough, enjoying a new lease of life on the green English wickets, collecting 10 for 62 against Worcester, but a shoulder injury incurred soon afterwards restricted his performances on the rest of the tour.

In another team, in another era, the resilient Atkinson, who underpinned his sound batting by bowling lively off-cutters and off-breaks, might have made a greater impact. Yet, for a man whose main interest was fishing until he left school, Atkinson developed a remarkable habit of involving himself in record partnerships: he established a ninth-wicket record of 106 with Robert Christiani on his inaugural trip to India in 1948-49, and shared in a record stand of 143 for the seventh wicket with Goddard on the tour of New Zealand in 1956 – performances which sandwiched his unforgettable partnership with Depeiza against Australia in 1955.

Career details

Born: *9 August 1926*
Role: *Right-hand batsman, right-arm medium pace and off-spin bowler*
Clubs: *Barbados, Trinidad*
First-class record: *[1946-60] 2,812 runs (28.40), including 5 centuries, and 200 wickets (26.73)*
Tests: 22
Test debut: *v India 1948*
Test runs: *922 (31.79); HS: 219 v Australia, Bridgetown, 1955*
Test wickets: *47 (35.04); BB: 7-53 v New Zealand, Auckland, 1956*
Tours: *India 1948-49; Australia and New Zealand 1951-52; New Zealand 1956; England 1957.*

Sheik Faoud Ahumul Bacchus

Having shown prodigious talent as a young batsman for Guyana, Faoud Bacchus was elevated to Test honours for the last two matche against Australia in 1978, after the withdrawal of the World Series cricketers.

The Guyanese had an unspectacular start to his Test career, but returned to his best territorial form on the subsequent tour to India. The discovery of the series, Bacchus hit 96 in the second game at Bangalore and 61, as the tourists followed on, in the fifth match in New Delhi. The youngster saved his real moment of glory for the sixth Test at Kanpur, where he scored a double century, single-handedly saving a game in which three Indians scored hundreds. His 250 was made in 512 minutes and was the highest individual Test score ever recorded on the ground.

Bacchus was included in Westindies' 1979 World Cup squad, but was surprisingly replaced by Lawrence Rowe for the trip to Australia and New Zealand later that year. He was back in favour for the subsequent three tours to England, Pakistan and Australia between 1980-82, and during that period was also selected to captain Westindies' under-26 side to Zimbabwe.

Clearly, Bacchus was regarded as a possible contender for the captaincy of the senior side but when, after playing in the one-day internationals against the Indian tourists in 1983, he was overlooked for the Tests, Bacchus seemed to give up hope of commanding a regular Test place.

The Guyanese was an attractive and positive batsman, although often prone to bouts of impetuosity. After the Packer schism had been resolved, Bacchus found himself competing for the opener's role with Gordon Greenidge and Desmond Haynes. Once their partnership had established itself, Bacchus was almost permanently on the periphery of a solid middle batting order.

India's game against Guyana during their 1983 tour could have provided Bacchus with an opportunity to impress the selectors but, when it was abandoned and he failed to make the party chosen to tour India at the end of that year, he turned his back on official Test cricket and joined the rebel team in South Africa in 1983-84.

In Zimbabwe in 1981, although the tourists won the only representative match to be completed, Bacchus, who was also qualified to play for Canada, was overshadowed by the batting of Everton Mattis, Timur Mohamed and Jeff Dujon. This perhaps further influenced Bacchus' decision to join the rebels and, after his defection, it was his vice-captain in Zimbabwe, Haynes, who replaced him in the Test side as opener and specialist short-leg, where Bacchus had performed admirably.

In South Africa Bacchus scored heavily, accumulating 664 runs from just 12 matches, confirming his ability which, with a little more patience, might have penetrated the formidable batting line-up of the full Westindies team.

Career details

Born: *31 January 1954*
Role: *Right-hand batsman*
Clubs: *Guyana, Border*
First-class record: *[1971-] 5,874 runs (35.17) including 8 centuries, and 8 wickets (24.50)*
Tests: 19
Test debut: *v India 1978*
Test runs: *782 (26.06); HS: 250 v India, Kanpur, 1979*
Tours: *India 1978-79; England (World Cup) 1979; England 1980; Pakistan 1980-81; Zimbabwe (under-26 side) 1981; Australia 1981-82; England (World Cup) 1983.*

*Bacchus, one
stindies' most
t batsmen*

Eldine Ashworth Elderfield Baptiste

A tall, slim right-handed all-rounder from Antigua, Eldine Baptiste made his first-class debut in England, when he appeared for Kent against Oxford University in 1981. The following year he played for the Leeward Islands.

Baptiste has a typically Westindian approach to his cricket, supplementing his medium pace bowling, with aggressive batting and spectacular fielding. In his first Test at Lord's in 1984, he ran out Geoff Miller with a blistering throw from deep fine leg to the far end, with the hapless Miller still well out of his ground!

Baptiste was nurtured at Kent and rewarded their faith in him with an outstanding season in 1983, including a career-best 136 not out against Yorkshire. This prompted Westindies' selectors to include him in the tour party to India in the autumn. Given limited opportunities, the lithe Antiguan did not live up to expectations on the sub-continent, but some worthy batting and bowling for the Leewards against the visiting Australians in 1984 secured his place in the side that toured Australia later that year.

In between, Baptiste played a crucial role in the overwhelming success Westindies achieved in England in the summer of 1984, making some important contributions after better known players had held the limelight. In the first Test at Edgbaston, Baptiste raced to an unbeaten 87, as he shared in a record ninth wicket stand of 150 with Michael Holding. He also collected eight valuable wickets in the series in his role as a stock bowler.

Baptiste is a gifted all-round cricketer, with the versatility to bolster the batting when the more distinguished players fail or the bowling when the strike bowlers are rested, allowing the Westindies cricket machine to continue at full throttle.

The young Antiguan was forced to miss the home series against England in 1986 through injury; but recovered in time to make the trip to Zimbabwe with the "B" team at the end of that year, where he topped the first-class bowling averages with 29 wickets at 14.06 each. He returned to the full Westindies team for the 1987 World Cup but, once again, had little chance to prove himself.

A supple athlete, Baptiste also plays football, tennis and volleyball, but it is at cricket at which he has excelled, winning the Viv Richards Schools Cricket Trophy for the Most Outstanding Cricketer in 1979, the same year as he was voted Sportsman of the Year in Antigua.

Baptiste, who showed further evidence of his superb all-round qualities as he eased the Leeward Islands into the final of the Shell Shield in 1987, lists his relaxations as watching movies, calypso music (to the extent that his team-mates call him "Soca") and meeting people. He has also worked as a sports officer in the Ministry of Education.

Career details

Born: *12 March 1960*
Role: *Right-hand batsman, right-arm medium-fast bowler*
Clubs: *Leeward Islands, Kent*
First-class record: *[1981-] 4,465 runs (29.76) including 3 centuries, and 356 wickets (26.26)*
Tests: *9*
Test debut: *v India 1983*
Test runs: *224 (24.88); HS: 87* v England, Edgbaston, 1984*
Test wickets: *15 (32.40); BB: 3-31 v England, Old Trafford, 1984*
Tours: *India 1983; England 1984; Australia 1984-85; Zimbabwe ("B" team) 1986; India and Pakistan (World Cup) 1987.*

Eldine Baptiste

Ivan Barrow

A wicket-keeper-batsman, Ivan Barrow's most memorable triumph came as he shared in a stand of 200 in 205 minutes with George Headley in the second Test against England at Old Trafford in 1933. Reaching his hundred, while the master remained on 99, Barrow beat Headley by a few minutes to the distinction of being the first Westindian to score a century in a Test in England. The two Jamaicans played resolutely against a barrage of short-pitched bowling, with Barrow displaying an uncharacteristic range of strokes as his 105 was his only score over 20 in the series.

Ivan Barrow: the first Westindian to score a Test century in England

The steady right-hander obviously enjoyed batting with his compatriot, Headley, as the pair put on 248 for the third wicket for Jamaica against Lord Tennyson's side at Kingston in 1932, with Barrow hitting his highest first-class score of 169.

Barrow made his Test debut as a 19-year-old, fresh out of Wolmer's Boys' School, against England in 1930. He appeared on his home ground at Sabina Park for the final Test, replacing Errol Hunte, who was unable to travel to the game. The youngster must have felt at home with seven other Jamaicans in the side, although his international baptism proved quite daunting, as it was in this game that the first Test triple hundred was recorded: 325 by England's Andy Sandham, an innings which contributed to the then highest-ever Test total of 849. Barrow stumped 50-year-old George Gunn off the bowling of his fellow Jamaican, Frank Martin, but failed with the bat, being bowled without scoring.

Nonetheless, the young man had made a sufficiently good impression with his tidy approach to be included on the first ever tour to Australia in 1930-31. He kept wicket in all five Tests and retained the position for the three matches against England in 1933, as well as opening the innings on each occasion with Clifford Roach. It seemed to be the practice in the 1930s to promote a succession of wicket-keepers to open the innings for Westindies, as they searched in vain for a stable first-wicket pairing.

Barrow's consecutive Test appearances were challenged by the emergence of Cyril Christiani, the Guyanese who had been the second-string wicket-keeper on the tour of England in 1933. Indeed, by the time of England's tour to the Caribbean in 1935, Christiani was preferred to Barrow, even though the latter returned as opening batsman for the final Test on his home ground. In that match Barrow, Christiani and the Barbadian wicket-keeper, Derek Sealy, filled three of the top four batting positions.

After Christiani's untimely death from malaria in 1938, Barrow was recalled to Test duty for the 1939 tour to England as a tried and trusted wicket-keeper-batsman. He had been living in the United States for a while and was short of top-class match practise. Even so, Barrow had flourished in English conditions on his first trip, making 54 dismissals and over 1,000 first-class runs, so his selection seemed a sensible gamble. Unfortunately, the neat and normally reliable Jamaican could not recover his earlier form and surrendered his position to Sealy after the first Test.

Barrow played for his island again in 1946 and later became the first cricket broadcaster in Jamaica.

Career details

Born: *6 January 1911*
Died: *2 April 1979*
Role: *Wicket-keeper, right-hand batsman*
Club: *Jamaica*
First-class record *[1928-46] 73 catches and 27 stumpings, and 2,551 runs (23.84) including 3 centuries.*
Tests: *11*
Test debut: *v England 1930*
Test catches: *17;* Test stumpings: *5*
Test runs: *276 (16.23); HS: 105 v England, Old Trafford 1933*
Tours: *Australia 1930-31; England 1933; England 1939.*

Carlisle Alonza Best

After three prolific seasons for Barbados in the Shell Shield, Carlisle Best catapulted himself into the all-conqueroring Westindies team in 1986. He had an unbelievable start to his Test career, opening his account with a hook for six off the incorrigible Ian Botham in the first Test against England at Kingston.

If the visitors had been following the progress of the Shield, they might have anticipated Best's confident start as, a few weeks earlier, in Barbados' deciding match against Jamaica, Courtney Walsh had received exactly the same treatment as the self-assured Bajan again got off the mark with a six.

Carlisle Best, who commentates to himself while batting

All Sport

24

However, after this flamboyant start in Test cricket, Best became more introverted and lost his confidence and his place after three games.

An orthodox right-hander, Best first distinguished himself as a school-boy by scoring over 800 runs in the Barbados Cricket Association's Division Two in 1976. His outstanding performances that year prompted his inclusion in the Barbados team for Westindies youth championships, where a hundred against Guyana secured his passage with the Westindies Youth team to England in 1978.

Best was encouraged by his father as a young cricketer and his ability was also nurtured by Irvine Harris, the cricket teacher at his secondary school. As he got older Best received invaluable help from Seymour Nurse, although his dad remains "probably my greatest fan". Best says of his father: "I don't think he has missed any of the matches I have played at any level."

Best made his debut for Barbados against Trinidad & Tobago in 1980, and carved a permanent place for himself in the side after the departure of several Bajan players on the rebel tours to South Africa. A cheerful and self-confident player, Best assumed the captaincy of his island in 1984, while the leading Barbadians were with the Test team in India and Australia. Best led his side to success in the Shield from the front, averaging 41.10 with the bat, which included his maiden first-class century, against the Windward Islands.

If his team couldn't sustain their performance the following year, Best's personal contribution was undiminished as he hit 437 runs, including centuries against Guyana and Jamaica, and secured his place on the short trip to Sharjah and Pakistan in November, although he didn't get a game on the tour.

In 1986, with all the Test players available for the domestic season, Best established his credentials once and for all as he topped the batting in the Shield for the second consecutive year with 518 runs, this time making hundreds against Trinidad & Tobago and Guyana.

Happiest in the opener's role, Best has to bat a number three when Gordon Greenidge and Desmond Haynes are available for Barbados and even lower in the formidable Test line-up, going in at number six. Nonetheless he has maintained his scoring momentum and helps himself concentrate by commentating on his own innings while at the crease! This unusual habit can be quite disconcerting to the uninitiated close fielders and, in one of his early games, after hooking Andy Roberts, he apparently remarked to himself: "Shot, Bessie...and that's Roberts!"

Chosen to captain the "B" tour to Zimbabwe at the end of 1986, Best was a model of consistency with the bat and led his side to success in the "Tests" and the one-day series.

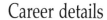
Carlisle Best

Best was schooled in the Barbados Cricket League, playing for West Ham as a youth, before joining the illustrious Empire Club. Unlike the majority of his team mates, however, cricket is not his life-blood. Educated at the University of the Westindies, Best has a Bachelor of Science degree in economics and works as an economist at the Barbados Central Bank.

In his endeavour to tread the tight-rope between his bank career and his cricket career, Best doesn't play for either a league or a county side in England. Nonetheless, he still appears for Empire, and certainly has the ability and the ambition to become a regular member of the Westindies team over the next few years.

Career details

Born: *14 May 1959*
Role: *Right-hand batsman*
Club: *Barbados*
First-class record: *[1980-] 2,481 runs (40.01) including 6 centuries, and 3 wickets (39.00)*
Tests: *3*
Test debut: *v England 1986*
Test runs: *78 (26.00); HS: 35 v England, Kingston, 1986*
Tours: *England (WIYC) 1978; Zimbabwe ("B" tour) 1986; India and Pakistan (World Cup) 1987.*

Keith David Boyce

Keith Boyce conducted his career under the shadow of premature comparisons with Learie Constantine, after a distinguished early career in Barbados, where he played primarily as a leg-spinner. His fiery bowling, hard-hitting batsmanship, and untiring enthusiasm in the field earned good reviews in the Press and heralded his great deeds in Test cricket in England in 1973.

Having joined Essex in 1966, Boyce soon demonstrated his all-round ability. In his maiden first-class match, he took nine wickets for 61 against Cambridge University and, five years later, set a Sunday League record when he took eight for 26 against Lancashire at Old Trafford. In 1975 he hit a century against Leicestershire in 58 minutes, before returning bowling figures of 12 for 73 and holding three catches in a match at Chelmsford. It was a typically robust performance which often brought him within reach of the coveted championship double of 1,000 runs and one hundred wickets. He came closest in 1972, when he scored 1,023 runs and took 82 wickets.

Boyce made his Test debut against India in 1971, although he saved his most memorable performance for the first Test against England at The Oval in 1973. Coming in at number nine, Boyce crashed 72 runs off the English bowlers and, sharing the new ball with Bernard Julien, returned match-figures of 11 for 147 to sweep Westindies to their first victory for four years. But, after this superb all-round performance, Boyce rarely shone with this brightness at Test level again.

When England visited the Caribbean the following year, Boyce failed to induce the life and bounce out of the pitches as he had done in England. The Barbadian took four for 42 in England's first innings in the first Test at Port-of-Spain, but he made little impression on the rest of the series.

Boyce was included on the trip to India in 1974-75, and made his most notable contribution in the second Test in New Delhi. There, the Barbadian rekindled old memories with his flamboyant batting as he hit a

Keith Boyce, a splendid all-rounder, was the first man to reach 1,000 runs and 100 wickets in limited-overs cricket in England

whirlwind 68, and shared in a century partnership with the confident young Viv Richards. In the bowling department, Boyce found himself opening the attack with another prodigious youngster, Andy Roberts.

After playing a decisive role in Westindies' World Cup final success in 1975, when he took four of the five Australian wickets to fall to bowlers, Boyce was included on the subsequent tour to Australia, even though Michael Holding had been selected as Roberts' new sparring partner.

The all-rounder showed that his abilities were far from exhausted, as he hit an unbeaten 49 in the second Test at Perth. Boyce saved his best form for the fifth match at Adelaide, when he scored 95 not out to save the follow-on almost entirely on his own, after Jeff Thomson's pace had subdued Westindies' earlier batsmen. But, even his second innings 69 could not stave off another defeat, in a disastrous trip which saw Thomson and Dennis Lillee annihilate the tourists by five games to one.

Despite these gallant efforts, hampered by minor, but niggling, injuries, Boyce's failure to score in his next innings at Melbourne signalled the end of his worthy and, occasionally, brilliant Test career.

Boyce's important contribution to Westindies cricket was that he filled a major vacuum in the bowling department after the departure of Wes Hall and Charlie Griffith from the Test scene, and before the next generation of pacemen were weaned into the international arena.

Boyce was one of the first, and one of the most popular, Westindian cricketers to play regularly on the English county circuit. He toured with Trevor Bailey's International Cavaliers and, during a distinguished career with Essex, he became the first player to reach 1,000 runs and one hundred wickets in limited-overs cricket.

Career details

Born: *11 October 1943*
Role: *Right-hand batsman, right-arm fast-medium bowler*
Clubs: *Barbados, Essex*
First-class record: *[1964-77] 8,800 runs (22.39) including 4 centuries, and 852 wickets (25.02)*
Tests: *21*
Test debut: *v India 1971*
Test runs: *657 (24.33); HS: 95* v Australia, Adelaide, 1976*
Test wickets: *60 (30.01); BB: 6-77 v England, The Oval, 1973*
Tours: *England 1973; India and Pakistan 1974-75; England (World Cup) 1975; Australia 1975-76.*

*Boyce's
ificent follow-
gh, captured on*

C.R. Browne
(B.G)

Cyril Rutherford "Snuffy" Browne

The splendidly named "Snuffy" Browne played in the inaugural Test series in both England and the Caribbean. But he made his real impact in the pre-Test days on the 1923 tour to England, as the third member of the visitors' seam attack. On that trip he collected 75 wickets, including six for 66 against Somerset and four for 41 as Westindies over-powered Surrey.

Then, in 1925-26, against the Hon. F. S. G. Calthorpe's touring MCC side, Browne was the main player to show any resistance, batting with Harold Austin, in Westindies' impoverished performance in the second representative match at Port-of-Spain. And, in the third game at Georgetown, Browne, who was suffering from a head injury after being hit by a rising delivery, scored a superb unbeaten 102, sharing in a large partnership with Claude Wight, which helped Westindies to hold their own in the three-match series.

By the time of the first official Test series in 1928, Browne was approaching 40 and past his best, and, with the advancement of Learie Constantine and the addition of Herman Griffith to the attack, his bowling contribution was somewhat redundant; while the inclusion of Joe Small to bolster the batting at number

Snuffy Browne, pictured on the far left with some members of the first Westindies Test squad to visit England in 1928

nine made Browne's position vulnerable on two fronts.

Nonetheless, the all-rounder rallied with the bat in the first Test at Lord's. After Westindies had followed on 224 runs behind, and then lost six second innings wickets for 55, the tail fought back with Small hitting 52 and Browne 44, as they bolstered the tourists' total to 166.

In 1923 Browne had taken 75 wickets (22.29) and, five years later, although his tally was lower, he still showed glimpses of his earlier skill as he took eight for 81 against Derbyshire and plundered a match-winning 103 in an hour against Kent.

In Westindies' first Test win in the third game against England at Georgetown in 1930, after a double century from Clifford Roach and a hundred in each innings from George Headley, Browne, batting sensibly but quickly, completed the assault by thrashing an unbeaten 70 off the English bowlers.

Even after his 40th birthday, Browne was still demonstrating his perennial abilities on the cricket field, as he took seven for 13 for Guyana against Barbados, as they slumped to 99 all out in the 1937-38 season.

A magistrate by profession, Browne later became the first black Westindian to be elected to honorary life membership of MCC.

Career details

Born: *8 October 1890*
Died: *12 January 1964*
Role: *Right-hand batsman, medium-pace spin bowler*
Clubs: *Barbados, Guyana*
First-class record: *[1908-39] 2,077 runs (19.97) including 3 centuries, and 278 wickets (22.40)*
Tests: *4*
Test debut: *v England 1928*
Test runs: *176 (25.14); HS: 70* v England, Georgetown, 1930*
Test wickets: *6 (48.00)*
Tour: *England 1928*

Basil Fitzherbert Butcher

Basil Butcher was one of a clutch of gifted young batsmen to emerge from Guyana in the mid-1950s, after Clyde Walcott went there as coach. Although Butcher established himself in the forefront of his country's batting, he had to wait for the retirement of Walcott and Everton Weekes before he got his chance at international level. When Test recognition finally arrived, in 1958, he struggled to establish himself in a batting line-up containing Conrad Hunte, Gary Sobers, Rohan Kanhai and Frank Worrell.

A less flamboyant batsman than many of his contemporaries, nonetheless, Butcher's methodical accumulation of runs made him difficult to dislodge. Considered unlucky to miss the trip to England in 1957, he was included on the tour to India and Pakistan in 1958-59. He hit his maiden hundred in the third Test at Calcutta, sharing in a fourth-wicket stand of 217 with his compatriot, Kanhai; and went on to make 142 out of a total of 500 in the fourth match at Madras. He never made less than fifty in any of the five Tests, ensuring a splendid first tour average of 69.42.

Yet, Butcher played in only two Tests against MCC the following season in the Caribbean. Omission from the tour to Australia in 1960-61 prompted him to contemplate making himself unavailable for international matches. Relatives calmed the incensed Butcher, persuading him to change his mind, which allowed him to establish himself at the highest level when he was recalled to the team, for the trip to England in 1963. He scored 1,294 first-class runs, including his famous innings of 133, featuring two sixes and 17 fours, which helped save the second Test at Lord's, after Westindies had lost five quick wickets. His efforts were especially commendable as he learned, during the game, that his wife had suffered a miscarriage.

He followed his rearguard action at Lord's with 78 at Headingley and 53 at The Oval, where he hit the winning run. He averaged over 40 on the tour which,

this time, was enough to ensure his inclusion in the side for the series against Australia, where he was instrumental in securing their first defeat in the Caribbean. He scored 71 in the first Test at Kingston, sharing in a stand of 160 with Sobers, before they were both run out. In Westindies' first innings in the second match at Port-of-Spain, Butcher top-scored with a magnificent 117.

Basil Butcher

Butcher seemed to save his heroic counter-attacks for the English and, in 1966, the setting was Trent Bridge, as the Guyanese came in with Westindies on 65 for two and still behind England's first innings total. When Butcher left, seven and three-quarter hours later, the score was 482 for five declared, and, with an unbeaten double century to his credit, he had set up victory for his side.

The right-hander was less successful against India later that year but, in the series against England in 1968 in the Caribbean, once again, he saved his team from defeat top-scoring with 52 in the second innings of the first Test at Port-of-Spain; and then hit two half centuries in the third match at Bridgetown. In the fourth game, again at Port-of-Spain, Butcher took five for 34 with his occasional leg-spinners, inducing Sobers to make his ill-judged second innings declaration. Setting England 215 runs to win in 164 minutes, the tourists romped home with seven wickets to spare, to take the match and, as it transpired, the series, as Butcher failed to reproduce his bowling magic.

Butcher was included in the ageing side sent to Australia and New Zealand in 1968-69. In the third Test at Sydney the tourists' batting collapsed around Butcher's admirable 101, while, in contrast, his century in the fourth match at Adelaide was part of an all-round effort which helped Westindies to a total of 616. On the New Zealand leg of the tour, Butcher hit three fifties.

The Guyanese made his last tour, to England in 1969, and was controversially dismissed in his final Test appearance, at Headingley. Chasing a total of 303 to win, with Butcher playing at his best, and the score on 219 for three, victory for Westindies seemed certain. But Butcher was given out on 91 in a hotly disputed catch by the wicket-keeper, Alan Knott, off Derek Underwood, and, when Barry Knight bowled Sobers immediately afterwards for a duck, victory evaporated into a 30-run defeat and the loss of the series.

The short right-hander, whose ready smile revealed a gold-capped tooth, was a popular and successful cricketer in the Lancashire league. At Test level, Butcher's value in holding the middle order together after the more extravagant players had failed was not, perhaps, as widely recognised as it should have been. Nonetheless, having finally established himself in the Westindies team, in 1963, he developed a reputation as a conscientious batsman, who was notoriously difficult to get out.

Career details

Born: *3 September 1933*
Role: *Right-hand batsman, right-arm leg-spinner*
Clubs: *Guyana, Lancashire League*
First-class record: *[1954-72] 11,628 runs (49.90) including 31 centuries, and 40 wickets (30.42)*
Test debut: *v India 1958*
Test runs: *3,104 (43.11); HS: 209* v England, Trent Bridge, 1966*
Test wickets: *5(18.00); BB: 5-34 v England, Port-of-Spain, 1968*
Tours: *India and Pakistan 1958-59; England 1963; England 1966; India 1966-67; Australia and New Zealand 1968-69; England 1969.*

George Stephen Camacho

After entering the Test arena for the 1968 series against England in the Caribbean, where he hit a solid 57 in the third match at Bridgetown, and played an even better innings of 87 in the fourth game at Port-of-Spain, it seemed that Steve Camacho would slip comfortably into Conrad Hunte's opening role.

He had a disappointing time in the subsequent series in Australia but, chosen for the tour to England in 1969, the bespectacled Guyanese replaced Joey Carew as Roy Fredericks' opening partner for the

Camacho

second Test at Lord's. He proceeded to help himself to a half century, sharing in a stand of 106 in the first innings, and 73 in the second, against some hostile short bowling from John Snow. It seemed that the successors to Allan Rae and Jeff Stollmeyer had emerged. Camacho confirmed his promise by hoisting another fifty in the subsequent Test at Headingley, where he helped Basil Butcher in a rearguard action which nearly secured the tourists a surprise win.

However, the notion that Westindies had solved their opening problem proved premature as Camacho, after topping the Test batting averages in England with 46.75, failed to turn his early accomplishments into regular, sound innings, and a succession of openers came and went before Fredericks was finally matched in an enduring partnership with Gordon Greenidge.

Camacho played in the home series against India in 1971, but only managed 68 runs from four innings and was obliged to make way for Lawrence Rowe.

The correct Guyanese, who collected his runs with uncharacteristic caution for a Westindian, had announced his arrival as a quality batsman with 106 against Trinidad at Port-of-Spain in his first innings in the Shell Shield in 1965-66. But, after promising much in the two series he played against England, he seemed unable to maintain his momentum and faded from the scene.

Later, Camacho contributed much to the administration of Westindian cricket, and is currently Secretary of the Westindies Board of Control.

Career details

Born: *15 October 1945*
Role: *Right-hand batsman*
Club: *Guyana*
First-class record: *[1964-79] 4,019 (34.86) including 7 centuries*
Tests: *11*
Test debut: *v England 1968*
Test runs: *640 (29.09); HS: 87 v England, Port-of-Spain, 1968*
Tours: *Australia and New Zealand 1968-69; England 1969.*

Michael "Joey" Conrad Carew

It was to take "Joey" Carew 10 years to live up to the early promise he had shown when, batting as a youngster for Trinidad, he made 114 against Jamaica in 1959 and the following season hit 102 not out and 70 in two matches against the touring MCC side.

A decade later Carew enjoyed his most prolific series at Test level on the tour of Australia and New Zealand in 1968-69. He and Rohan Kanhai got the visitors off to a promising start as they put on 165 for the second wicket in the first Test at Brisbane, exploiting an Australian attack which, unusually, lacked a quality fast bowler. The pair were dismissed with successive balls with Carew being run out for 83, as the rest of the side could only muster a total of 296.

Australia's first innings reply fell 12 short of Westindies' score. When the tourists batted again they were reduced to 178 for six and a lead of just 190, before Clive Lloyd and Carew, who had dropped down the order to number seven because of injury, shared in a stand of 120 to build the foundations of Westindies' solitary victory in Australia.

In the fourth Test at Adelaide Carew mastered John Gleeson's peculiar style of spin bowling by hitting him straight in Westindies' second innings, as he went on the attack after the visitors found themselves 257 runs adrift. Carew galloped to 90, his highest score of the series, helping Westindies to a morale-boosting 616 and the safety of a draw.

In the fifth match at Sydney the Trinidadian shared in a century opening partnership with Roy Fredericks. Carew contributed 64, but this time it was in vain as Westindies slid to a decisive defeat. Yet, Carew, the surprise choice for the trip, proved to be the surprise success, scoring over 1,200 runs in the first-class matches, for an average of 45.25.

By the New Zealand leg of the tour, Carew, the in-form batsman, had become even more confident and registered the only Test hundred of his career in the first match at Auckland, adding 172 for the second wicket with Seymour Nurse. The pair took the score

to 195, before a massive collapse by the rest of the Westindian batting saw only another 81 runs added to the total. In the end it took a stupendous innings of 168 from Nurse to shift the balance in Westindies' favour.

In the third and final Test at Christchurch, Carew and Nurse shared in a stand of 231, the former being more restrained as he took a little over five hours compiling 91, while the latter pulverised the bowling. As in Auckland, the batting hinged on the efforts of this illustrious pairing, as they built a lead of 200 for the tourists and, even though the third wicket did not fall until the total was on 326, the innings closed on a mere 417.

After years of trying to graft a regular place in the Test side, Carew seemed to have established himself at the highest level before, strangely, his most successful series heralded his demise, as the enterprising left-hander became a casualty of several

Joey Carew

selectorial vagaries that year.

Carew made the trip to England in 1969, when bad weather hampered the tourists' early preparations. But after failing in the first innings of the first Test at Old Trafford – both he and Fredericks were out with the total on five – Carew was replaced by Steve Camacho, despite making amends in the second innings, as he added 92 with Fredericks. Generally, Carew was not seen at his best on English wickets, although he made 677 runs in 12 matches on the tour, including three centuries, in spite of an injury to his hand. When India visited the Caribbean in 1971, Carew was recalled, this time to partner Camacho in the second Test at Port-of-Spain, where they shared in an opening stand of 119.

Carew had been drafted into the Test side originally for the tour of England in 1963, in place of the Barbadian Cammie Smith, but, like his predecessor, Carew had a reputation for early impetuosity, and he was frequently dismissed before he accustomed himself to the prevailing conditions.

Apart from his vintage series against Australia and New Zealand, which ironically came at a time when the rest of the team were struggling, Carew was never able to reproduce the impressive form he showed for Trinidad at the highest level. In 1971 and 1972 this lithe athlete, who is best remembered for his attacking qualities, as well as for his handy off-break bowling, led his regional side to consecutive Shell Shield titles.

After he retired from the first-class game, Carew continued to be heavily involved with Westindian cricket, serving them further as a Test selector. He also has a keen interest in youth cricket, and follows the progress of his two sons closely, who have both shown immense promise for Trinidad.

Career details

Born: *15 September 1937*
Role: *Left-hand batsman, right-arm spin bowler*
Club: *Trinidad*
First-class record: *[1956-74] 7,810 runs (38.47) including 13 centuries, and 108 wickets (29.76)*
Tests: *19*
Test debut: *v England 1963*
Test runs: *1,127 (34.15); HS: 109 v New Zealand, Auckland, 1969*
Tours: *England 1963; England 1966; Australia and New Zealand 1968-69; England 1969.*

George Challenor

Perhaps the saddest irony of George Challenor's prolific batting career was that, for someone who arguably did more than any other individual to hasten Test status for Westindies, he was too old

George Challenor, widely recognised as the "father" of Westindian batting

when it finally arrived, in 1928, to make the impact he undoubtedly would have in his prime.

On his first tour of England in 1906, the teenaged Challenor lived up to his reputation as the best young batsman on the trip, as he hit a century against Nottinghamshire, one of the strongest sides in the country, and an exhilarating 90 against Scotland.

It was another 17 years before he visited English shores again, but the touring MCC side of 1912-13 had a gentle reminder of his batting prowess, as he hit two centuries for Barbados in successive matches.

The First World War postponed his next encounter with the English, but, it was worth the wait. Selected for the 1923 tour of England, he scored 1,895 runs, featuring eight hundreds, including 155 not out against Surrey as he carried his bat and his side to victory by 10 wickets.

Gordon Ross in *A History of West Indies Cricket* says: "Challenor was in a class by himself as a batsman. He had everything – a classical style and aggression, reinforced by a solid, technically sound defence." The consensus of opinion at the time was that he was the best batsman to visit England between Victor Trumper and Don Bradman.

Masterful batting during the summer of 1923 resulted in his special election to the membership of MCC; while a superb 124 for Barbados against the next touring MCC side, convinced the English of the calibre of Westindian cricket and paved the way for their elevation to Test match status.

Despite his excellent batting in England, Challenor played many of his most outstanding innings in the Caribbean, establishing an enduring opening partnership for Barbados with Tim Tarilton. In the 1927 domestic series Barbados scored 700 against both Guyana and Trinidad. In the first match, the pair shared in an opening stand of 183, as Challenor hit 105 and Tarilton 120; then against Trinidad they shared in a spectacular 292-run partnership, in which Challenor made 220 and Tarilton 123. Even though they had opened together for Barbados as early as 1906, it was not until 1920 that they scored the first of their many century partnerships, putting on 180 against Trinidad at Port-of-Spain. On that occasion, Challenor scored 103, before Tarilton went on to make the maiden first-class triple hundred in the

Caribbean.

Often described as the "father" of Westindian batting, Challenor was born, according to many commentators, 20 years too early. By the time he had his first taste of Test cricket, in his 41st year, he was an imitation of his former self. Even so, during Westindies' inaugural series against England, in England in 1928, he shared in a stand of 86 with Frank Martin in the first Test at Lord's and, in the third and final Test at The Oval, he and Clifford Roach put on 91 in just over an hour, with Challenor making an impressive 46 against the fearsome pace of Harold Larwood.

Inevitably, his first-class career, which spanned 25 years, and saw him make nearly 40 runs every time he went to the wicket, is infinitely more reflective of his ability than his miserly Test average.

If one of the most fluent and powerful batsmen of his age happened to be in the wrong place at the wrong time, it is comforting to know that Challenor's influence on Test cricket wasn't entirely negligible. As a teacher in Barbados, he encouraged outstanding players, such as the young Frank Worrell and Clyde Walcott, to take their game seriously, and was influential in shaping their batting skills.

Career details

Born: *28 June 1888*
Died: *30 July 1947*
Role: *Right-hand batsman*
Club: *Barbados*
First-class record: *[1905-1930] 5,822 runs (38.55) including 15 centuries, and 54 wickets (23.87)*
Tests: *3*
Test debut: *v England 1928*
Test runs: *101 (16.30); HS: 46 v England, The Oval, 1928.*
Tour: *England 1928*

Robert Julian Christiani

Born in a different generation, or even 10 years earlier, Robert Christiani would undoubtedly have made a greater impact in Test cricket than he did, batting in the distinguished company of Everton Weekes, Clyde Walcott, Frank Worrell, Jeff Stollmeyer and Gerry Gomez.

Yet the 5ft 10in Guyanese, who monopolised his island's batting records during his prime, had an encouraging start to his international career when he made 99 in the second innings of the match against England in 1948 – even if his untimely departure caused him to shed tears of disappointment in the dressing room. In the next game at Georgetown, Christiani hit a masterful half century as Westindies swept to victory by seven wickets.

His sound performances against England ensured his selection for the tour to India in 1948-49 and, during the first Test in New Delhi, Christiani scored his maiden century and then snapped up three Indian wickets. In the second match at Bombay, the Guyanese hit an attractive 74, although Westindies' batting strength was such that he could not find a place in the top half of the order.

Like his elder brother, Cyril, who died prematurely from malaria in 1938, Robert was a capable wicket-keeper and stood in for Walcott during his temporary illness in the third game at Calcutta, making one catch and two stumpings. Altogether it was a successful tour for the bespectacled Christiani, whose good footwork and wristy stroke-play brought him 984 runs at an average of 41.31.

Despite scoring over 1,000 first-class runs on the tour to England in 1950, batting at number seven in the Tests, he came in too late to show his true class, but was retained for the trip to Australia and New Zealand the following winter in preference to both Roy Marshall and Kenny Trestrail. His experience showed through on several occasions in Australia when, as the front-line batting floundered, he top-scored with 76 in the second Test at Sydney and hit the winning run at Adelaide to notch up Westindies' solitary victory in the series.

After this trip his international career was restricted to occasional appearances at home, against India in 1953 and England in 1954, but, by this time, he was past his best and in the twilight of his playing days.

In his first-class career, the hard-hitting Christiani averaged over 40 and, besides his fluent batting, is remembered for his sharply-turning leg-breaks and agile fielding.

Robert Christiani stumped in Westindies' match against MCC on their 1950 tour

Career details

Born: *19 July 1920*
Role: *Right-hand batsman, wicket-keeper, off-break bowler*
Club: *Guyana*
First-class record: *[1938-1954] 5,103 runs (40.50), including 12 centuries, 97 catches and 12 stumpings, and 18 wickets (60.44)*
Tests: *22*
Test debut: *v England 1948*
Test runs: *896 (26.35); HS: 107 v India, New Delhi, 1948*
Tours: *India 1948-49; England 1950; Australia and New Zealand 1951-52.*

Dr. Carlos Bertram Clarke

*e Clarke:
vned for his
y*

A tall, gangling man, Bertie Clarke was a surprise choice for the 1939 tour to England at the age of 21, after being recommended by George Headley. The youngster's skilful slow leg-break bowling met with great success, as he captured 87 wickets (21.18). Clarke says: "I'd read all about the English stars, the Huttons and the Comptons and came here on tour with a great feeling of deference. To my amazement, I found myself getting these stars out!"

Unlike Wes Hall and Charlie Griffith after him, Clarke began life as a fast bowler but later learned the secrets of spin bowling from a library book as a school-boy. Soon afterwards he collected five wickets in a school match, prompting the captain of the First

X1 to remark on his famous googly. Clarke remembers: "I didn't know what he meant at the time, but I had already gained a reputation."

The Second World War effectively closed the door on his Test career, but Clarke played regular wartime cricket in England, where he had also enrolled as a medical student at Guy's hospital. In 1942 he began his freelance contributions to the BBC's Westindian service, which included cricket commentaries.

The jovial doctor played for Northamptonshire between 1946-49 (during which time he took 156 wickets) and for the BBC on Sundays. He appeared for Essex in 1959 and 1960 and continued playing club cricket well into his sixties, including taking part in a celebrated veterans' match at The Oval. Clarke was regarded as one of the best exponents of his type of bowling in the country. He once described his renowned googly as: "looking like a full toss until it turns, then, as a bonus, dips a little..." He was also a typically hard-hitting batsman and a nimble fielder.

In 1948, he was invited to join the Westindies to play the English tourists in the first post-War Test series. But, as Clarke was not sure of retention for the entire series, he opted to stay in England where the National Health Service was being set up, in the interests of his long-term medical career.

In 1956 Clarke took 380 wickets playing for the BBC which prompted his brief return to county cricket. He has a long and illustrious association with the BBC club and last year collected their trophy for the best bowling performance for the 30th time in his distinguished career.

He was awarded the OBE for his voluntary social work.

*e Clarke keeps
guessing in his*

Career details

Born: *17 April 1918*
Role: *Right-arm leg-spinner*
Clubs: *Barbados, Northamptonshire, Essex*
First-class record: *[1937-61] 333 wickets (26.37) and 1,292 runs (12.30)*
Tests: *3*
Test debut: *v England 1939*
Test wickets: *6 (43.50)*
Tour: *England 1939.*

Sylvester Theophilus Clarke

A tall, broad-shouldered man, Sylvester Clarke is the ideal build for a fast bowler and has been terrorising batsmen ever since he burst on to the first-class scene in 1978, when he made his debut for Barbados and got a hat-trick against Trinidad in his first season.

Although none of his family play cricket, the youngster learned the game at school. "Then", he says, "I progressed to play First Division cricket in Barbados. I didn't have any coaching, although I was helped by Vanburn Holder."

The hostile right-armer also made his Test debut in 1978. He opened the bowling in his first match against Australia at Georgetown and, despite several dropped catches, he took six wickets in the game. Only injury, which has dogged Clarke throughout his career, curtailed his involvement in the series.

The Barbadian was included in the tour party to India the following year, where he topped the Test bowling averages with 21 wickets (33.85), which included five for 126 in an innings in the second match at Bangalore and four for 75 in the fourth game at Madras.

After the Packer players returned to the fold, Clarke was dropped, but was recalled for the trips to Pakistan in 1980-81 and Australia in 1981-82. He was at his best in Pakistan, after he replaced the injured Michael Holding, and made his mark by collecting 14 wickets (17.28) in four Tests. He also hit a vital unbeaten 35 in 30 balls, an innings which included three consecutive sixes, in the second Test at Faisalabad.

The normally placid Clarke was involved in a nasty incident in the fourth match at Multan when, after being showered by oranges and other debris while fielding on the boundary, he retaliated by throwing a brick, being used as a boundary marker, into the crowd which resulted in serious injury to a student leader. Thankfully the spectator recovered and Clarke escaped with a suspension from the Westindies Cricket Board.

The spearhead of Surrey's attack for many years, Clarke took a hat-trick against Nottinghamshire in 1980. He was instrumental in their victory in the Benson & Hedges Cup in 1982 and finished the season with 85 county championship wickets at 19.95 runs apiece. In 1986 "Silvers" finished fourth in the

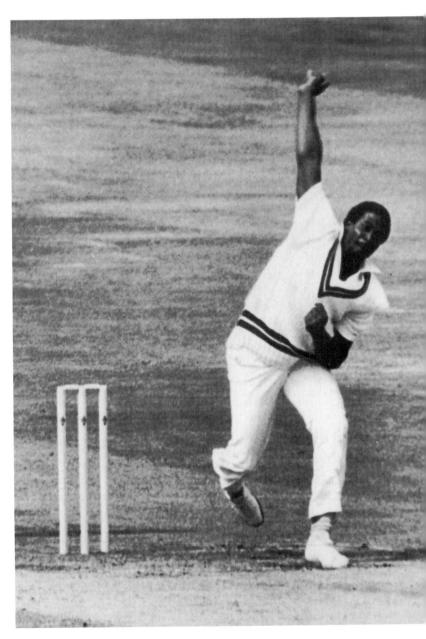

Sylvester Cla

national averages with 48 victims at 16.79 each and returned his career-best bowling figures of seven for 31 against Essex at The Oval in 1987, as he continued to torment batsmen on the English county circuit. One of the most feared bowlers around, some believe that Paul Terry's performances against the Barbadian in 1984 prompted the former's elevation to Test honours.

However, Clarke's own Test aspirations ended when he signed for Transvaal and joined an unofficial Westindian team on their tour of South Africa in 1983. Seemingly unaffected by the political controversy surrounding his decision, Clarke enjoyed great success and equalled the Currie Cup record in 1984-85 with 58 wickets at 13 runs apiece.

Clarke was immobilised by a serious back injury which stopped him from playing for Surrey in 1985 but, like other gifted fast bowlers, he bounced back to prosper with both Surrey and Transvaal.

There can be no doubt that, in the prime of his career, Clarke was one of the key losses to the Westindies Test side when he defected to South Africa. But, the relaxed bowler, who is as gentle off the field as he is aggressive on it, has no regrets about his decision. He says: "I don't think I was fairly treated by Westindies' selectors. I got the most wickets in India and then they picked Malcolm Marshall for the next tour to Australia. Then I was banned for a whole series for the brick-throwing in Pakistan. All I want to do is play cricket."

Away from the cricket field, Clarke likes to relax with friends, and listen to reggae and calypso music. The Barbadian is also a keen follower of tennis: "I especially enjoy watching Boris Becker", he says, with a glint in his eye.

Career details

Born: *11 December 1955*
Role: *Right-arm fast bowler*
Clubs: *Barbados, Surrey, Transvaal*
First-class record: *[1978-] 825 wickets (19.89) and 2,825 runs (14.94) including 1 century*
Tests: *11*
Test debut: *v Australia 1978*
Test wickets: *42 (27.88); BB: 5-126 v India, Bangalore, 1978*
Test runs: *172 (15.63); HS: 35* v Pakistan, Faisalabad, 1980*
Tours: *India 1978-79; Pakistan 1980-81; Australia 1981-82*

Sir Learie Nicholas Constantine (Lord, Baron of Maraval and Nelson)

Learie Constantine, who is remembered a much for the way h played his cricket, a for the deeds themselves

Learie Constantine was the first Westindian to receive widespread recognition from the cricketing public at large. His zest for the game and legendary enthusiasm on the field, which has never been surpassed, enabled him to personify the Caribbean spirit.

Learie Constantine was the son of Lebrun, a foreman on a cocoa plantation in Trinidad and himself the son of a slave, who had toured England in 1900 and who became the first Westindian batsman to score a century in England. Cricket was deeply ingrained on both sides of his family and the young Learie was shown the basics of the game by his mother's brother, Victor Pascall.

Constantine captured the family atmosphere that imbued his cricket from his earliest days when he wrote in *Wisden:* "My mother could keep wicket almost as well as a Test 'keeper; my sister had as much aptitude for batting as I had; one of my uncles was an international player and another was just as skilled. When we small boys were not playing in bigger games, we incessantly opposed each other, using oranges for balls and coconut branches for bats."

Father and son played their first match together for Trinidad in an inter-colonial game in 1922 and, after just three first-class matches, the youngster was selected for the trip to England in 1923. On that tour he attracted attention with his splendid fielding in the covers, and showed prodigious talent with the ball, taking 48 wickets as first or second change bowler; and shone with the bat, as he helped himself to 60 in a total of 97 in Westindies' fixture against Derbyshire, which was spoilt by the weather.

Constantine was a gifted, although erratic, batsman, but it was as a bowler of varying pace for which he was most noted. As a young man, he was one of the fastest bowlers in the world and, according to Jack Hobbs, who had faced the lethal Australian pace duo of Ted McDonald and Jack Gregory at their peak, Constantine's first few overs against him in the 1928 Test series were as quick as anything he had faced. As he got older, Constantine adapted his bowling style to reflect his advancing years, but he remained consistently effective throughout his career.

On the 1928 tour, Constantine was the leading wicket-taker with 107, the leading batsman with 1,381 runs, and the leading fielder with 33 catches but, inexplicably, he performed only moderately in the Tests, scoring just 89 runs in six innings and collecting a mere five wickets.

He did, however, claim the first wicket by a Westindian in a Test: Charles Hallows in the first session of the inaugural match at Lord's and finished with figures of four for 82. He also confirmed his brilliant fielding ability by catching out the top three scorers on the first day, prompting C.L.R. James to remark: "Constantine is probably the only all-rounder in cricket who could win his place in a Test side by fielding alone."

But Constantine saved his most magical performances for the games against the counties. In their match against Middlesex, the home side reduced the visitors to 79 for five, after scoring 352 for six themselves. Then Constantine arrived at the wicket and collected fifty runs within 20 minutes, and went on to a top-score of 86 in Westindies' total of 230, before snapping up seven Middlesex wickets for 57, which included a spell of six for 11 off 39 balls. As if that were not enough, Westindies' batting collapsed a second time to 121 for five, leaving Constantine to bring off a remarkable three wicket victory, as he hit 103 out of 133, with two sixes and 12 fours.

Later on in the season, he repeated his one-man show against Northamptonshire as his pace broke through their batting to give him figures of seven for 45; whereupon he turned on them with his bat, racing to 107 in 90 minutes, before a second innings hat-trick brought his side victory and Constantine 13 wickets in the match.

He revealed his abilities more accurately at the highest level in the first Test played in the Westindies, against England at Bridgetown in 1930. Opening the bowling with Herman Griffith, in the absence of George Francis, he removed Les Ames, Andy Sandham and the Hon. F.S.G. Calthorpe without the help of any fielder, and held three catches; then in the second Test at Port-of-Spain, he top-scored with 58. In the long-awaited victory at Georgetown, Constantine played a crucial role, as he

broke through England's batting on the first day to collect four wickets for 35, before completing the rout in the second innings by taking five for 87. Constantine missed the final Test at Kingston as he couldn't get time off from his job, which was quite a common occurrence, even for leading players, in those days.

Constantine again failed to shine in the international matches against Australia in 1930-31, yet he treated several state sides with the same disdain he had showed against Middlesex a couple of years earlier, including taking six for 45 against the Sheffield Shield champions, New South Wales.

In the Tests, in the third match at Adelaide, Don Bradman was dropped off Constantine's bowling on four and went on to make 223. Yet Constantine's own athletic prowess and attitude on the field were predictable talking-points. He explained his approach: "I watched the bowler run-up, watched him deliver the ball and as soon as it was in the air, I followed it to the pitch and then watched the batsman's movement, so that my anticipation took me to where the ball was directed and played by the batsman." His phenomenal catching record was doubtless nurtured, too, by his family's penchant for throwing crockery at each other as they washed up!

Constantine was one of the first Westindians to make his mark in the Lancashire League, which in those days provided Westindians with their only chance of regular competition. The Trinidadian endeared himself to the northern crowds and, by the time he and George Headley were entertaining them with their exceptional talent in the 1930s, they were already international celebrities. For C.L.R. James, Constantine was not a Test cricketer who played league cricket, but a league cricketer who played Test cricket.

Indeed, his league commitments were such that he was only released for the second Test against England at Old Trafford in 1933, where he was the highest scorer in Westindies' second innings with 64; and subjected the English to some of their own medicine as he and Manny Martindale bowled body-line at the home side, after "Nobby" Clarke had attempted the same against the tourists. Constantine played a key role in securing a draw for the visitors,

Learie Constantine

who were overwhelmed by an innings defeat in the other two Tests in which he did not play.

England's second trip to the Caribbean in 1935 coincided with the peak of Constantine's career. He missed the first Test at Bridgetown, played in notoriously boggy conditions, where he might have been able to pull off an unlikely win bowling in tandem with Martindale. But, he played an important role in the next match at Port-of-Spain, scoring a scintillating 90 in Westindies' first innings, before he removed two batsmen as the tourists slumped to 28 for five. Even though England eventually rallied to 258, they failed to stave off defeat as, with the penultimate ball of the game, Constantine trapped Maurice Leyland LBW to level the series, and give himself bowling figures of three wickets for 11 runs.

In their historic win at Kingston, after being instrumental with Martindale in enforcing the follow-on, and taking an exhilarating catch to end Ames' rearguard innings of 126, Constantine had the satisfaction of leading the side as Westindies won their first ever Test series, after Jackie Grant had retired with an ankle injury. Soon after he took over the reins of captaincy, Constantine introduced Derek Sealy into the attack so he and Martindale could change ends. Sealy obligingly dismissed Errol Holmes, after which the acting captain removed three other batsmen before the rains came.

Throughout his career, Constantine's standards remained extraordinarily high. In the 1939 series against England, the 36-year-old maestro bowled more overs (651.2) and took more wickets (103 at 17.77 apiece) than anyone else.

In the first Test at Lord's he was the only bowler to stand up to the assault from the English, and collected four wickets in the second match at Old Trafford, before his swan-song at The Oval. There, he took five wickets for 75 and hit a brilliant 79 out of 103 added in an hour, as he stroked the ball to all parts of the ground, in a fitting end to a great career.

Constantine played for the Dominions during the War, and captained them when they defeated England at Lord's in 1945; but on the resumption of international matches, three years later, he was too old to be considered.

After his playing days were over, Constantine

carried his fighting spirit into the political arena, working incessantly against racial discrimination. He promoted the cause of black people in England and, at the outbreak of the Second World War, he went to work in the Ministry of Labour's Welfare Office, looking after the interests of his fellow Westindians. In 1944 Constantine received damages from the Imperial Hotel of London, as they refused to accommodate him because of his colour.

He studied law, and in 1954 he was called to the Bar by Middle Temple. He became an MP in Trinidad's first democratically elected parliament after the country gained independence in 1962, and later became the Minister of Works in the Trinidadian government. Between 1962-64 he was High Commissioner for Trinidad & Tobago in London.

After the War in 1945, he was made an MBE, then in 1962 he was knighted before finally being created a life peer in 1969. Among the various posts he held, he was a Rector of St. Andrews, a member of the Race Relations Board and also the Sports Council, and became a Governor of the BBC.

In 1963 he was made an honorary Master of the Bench. He wrote and broadcast on cricket, and when he died in 1971 his country posthumously awarded him its highest honour, the Trinity Cross.

Despite his wealth of achievements in the political and social arena, it is perhaps indicative of his calibre as a cricketer, that it is his exploits on the cricket field for which Constantine is most remembered and most loved.

Career details

Born: *21 September 1902*
Died: *1 July 1971*
Role: *Fast bowler, medium-pace bowler, right-hand batsman*
Clubs: *Trinidad, Barbados, Lancashire League*
First-class record: *[1922-45] 424 wickets (20.61) and 4,451 runs (24.32) including 5 centuries*
Lancashire League record: *[1929-37] 6,673 runs (38.35) and 790 (9.90) wickets*
Tests: *18*
Test debut: *v England 1928*
Test wickets: *58 (30.10); BB: 5-75 v England, The Oval, 1939*
Test runs: *635 (19.24); HS: 90 v England, Port-of-Spain, 1935*
Tours: *England 1928; Australia 1930-31; England 1933; England 1939.*

Colin Everton Hunte Croft

Colin Croft was a large, thickly-set pace bowler, who seized the opportunity to establish himself at Test level when he and Joel Garner were summoned to the Westindies side for the series against Pakistan in 1977, after injuries to Michael Holding and Wayne Daniel.

Having achieved considerable success for Guyana in the Shell Shield, Croft made his Test debut against the strong Pakistani batting side in the first match at Bridgetown, where he took four for 47 in the tourists' second innings. In the second game at Port-of-Spain, his lift and movement off the pitch made him unplayable and he returned the historic figures of eight for 29. In a devastating opening spell, Croft forced Sadiq Mohammad to retire, before removing Haroon Rashid, Asif Iqbal and Mushtaq Mohammad. Majid Khan and Wasim Raja steadied the innings briefly, but no-one could prevent the Guyanese from surpassing Holding's record of six for 57, set against England in 1976. Five of Croft's victims fell for just nine runs in 10.5 overs in one of the most spectacular bursts of fast bowling ever seen. He eventually finished the series with 33 wickets, equalling Alf Valentine's record for a Westindian bowler, and achieved his twin ambitions of establishing himself in the Test side and winning a contract with an English county, when he signed for Lancashire the following year.

1978 was also the year of the Packer crisis. Croft became one of the World Series contracted players and, along with Andy Roberts and Garner, humbled the Australian tourists in the first two Tests of that season. However, with the deterioration of relations between the WSC players and the Westindies Board of Control, the former were obliged to withdraw from the third match at Georgetown on a matter of principle. When the rift was finally healed, Croft, unlike the other WSC players, had to wait until the 1979 World Cup for a recall to international honours.

Croft was included in the party for the tour of

Colin Croft

Australia and New Zealand in 1979-80 where, as the leading wicket-taker in Australia, with 16 victims, he was instrumental in securing Westindies' first series victory on Australian soil, as 55 of the 56 wickets which fell succumbed to the visitors' pace quartet. On the bad-tempered New Zealand leg of the tour, Croft lost his patience after some poor umpiring decisions and charged into umpire Fred Goodhall on his run-up, before both he and the Westindies Board apologised to the New Zealanders.

The Guyanese toured England with Westindies in 1980, and was selected for the trip to Pakistan later that year. In the five-match series against England in the Caribbean in 1981 he took 24 wickets at 18.95 each, before enduring a lean spell in Australia in 1981-82, mustering just seven wickets at 51.57 apiece from three Tests.

Croft's Test career came to an abrupt end when he went on the rebel tour to South Africa in 1983 (where he provoked a controversy when he was removed from a 'whites only' carriage on a train). It was an early exit for a bowler who, even in the esteemed company of Roberts and Holding, invariably finished as the leading wicket-taker in the series in which he played. He had an incomparable strike-rate, and regularly produced the unplayable delivery. The moody Guyanese worried most batsmen, with his exceptional lift and movement off the pitch. Croft was also a useful nightwatchman and, in a celebrated innings in the first Test against Australia at Brisbane in 1979, he scored two not out in 80 minutes.

The tall, hostile paceman could have played several more Tests but, perhaps feeling that he was past his peak when, at the age of 30, the offer to tour South Africa came, he turned his back on official international competition and terminated his career with Westindies.

A qualified airline pilot, Croft now lives in the United States.

Career details

Born: *15 March 1953*
Role: *Right-arm fast bowler*
Clubs: *Guyana, Lancashire*
First-class record: *[1971-84] 428 wickets (24.60) and 865 runs (10.55)*
Tests: 27
Test debut: *v Pakistan 1977*
Test wickets: *125 (23.30); BB: 8-29 v Pakistan, Port-of-Spain, 1977*
Tours: *England (World Cup) 1979; Australia and New Zealand 1979-80; England 1980; Pakistan 1980-81; Australia 1981-82.*

Wayne Wendell Daniel

Wayne Daniel, an amiable fellow, built in the mould of Charlie Griffith, has become such a familiar face at Lord's, it is difficult to imagine a time when 'Diamond' wasn't there to spearhead Middlesex's attack. He has helped the club to five county championships since joining them in 1976. Indeed, it has been Middlesex's good fortune that their leading strike bowler has been consistently overlooked by the Westindies selectors.

The softly-spoken Bajan, whose mild voice and manner are in marked contrast to his bowling, is philosophical, if obviously disappointed, about why he has found such little favour. He says: "I think as far as the Westindies side is concerned, there are 'in' people and there are 'out' people and, unfortunately, I fell on the wrong side of the line." Certainly, there can be no question over his fitness, as his phenomenal championship record proves, having played in over 150 games, with a best bowling performance of nine for 61 against Glamorgan in 1982.

Like most pacemen, Daniel has an extra sparkle in his eyes when he talks about the thrill of bowling fast. "I've always been able to bowl quickly," he says. "I used to bowl every day at school: cricket was on the menu for breakfast, lunch and tea; and it was while I was still at school that I came under the influence of Charlie Griffith, whom I have always admired."

But, it was another Griffith, Bosco, his geography teacher, who prevented the raw youngster from giving up the game when, at about 16, Daniel could not see how his cricket could earn him a living. The Barbadian remembers: "He gave me a lot of encouragement at a crucial time. I played in a strong school side for Princess Margaret's in St. Philip and he would take me to cricket every Saturday afternoon. Eventually I progressed to play for Spartan, who were one of the top clubs in Barbados in the early Seventies."

Daniel toured England with Westindies Young Cricketers in 1974, which was when he first came to the notice of Middlesex, who invited him to play

Wayne Daniel

some qualifying games in their second team the following season.

In 1976 he fulfilled his early promise being selected for Barbados, Middlesex and finally Westindies. He made his Test debut against India at home early that year and, on the subsequent tour of England, he took 52 wickets bowling in the company of Michael Holding, Andy Roberts, Vanburn Holder and Bernard Julien. Tony Cozier wrote of the young firebrand: "He was the least experienced of the lot, (and) accordingly the wildest but, on occasion, the fastest."

Daniel was fortunate to come under the watchful eye of some of Westindies' former Test stars. He says: "As a youngster, I had great admiration for Wes Hall; and Seymour Nurse helped me a lot in my junior years with the Barbados team. It was also in the early Seventies that I came under the wing of George Rock, who was a terrific coach with a good eye. For about three years, from the age of 19, he spent hours with me on a one-to-one basis coaching me and helping me to develop the right mental attitude."

Cricket has taken him all over the world, but Daniel still regards his native Barbados, where his family and many of his friends live, as home. Indeed, it is rumoured that he has never seen a snowflake, although that seems unlikely, having turned out for Middlesex on many less than spring-like April days.

In 1987 Daniel signed a two-year contract with Middlesex, which is indicative of the faith that one of the most successful English sides of the Seventies and Eighties have in a man who remains, on his day, one of the quickest in county cricket. During his benefit year, in 1985, the Barbadian finished as their leading wicket-taker.

It is difficult to know what will be missed most about Daniel when he finally hangs up his boots: maybe it will be his shining smile, or his wicked narrated mimes which have had the dressing room in hysterics on many wet Tuesday afternoons. But, probably, he will be remembered best for always putting his heart and soul into his bowling.

Career details

Born: *16 January 1956*
Role: *Right-arm fast bowler*
Clubs: *Barbados, Middlesex, Western Australia*
First-class record: *[1976-] 865 wickets (22.48) and 1,553 runs (11.67)*
Tests: *10*
Test debut: *v India 1976*
Test wickets: *36 (25.28); BB: 5-39 v India, Ahmedabad, 1983*
Tours: *England (WIYC) 1974; England 1976; Zimbabwe (under-26 side) 1981; England (World Cup) 1983; India 1983.*

Charles Alan Davis

Charlie Davis hooking during his century against England at Lord's 1969

Charlie Davis was something of a school-boy prodigy, as he showed when, at the age of 16, he hit 115 in a Beaumont Cup match for North Trinidad in 1960, and then attracted considerable attention by scoring heavily for Trinidad in inter-territorial games.

However, elevation to the Test side curbed his dashing stroke-play of the domestic competitions, as he found himself in situations that demanded a more restrained approach. The slim Trinidadian captured the selectors' attention with an unbeaten 158 for the President's X1 against the visiting MCC side in 1968; but it was not until the subsequent series in Australia that Davis got his first opportunity at international level. Ironically, he failed with the bat on that trip but headed the bowling averages with 24 wickets, including his career-best bowling of seven for 106 against South Australia at Adelaide.

It wasn't until the tour of England in 1969 that Davis came of age as a batsman at the highest level, when he averaged over 40. His first big score was made in dire circumstances during the second Test at Lord's. The Trinidadian was involved in a mix-up with one of his cricketing heroes, Gary Sobers, which resulted in the latter's premature departure, leaving the young Davis to atone for the error by crawling to his maiden Test century in six-and-a-half hours.

Davis was the outstanding Westindian batsman during the series against India in 1971, scoring 529 runs (132.25) in four Tests. In the second Test at Port-of-Spain Davis was the mainstay of both innings, as he fought a lone battle in a losing cause. He batted with resolution against the spinners, Erapalli Prasanna and Srinivasan Venkataraghavan, to finish unbeaten on 71 and 74 respectively. He followed this with an undefeated 125 in the third match at Georgetown and contributed 79 in a total of 501 for five declared at Bridgetown, before hitting another hundred on his home territory in the fifth and final Test at Port-of-Spain.

A year later he made 466 runs (58.25) in the series against New Zealand, hitting 90 in the second Test at Port-of-Spain, as many of his colleagues fell to injudicious strokes; and followed this with his highest Test score of 183 in the third match at Bridgetown, in a happier partnership with Sobers that saw the pair put on 254 for the sixth wicket. Davis' marathon innings lasted for 10 hours, after he had been dropped in the slips on 18.

Given his fine batting displays of the previous three years, it was strange that Davis was omitted from the next series against Australia and failed to make the tour to England in 1973. Selectorial idiosyncrasies brought his Test career to a seemingly abrupt end, leaving him with one of the highest batting averages by a Westindian.

His older brother, Bryan, also played for Westindies, against Australia in 1965.

Career details

Born: *1 January 1944*
Role: *Right-hand batsman, right-arm medium pace bowler*
Club: *Trinidad*
First-class record: *[1960-1976] 5,538 runs (41.32), including 14 centuries, and 63 wickets (39.36)*
Tests: *15*
Test debut: *v Australia 1969*
Test runs: *1,301 (54.20); HS: 183 v New Zealand, Bridgetown, 1972*
Tours: *Australia and New Zealand 1968-69; England 1969.*

Winston Walter Davis

It comes as a surprise that Winston Davis, rather than one of Westindies' more recent consistent front-line bowlers, should be the proud owner of two notable bowling records: namely, the most wickets for a Shell Shield season, when he took 33 wickets at 18.78 apiece in 1983 and later, the same year, the best bowling analysis in the World Cup, when he snapped up seven for 51 in Westindies' clash with Australia at Headingley.

The wiry Vincentian remembers: "I was taking severe punishment from Kim Hughes and David Hookes and, at one time, it looked like I wouldn't finish my 10 overs, as my first five had been hit for 33 runs; but then it all started to happen and I took seven wickets for 18 in my last five overs to clinch the record."

The slightly built Davis, who does not appear to be in the traditional mould of fast bowlers, has, however, had no problems in generating a tremendous amount of pace as Hampshire and former England opener, Paul Terry, found out when he suffered a clean break to his arm facing up to Davis during the 1984 Test series.

After he left school, Davis helped Sion Hill Cricket Club to the First Division championship in 1977; while all three of his brothers played for the Second X1. But it wasn't until 1978 that the young paceman received any formal coaching, when he and Linton Lewis were sent to the Alf Gover School in London, courtesy of their government and other well-wishers.

Davis' potential had already been spotted in 1976 when he performed well in a youth tournament in St. Vincent, which led to his inclusion in the Windward Islands team, who were taking part in an under-19 tournament. Further impressive performances saw him selected for the Westindies Young Cricketers side to play the touring England Young Cricketers. He was then included on the Westindies Young Cricketers tour to England in 1978, the same year that he won his scholarship to the Alf Gover School.

In 1980 Davis made his Shield debut for the Combined Islands. He says: "It was my first real taste of top competition and, as with my Test career, I didn't have a particularly promising start." But he impressed sufficiently to be included in Westindies' under-26 tour party to Zimbabwe in 1981, paving the way for his successful Shield year in 1982, when he collected 22 wickets at 22.77 each.

It seemed only a matter of time before Davis was offered terms by a county. The offer came from Glamorgan in 1982 after Ezra Moseley was troubled with a back injury. Ironically, it was Moseley's back problem which had made space for Davis on the tour to Zimbabwe.

His record-breaking Shield season in 1983, when he took five wickets in an innings against Guyana, Jamaica and the Leeward Islands, together with five wickets against the Indian tourists in Grenada, clinched his place in the Westindies side for the fifth Test in St. John's. He took a couple of wickets in each innings, which was enough to secure his place in the World Cup squad and a three-year contract with Glamorgan. His vintage year was made complete when he recorded his best bowling figures in the county championship, as he took seven for 70 for Glamorgan against Nottinghamshire at Ebbw Vale.

Davis had to wait until the fourth Test at Old Trafford in 1984 for his maiden Test appearance in England. He was called up as the emergency replacement for Malcolm Marshall, who had injured his back. Strangely, Davis made more impact with the bat than with the ball, as he joined Gordon Greenidge late on the first day as nightwatchman. They took the score from 267 for four to 437 before Davis was bowled for 77, during the soggy second afternoon.

Davis was included in the Westindies side to Australia in 1984-85, and was selected for two Tests against the touring New Zealanders in 1985, where he collected his best bowling figures of four for 19 in Kingston. In 1985-86 he played for Tasmania in the Sheffield Shield, but a recurring hamstring injury and longer intervals between matches than he was used to, meant that Davis didn't perform as well as he might have. A season of Lancashire League cricket with Rishton in 1986, and a return to full fitness, revived his appetite as he took 102 wickets for the northern club.

The north of England obviously suits Davis who had no hesitation in joining Northamptonshire in 1987 as their second Westindian player, after Roger Harper.

With his thirties looming, Davis knows he can't be a fast bowler forever and he is already planning for the future. He says: "I think it is sensible to think about what you will do after your cricket days are over while you are still playing. I am keen to start my own business and, hopefully, enjoy an affluent second career."

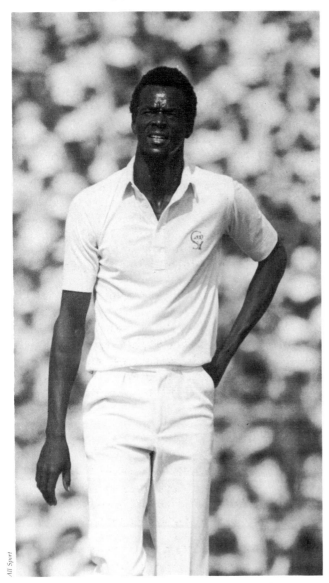

Winston Davis, who holds the record for the most wickets in a Shell Shield Season and the best bowling analysis in the World Cup

Career details

Born: *18 September 1958*
Role: *Right-arm fast bowler*
Clubs: *Windward Islands, Glamorgan, Tasmania, Northamptonshire, Lancashire League*
First-class record: *[1980-] 403 wickets (28.36) and 1,434 runs (14.48)*
Tests: *11*
Test debut: *v India 1983*
Test wickets: *32 (33.81); BB: 4-19 v New Zealand, Kingston, 1985*
Test runs: *157 (19.62); HS: 77 v England, Old Trafford, 1984*
Tours: *England (WIYC) 1978; Zimbabwe (under-26 side) 1981; England (World Cup) 1983; India 1983; England (as a replacement) 1984; Australia 1984-85.*

Cyril Clairmonte Depeiza

An accomplished wicket-keeper, Clairmonte Depeiza nonetheless is remembered above all for his world record seventh wicket partnership of 348 with his captain, Denis Atkinson, in the fourth Test against Australia at Bridgetown in 1955. After the tourists had compiled 668 runs, Westindies were reduced to 146 for six before Depeiza, without even a first-class fifty to his name, joined Atkinson at the wicket. In the event, the two Barbadians batted on and on for over a day in front of their home crowd, as they both went on to their career-best performances: Atkinson with 219 runs and Depeiza with 122.

Although the pair failed to avert the follow-on, the opposing bowlers, spearheaded by Ray Lindwall and Keith Miller, were so tired that the visitors could not risk another session in the field immediately, and the game fizzled out into a draw. Lack of time meant that the Australian captain, Ian Johnson, could not make a realistic second innings declaration and, fittingly, Atkinson and Depeiza played out the last half hour.

It was a truly remarkable feat and the two local batsmen were the talk of the island for weeks afterwards. Atkinson was the dominant partner, while Depeiza defied the bowlers with a studious forward defensive push which prompted someone to christen him "the Leaning Tower Depeiza". When they finally parted company, in the first over of the fifth day, they had overhauled the previous seventh wicket record, set in 1902, by four runs.

Depeiza, a customs clerk, had only been drafted into the side as wicket-keeper for the third Test at Georgetown, after Jamaica's Alfie Binns had been tried for the first match in Kingston and the Guyanese, Clifford McWatt, had played in the second at Port-of-Spain. But once Depeiza got into the team, he was retained for the rest of the series.

Depeiza and Binns were both selected for the tour to New Zealand in 1956, before Gerry Alexander eventually introduced some security of tenure to the wicket-keeping position following his surprise selection for the 1957 tour to England. Depeiza played in two Tests on the New Zealand trip, 'keeping in one and bowling in the other, with Binns behind the stumps. Indeed, it was thanks to Depeiza's efficient work in the second match at Christchurch that the spinners, Alf Valentine and Sonny Ramadhin, were able to bring the tourists such a conclusive victory. There were three Westindian wicket-keepers in that game, as New Zealand's 'keeper, Simpson Guillen, a former Trinidad and Westindies Test player, had settled there after Westindies' tour in 1952.

Depeiza, Binns and McWatt were all rated ahead of Alexander as wicket-keepers, so the latter's selection over the more naturally gifted trio, not to mention the omission of the outstanding Jackie Hendriks, caused something of a stir in 1957. It has been suggested that some of the selectors were apparently under the impression that Depeiza, who enjoyed an enviable regional reputation, had been chosen but, in the end, did not make the tour because his whereabouts were unknown. This seems particularly strange given that both he and the other surprise omission from the 1957 party, Conrad Hunte, were both available for English sides.

Nonetheless, Depeiza had left an indelible mark on international cricket, ironically as a batsman rather than as a wicket-keeper. Having played for the same Empire club as Frank Worrell and Everton Weekes, Depeiza later met with great success as a bowler in Scotland and the Lancashire League, where his distinctive round-arm action brought him hundreds of wickets.

Career details

Born: *10 October 1927*
Role: *Wicket-keeper, right-hand batsman*
Clubs: *Barbados, Scottish and Lancashire Leagues*
First-class record: *[1951-57] 31 catches and 9 stumpings, and 623 runs (32.78) including 1 century*
Tests: *5*
Test debut: *v Australia 1955*
Test catches: *7; Test stumpings: 4*
Test runs: *187 (31.16); HS: 122 v Australia, Bridgetown, 1955*
Tour: *New Zealand 1956.*

Peter Jeffrey Leroy Dujon

The latest in a long line of Westindian Test wicket-keepers from Wolmer's Boys' School in Kingston, Jeff Dujon is probably the most acrobatic of them all, brought up in an era of a four-pronged pace attack and incessant one-day cricket.

Dujon hails from a cricketing family: his father played first-class cricket and his brother, Dean, seemed to have the makings of a top cricketer until he opted to pursue a career in medicine in Canada. But it was young Jeffrey (who as a toddler pestered the players at Kingston Cricket Club to practise with him) who took up where his father left off when he made his first appearance for Kingston at the age of 13.

Dujon was still at school when he made his first-class debut for Jamaica at 18, and two years later hit his maiden century, having already impressed on Westindies Young Cricketers tours to England in 1974, where he top-scored with 62 in the one-day game at Lord's.

After this, Dujon's rise was rapid. He performed well with Westindies' under-26 side in Zimbabwe in 1981, and his batting ability earned him selection as deputy wicket-keeper to David Murray in front of his rivals for the short tour of Australia in 1981-82. Indeed, he prospered so much as a batsman in the early games on that trip, scoring an undefeated century against New South Wales, that he was selected for the Tests as a batsman where he averaged 45.40. Dujon enjoyed particular success in the third game at Adelaide, where he kept wicket, after Murray had injured his finger. He took three catches in each innings, compared to several dropped chances by the opposition, and also registered his first Test fifty.

It was a timely moment for Dujon to make his mark as, before the next series against India in 1983, Murray had joined the rebels in South Africa. This paved the way for the accomplished Jamaican to secure the long-term succession to Deryck Murray as Westindies' first choice wicket-keeper. Just to make

sure, Dujon underlined his pedigree with a century for Jamaica against the Indians in the opening match of their tour, celebrating his graduation to the captaincy after Lawrence Rowe had defected to lead the rebel Westindians in South Africa.

In the fifth Test against India, at St. John's, Dujon became the first Westindian wicket-keeper in over 20 years to score a hundred, as he shared in a double century stand for the fifth wicket with Clive Lloyd. Earlier, in the first match of the series in Kingston, Dujon equalled the record for the most catches in an innings by a Westindian 'keeper -- a feat he repeated against England at Bridgetown in 1986 – and then won the game for Westindies by hitting a six over square-leg in the last over, to the delight of his home crowd.

The masterful Dujon maintained his batting momentum into the next home series against the Australians in early 1984, when he helped himself to 130 in the second Test at Port-of-Spain: a splendid innings which brought him two successive hooked sixes off Rodney Hogg and 15 fours. He also established a record for a Westindies wicket-keeper by making 20 dismissals in the series.

Dujon was on the attack against the Australians again, this time in Australia at the end of 1984, when he hit 139 in the first Test at Perth, having retired hurt after being hit on the head by a bouncer before he had scored. He put on 147 for the fourth wicket with Larry Gomes and 160 for the same wicket with his skipper, Clive Lloyd, in the third game at Adelaide, as he followed his first innings 60 with an unbeaten 120, and finished a mightily successful series with fifty at Melbourne.

Sandwiched between these two series against the Australians, Dujon toured England in the summer of 1984, once again impressing with his athletic wicket-keeping and outstanding batsmanship. Dujon rates his century in the fourth Test at Old Trafford, when he added 197 for the fifth wicket with Gordon Greenidge, as one of the best moments of his career. He told *The Cricketer:* "A lot had been said about hitting through the line and the moving ball giving me trouble, so having made a hundred removed all the doubts. I was never in doubt!"

The editor of *The Cricketer* was also impressed by

Jeff Dujon: the most acrobatic of wicket-keepers

All Sport

his performance. He wrote: "Dujon, simply, is a batsman of high class, a classical player with all the strokes, not least the late cut which he was able to play with delicate precision all too often by (Nick) Cook and (Pat) Pocock."

Dujon is one of the few Westindian Test stars seemingly uninterested in playing county cricket, although he had a brief association with Swansea in 1977. This was on the initiative of a Welsh sports teacher, Ron Jones, who had helped the Jamaican as a youngster. But Dujon returned home early after there was an attempt to turn what had been an informal arrangement into a full-time contract.

As a batsman, Dujon struggled against Pakistan in 1986, collecting a pair in the first Test at Faisalabad, although he was almost back to his best in the subsequent series against New Zealand, finishing second in the averages with 36.

With an overall batting average approaching 40 and 142 dismissals from 43 Tests, Dujon remains the outstanding contemporary wicket-keeper-batsman, which was reflected in his invitation to keep wicket for the Rest of the World X1 in MCC's bi-centenary Test in 1987.

Dujon is married to a Barbadian and now lives in Barbados, the birthplace of Frank Worrell and Gary Sobers, two players who influenced the Jamaican as a youngster, although the quiet wicket-keeper has always fostered his own style.

A splendid batsman, "Dooj", as he is known to his team-mates, is equally at home against spinners or fast bowlers. Some believe that Dujon is such a gifted batsman that, should he be allowed to concentrate on this alone, he could prove an invaluable asset in the middle order in years to come.

Career details

Born: *28 May 1956*
Role: *Wicket-keeper, right-hand batsman*
Club: *Jamaica*
First-class record: *[1975-] 252 catches and 14 stumpings, 5,874 runs (40.23) including 14 centuries, and 1 wicket (44.00)*
Tests: *43*
Test debut: *v Australia 1981*
Test catches: *139*; Test stumpings: *3*
Test runs: *2,020 (38.11); HS: 139 v Australia, Perth, 1984*
Tours: *England (WIYC) 1974; Zimbabwe (under-26 side) 1981; Australia 1981-82; England (World Cup) 1983; India 1983; England 1984; Australia 1984-85; Pakistan 1986; New Zealand 1987; India and Pakistan (World Cup) 1987.*

Jeff Dujon, Westindies' gifted wicket-keeper-batsm

54

Richard Martin "Prof" Edwards

"Prof" Edwards, a quietly spoken and unassuming man with sparkling green eyes, was taken as understudy for the ageing bowling partnership of Wes Hall and Charlie Griffith on the 1968-69 tour of Australia and New Zealand.

Edwards decided to become a fast bowler after seeing the Australian, Ray Lindwall, perform. He says: "I saw him in 1960 with E.W. Swanton's touring team and I played against him and he encouraged me. He was the best fast bowler in the world at the time. Generally, though, I didn't get a lot of coaching; the older players used to tell me to watch and learn."

The promising youngster was taken under the wing of the Atkinson brothers, Denis and Eric, at Wanderers Cricket Club, and after he left school Edwards quickly progressed to playing First Division cricket. He remembers: "In a match against Empire, which included four or five island players, I took 14 wickets for 70 runs and things developed from there."

Normally a strong, lively bowler, Edwards struggled on the Australian pitches on his first tour, and could only muster 14 expensive wickets. His figures were not helped by some indifferent fielding, particularly in the second Test at Melbourne, when Ian Chappell was dropped off his bowling on 10 and went on to 165, and then Bill Lawry enjoyed the same luck as he was missed off the unfortunate Edwards on 132, before going on to a double century.

By the New Zealand leg of the trip Edwards seemed to have recovered his zest, as he captured six wickets for 129 in the first Test at Auckland and returned seven for 126 in the second at Wellington, including five for 84 in the first innings. Although the Barbadian finished as the leading wicket-taker with 15 (23.48) his surge of form came too late, with the selectors having already decided on a new-look pace attack, and he was left out of the tour party to England in 1969. Even so, Edwards excelled in English conditions when he played in the Rothman

Cavaliers knock-out tournament that summer.

A stalwart of the Wanderers club in Barbados, where his son plays, Edwards takes a keen interest in the development of the current batch of youngsters.

Now working as a building contractor, the genial Edwards keeps fit by jogging and weight-training, and relaxes by deep-sea fishing. He is also a familiar face at the various cricket festivals held in Barbados.

Career details

Born: *3 June 1940*
Role: *Right-arm fast bowler*
Club: *Barbados*
First-class record: *[1961-70] 78 wickets (36.29) and 389 runs (11.78)*
Tests: *5*
Test debut: *v Australia 1968*
Test wickets: *18 (34.77); BB: 5-84 v New Zealand, Wellington, 1969*
Tour: *Australia and New Zealand 1968-69.*

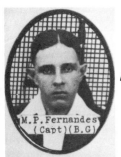

M.P.Fernandes
(Capt)(B.G)

Marius Pachaco "Maurice" Fernandes

"Maurice" Fernandes had the distinction of being the first Westindian captain to lead his side to victory in a Test match, against England at Georgetown in 1930. In that series Westindies fielded 28 different players against the tourists, with one of the main criteria for selection being accessibility to the ground.

Earlier, on the 1923 tour of England, Fernandes had been one of the key batsmen and, despite a bout of malaria, still managed to score 523 runs (34.86), including a superb innings of 110 against Leicestershire.

When the Hon. F.S.G. Calthorpe brought his side to the Caribbean in 1925-26, Fernandes scored 120 for Guyana against the tourists, to balance an earlier century by Wally Hammond, as the game fizzled out into a high-scoring draw. But, by the time of the first official Test series, against England in 1928, Fernandes was past his best and, although he played in the inaugural match at Lord's, he had a generally disappointing trip, averaging under 20.

Fernandes' fortunes improved by the time Westindies met England in 1930, this time on their own soil, as he led them to success in the third Test at Georgetown. After Learie Constantine and George Francis had humbled the tourists in their first innings, Fernandes rested his bowlers rather than enforce the follow-on, before the revitalised Constantine returned to complete his work, taking five wickets for 87 and Westindies to victory by 289 runs.

In keeping with the practice of the time, Fernandes was not chosen to play in a Test outside Guyana, although the elegant right-hander enjoyed considerable success in the domestic championship that year, scoring centuries against Barbados and Trinidad.

Career details

Born: *12 August 1897*
Died: *8 May 1981*
Role: *Right-hand batsman*
Club: *Guyana*
First-class record: *[1922-32] 2,087 runs (28.20) including 4 centuries*
Tests: *2*
Test runs: *49 (12.25); HS: 22 v England, Georgetown, 1930*
Tour: *England 1928*

Maurice Fernandes, who led Westindies to their first Test victory, against England at Georgetown in 1930

Thaddeus Michael Findlay

An excellent wicket-keeper, with superb reflexes, Mike Findlay was only the second player from St. Vincent to distinguish himself at international level since Charles Ollivierre, two generations earlier.

Findlay had an impressive first-class debut against the Australian tourists in 1965 but, nonetheless, was a surprise choice for the tour to Australia and New Zealand three years later, when he was taken as deputy wicket-keeper to Jackie Hendriks, ahead of the prodigious Deryck Murray.

Findlay and Grayson Shillingford from Dominica set a precedent as representatives from the Windward Islands, when they were included in the tour party to England in 1969. On that trip, Findlay took over from Hendriks as the first choice wicket-keeper for two of the three Tests.

But the wicket-keeping position was far from secure, and the lithe Vincentian, who was only an average batsman, relinquished his place to Desmond Lewis for the final three Tests against India in the Caribbean in 1971. Lewis was a specialist opener who kept wicket, but the home team fared no better with

this alteration and Findlay was recalled for the trip to New Zealand in 1972.

He retained the position for the first Test at Kingston against Australia the following year, but with Murray now out of university and watching his pretender have an indifferent game from the pavilion, Findlay lost his place for good. The likeable Findlay made the triumphant tour to England in 1976 but, despite performing well, he could not lever the Trinidadian out of the Test side, and faded from the scene.

A first-rate sportsman, Findlay also represented St. Vincent at soccer, where he used his enviable agility to keep goal.

Career details

Born: *19 October 1943*
Role: *Wicket-keeper*
Club: *Windward Islands*
First-class record: *[1964-78] 209 catches and 43 stumpings, and 2,927 runs (20.18)*
Tests: *10*
Test debut: *v England 1969*
Test catches: *19*; Test stumpings: *2*
Test runs: *212 (16.30)*
Tours: *Australia and New Zealand 1968-69; England 1969; Australia 1973; England 1976.*

Findlay keeping ... during the ...d Test against ... and at Lord's in ... John ... pshire is the ... man

Maurice Linton Churchill Foster

Tests: *14*
Test debut: *v England 1969*
Test runs: *580 (30.52): HS: 125 v Australia, Kingston, 1973*
Tours: *England 1969; England 1973.*

Maurice Foster

Maurice Foster was a resolute right-handed batsman and useful off-break bowler from Jamaica. A product of the illustrious Wolmer's Boys' School, he made his first appearance against International Cavaliers in 1963-64 and immediately established his credentials by scoring 136 not out in the second game.

Foster, who captained Jamaica for several seasons, toured England in 1969 and buttressed the middle order with a less exuberant approach than many of his contemporaries.

He hit his only Test hundred in the first match against Australia at Kingston in 1973, adding 210 for the fifth wicket in as many minutes with Rohan Kanhai, and went on to enjoy his most prolific series, averaging 43.66.

Foster would have had two Test centuries to his credit if he had not had the misfortune to play Abid Ali into his stumps when on 99 in the fifth match against the Indians at Port-of-Spain in 1971. He was included in the tour party to England in 1973, where he enjoyed a prolific summer, even though he only played in one Test.

If the Jamaican had accepted the invitation to tour India in 1974-75, he might have played more at the highest level. Even so, he remained on the Test scene until 1978 but, in the end, had to make way for the remarkable middle-order batting talent that mushroomed under the captaincy of Clive Lloyd.

A loyal servant of Caribbean cricket, Foster was also Westindies' table tennis champion, a game at which other members of his family excelled.

Career details

Born: *9 May 1943*
Role: *Right-hand batsman, off-spinner*
Club: *Jamaica*
First-class record: *[1963-78] 6,731 runs (45.17) including 17 centuries, and 132 wickets (30.72)*

George Nathaniel Francis

George Francis made his mark on the 1923 Westindies tour of England, as his devastating speed set new standards for fast bowlers. He shared the new ball with the veteran Trinidadian, George John, as the two pacemen wreaked havoc against the English counties.

The new boy, Francis, who lacked any first-class experience, but who had been included in the party on the wishes of the captain, Harold Austin, immediately justified his selection by collecting 10 wickets in the game against Sussex at Hove. He then took six for 34 in an innings against Middlesex, before helping himself to another 10 wickets for 76 in the match against Surrey at The Oval, setting up a magnificent victory for the tourists.

The brilliant young Barbadian then left a final indelible mark on the trip, as he played a decisive role in Westindies' historic end-of-tour match against H.D.G. Leveson-Gower's X1 at Scarborough. For this festival game, the English fielded as powerful a batting line-up as any they turned out in the next 30 years, including Jack Hobbs, Ernest Tyldesley, Percy Chapman, Johnny Douglas, Wilfred Rhodes and Percy Fender.

Predictably, this splendid array of batting talent secured a first innings lead of 108, and eventually required just 28 runs for victory in the fourth – seemingly a formality. But, perhaps, complacency had gripped the English, as the undemonstrative Francis began the rot by dismissing Hobbs with only three runs on the board, before he and John combined to reduce the home side to 19 for six, to put Westindies on the verge of a remarkable win. In the end, the Englishmen crept home by four wickets, as Francis bagged four for 12 in a match which, arguably, more than anything else contributed to the elevation of Westindies to Test match status.

As if to underline their readiness for Test recognition, when the Hon. F.S.G. Calthorpe took the strongest-ever MCC side to the Caribbean in 1925-26 to test the waters further, they were met by Francis and Herman Griffith, Barbados' dynamic new-ball pairing. In their first match against the Englishmen, the opening bowlers collected nine wickets each to inflict the only defeat of their trip on the tourists, dismissing them for 151 and 65. Francis and Griffith probably represented one of the quickest opening attacks ever seen at that time, and in Barbados' second drawn game with MCC, Francis nearly manufactured another victory as he took seven first innings wickets.

When Francis first visited England in 1923, he was regarded as the junior partner to George John, even though the former subsequently returned the more impressive analyses, as he was far and away the leading bowler capturing 96 wickets at 15.32 apiece. As a contemporary of Learie Constantine, Francis enjoyed a similar reputation, although the passage of time has seen him slip in comparison.

In the first Test series between England and Westindies in 1928, Francis could not reproduce his form of five years earlier, as this time he compromised his accuracy for speed. Nonetheless, it was appropriate that, given his pedigree, Francis bowled the first ball by a Westindian in Test cricket, at the home of cricket in the inaugural match at Lord's. His first Test victim was the illustrious Herbert Sutcliffe, and he also accounted for Tyldesley, the first player to score a century against Westindies. After Hobbs and Sutcliffe had shared in an opening stand of over a hundred in the third

George Francis

match at The Oval, Francis removed both players, paving the way for Griffith to snap up five quick middle-order wickets. Although he was past his peak, Francis still took 60 wickets at 31.33 each, even though only six of those were Test victims.

When England toured the Caribbean in 1930, they only had to face Francis in the third Test at Georgetown as the Barbadian could not get any more time off from his job. Francis must have been delighted to have played in this game, which saw Westindies' first Test victory.

A splendid effort from the home side's batsmen provided the platform from which the pacemen could launch their assault. Francis began by inducing 50-year-old George Gunn to hit his wicket, before he claimed another three wickets to give him four for 40 in 21 overs as, between them, Francis and Constantine dismissed the tourists for an impoverished 145. In the end Westindies cut their victory fine, winning with just a few minutes to go, as England batted with more application second time round; but after Francis had removed Gunn again, he completed their first win by dismissing Bill Voce.

With several years of international competition behind him, the experienced Francis was included in the first ever Westindies team to tour Australia in 1930-31; it was a tough baptism, as the visitors were comprehensively beaten in the first four Tests.

In the final match at Sydney, attempting to bring off a clean sweep of victories, Australia again fielded their strongest side. Westindies made 350 for six declared, which gave their bowlers a good score to defend. Francis and Griffith seemed to be saving themselves for such a moment, as they fired together for the first time in the series, with Francis claiming four wickets, to increase his Test tally by more than a third to 11, and help the tourists to their first ever lead in Australia of 126.

Jackie Grant made his second declaration of the match when Westindies' second innings had reached a precarious 124 for five, and put complete faith in his rejuvenated bowlers. Happily, they repaid him by taking Westindies to victory by 30 runs, to round off a rigorous and exhausting tour on a high note.

On Westindies' tour of England in 1933, the visitors were hampered in the field as two of their leading strike bowlers, Francis and Constantine, were unavailable for much of the time because of their league commitments in Lancashire. Francis' sole Test appearance came at Lord's; with the only regular fire-power coming from Manny Martindale. Had the gifted Martindale been partnered by either Francis or Constantine throughout the series, the result might have been different, or at least more closely fought.

Nonetheless, as two of the earliest Westindians to take part in league cricket in England, Francis with Radcliffe in the Central Lancashire League and Constantine with Nelson in the Lancashire League, they were able to pass on the invaluable knowledge they had gained from their experiences to the next generation of Westindians.

A comparatively short man for a quick bowler, Francis bowled fast and straight and, as he reached the wicket, he had a great leap in his delivery stride, which was often as disconcerting to the batsman as the delivery itself. This combination of factors meant that he was almost always invited to open the bowling regardless of the composition of the rest of the team, as he moved the ball late and was famous for his thundering yorker, as well as his enthusiastic fielding.

As with so many of the earlier players, Francis' Test figures do not reflect the real ability of a man who did so much to bring about Test status, but who was past his best when it finally arrived. At the end of his first-class career, Francis became a groundsman at the Pickwick club in Barbados.

Career details

Born: *7 December 1897*
Died: *12 January 1942*
Role: *Right-arm fast bowler*
Clubs: *Barbados, Central Lancashire League*
First-class record: *[1922-33] 223 wickets (23.11) and 874 runs (12.85)*
Tests: *10*
Test debut: *v England 1928*
Test wickets: *23 (33.17); BB: 4 for 40 v England, Georgetown, 1930*
Test runs: *81 (5.78)*
Tours: *England 1928; Australia 1930-31; England 1933.*

Roy Clifton Fredericks

Roy Fredericks, a small, courageous opening batsman is probably best remembered for two contrasting Test innings he played within three years of each other. The first came in the second Test against England at Edgbaston in 1973, when his eight-and-a-half hour 150 was criticised as one of the most tedious innings of modern cricket but, which, nonetheless, secured the series for the tourists; and the second, in the second Test against Australia at Perth in 1975, when he savaged Dennis Lillee and Jeff Thomson for 169 runs in 217 minutes, off 145 balls, with one six and 27 fours, in one of the great innings of Test cricket.

These two performances reflect the two phases in Fredericks' career, the former, before 1974, when he was more restrained in his approach, and the latter when he loosened up, giving full vent to the superb range of strokes he had at his disposal.

Fredericks made his Test debut on the trip to Australia in 1968-69. A relatively unknown player, the Guyanese owed his selection largely to two centuries he scored against Barbados in the Shell Shield in 1967. The compact little man, who was never afraid to take the attack to his opponents, impressed with several determined innings against stiff opposition. He established himself on the subsequent short tour of England, underlining his ability with 63 and 60 in the second Test at Lord's.

Yet, after grafting a place for himself in the side, Fredericks fell away in the rubber against India in the Caribbean in 1971; although, after making a golden duck in the first innings of the second Test at Port-of-Spain, he hit 80 in the second, as India won by seven wickets to clinch their first-ever series against Westindies.

When New Zealand visited the Caribbean in 1972, Fredericks returned to his earlier form, posting his maiden Test century in the first match at Kingston. His 163 was an entertaining innings of original stroke-play, second only to the masterly double century by the prodigious debutant, Lawrence Rowe, as the pair entertained the Sabina Park crowd with a

Fredericks hooks Snow during magnificent ... ry against ... nd at ...ingley in 1976

61

stand of 269 runs.

When Australia visited the Westindies the following year, Fredericks scored 98 in the second Test at Bridgetown, and played well for 76, adding 102 for the second wicket with Alvin Kallicharran, in the third match at Port-of-Spain.

After Westindies lost that game, Fredericks appeared to re-think his approach and became determined to transform his occasional outstanding innings into regular big scores. At that time the Guyanese was suffering both from his own inconsistency and the lack of a regular opening partner.

After his century at Edgbaston in 1973, Fredericks scored over fifty runs six times in his next seven Tests. It is likely that the wiry left-hander's performances were enhanced by the spell he had in English county cricket, when he played for Glamorgan between 1971-73. He scored a phenomenal 1,377 runs in his first season and, in his second, featured in a record opening stand of 330 with Alan Jones against Northamptonshire, finishing unbeaten on 228.

England suffered at the hands of the Guyanese once more when they visited the Caribbean in 1974, as he put on a record 206 with Rowe in the second Test at Kingston. Fredericks fell six short of his century then, only to be dismissed in the nineties again in the third game at Georgetown.

When Westindies visited India in 1974-75, Fredericks was determined to make up for his earlier disappointments on the sub-continent. He hit a hundred in the third Test at Calcutta, to help Westindies to a first innings lead, while his 104 in the fifth and deciding match at Bombay was crucial in steering his side to victory. But, perhaps, one of the most important developments of the series was the blooding of Gordon Greenidge, whose partnership with Fredericks became the most solid Westindies had known since that of Allan Rae and Jeff Stollmeyer.

However, the partnership was not without its problems, most notably when Greenidge lost his form and then his confidence on the tour of Australia in 1975-76. During that series, Fredericks found himself opening with Bernard Julien, Kallicharran

and finally Viv Richards, as Westindies only once scored over fifty for the first wicket. When the Indians visited the Caribbean in 1976, Fredericks had yet another partner for the fourth Test at Kingston, opening with Rowe again, as the two of them shared in a stand of 105, which set up victory in the match and the series.

In England later that year, Fredericks' sparkling play in the second Test at Lord's momentarily revealed the possibility of a result, after rain and slow batting by England seemed to have precluded it. But when the Guyanese was caught in the deep, off his favourite hook shot, for 138, the match fizzled out into a draw.

In a way, Fredericks made the hook shot his own. In the 1975 World Cup final, he played the stroke to despatch a delivery off Dennis Lillee over the boundary ropes – only to dislodge a bail with his foot. The use of the shot either paid him rich dividends, as when he sent the unfortunate Lillee's second ball into the crowd at Perth at the start of his famous innings earlier in 1975, or led to his early demise, such as his dismissal for a duck in the first innings of the third Test at Old Trafford, after his century at Lord's.

Thereafter, the partnership between Fredericks and Greenidge came of age as they added 116 in the second innings of the game in Manchester, before Fredericks hit his own wicket again. They both scored centuries in the fourth Test at Headingley, thrashing 192 off the English attack, with 147 of the runs coming off 27 overs on the first morning. Fredericks concluded the series with a partnership of 159 with Richards in the first innings of the final Test at The Oval, and an unbeaten stand of 182 with Greenidge in just over two hours in the second, to pulverize England by three games to nil, as both openers topped 500 runs for the series.

Westindies' batting, with the notable exception of their openers, was less secure against the Pakistanis when they visited the Caribbean in 1977. Fredericks opened his account with 52 in the first Test at Bridgetown, adding 130 for the second wicket with Richards, and followed this up with 120 in the second game at Port-of-Spain. He got an unbeaten half century in front of his home crowd in the third match at Georgetown, and, when Pakistan levelled the series by winning the fourth at Port-of-Spain, everything depended on the fifth game at Kingston. Fredericks had announced his imminent retirement and, suitably, he and Greenidge shared in a match-winning stand of 182, before they were dismissed in successive overs: an appropriate epitaph for one of the great opening partnerships in Test cricket.

After his retirement, Fredericks became involved in politics and was made Minister for Sport in Guyana, with responsibility for youth affairs and recreation. When he made a brief return to first-class cricket as player-manager for the victorious Guyana Shield team in 1983, Fredericks showed that he had lost none of his flair by scoring 103 against Trinidad & Tobago and 217 against Jamaica in his only innings.

Fredericks was called into the Westindies side at a time of transition and, in his 59 Tests, shepherded the team from the jubilant era under the leadership of Frank Worrell and Gary Sobers to the splendidly successful years under Clive Lloyd. Like Conrad Hunte before him, Fredericks' performances are all the more worthy when one remembers that, for many years, he was without a regular partner.

Career details

Born: *11 November 1942*
Role: *Left-hand batsman*
Clubs: *Guyana, Glamorgan*
First-class record: *[1963-83] 16,384 runs (45.89) including 40 centuries, and 75 wickets (37.94)*
Tests: *59*
Test debut: *v Australia 1969*
Test runs: *4,334 (42.49); HS: 169 v Australia, Perth, 1975*
Tours: *Australia and New Zealand 1968-69; England 1969; England 1973; India and Pakistan 1974-75; England (World Cup) 1975; Australia 1975-76; England 1976.*

Joel Garner

Joel Garner is one of the tallest men ever to have played Test cricket and he has put his phenomenal 6ft 8in height and huge frame to very good use.

Of normal height until he was 13, the "Big Bird", as he is universally known, after the Sesame Street character, bowls with remarkable control. He has a good action off a short run, and his height and long arms help him to achieve excessive bounce. Garner is a formidable prospect for any batsman as he varies his pace, before unexpectedly producing his deadly yorker. Both as an economic and as a penetrative bowler, Garner was acknowledged as the best bowler of his type in the world for many years.

The Barbadian developed his talents under the experienced eyes of Seymour Nurse and Wes Hall at the Boys' Foundation School, before Barbados' coach, Charlie Griffith, advised a change in his action which transformed him from a promising youngster into a world class bowler.

Garner shared the new ball with Wes Hall in the Cable & Wireless cricket team in the Intermediate Division of the Barbados Cricket Association. After the youngster had collected 95 wickets from 11 matches, he forced his way into the Barbados youth team and gained the attention of the First Division clubs, where he began playing for the Young Men's Progressive Club. Yet, because of the intensity of the competition, Garner did not make his first-class debut until 1975 when he was 23 years old, and that was prompted by the absence of Keith Boyce and Vanburn Holder who were on tour in Australia.

Two years later the gentle giant performed soundly for the President's X1 against Pakistan, and excelled for Barbados against Jamaica and Trinidad & Tobago. This prompted his selection for the first Test at Bridgetown against the Pakistanis, after injuries to Wayne Daniel and Michael Holding. Despite having little first-class experience to draw on Garner had a happy start to his international career as he finished his inaugural series with 25 wickets (27.32), including a splendid eight for 148 in the third match at Georgetown.

Originally chosen to bridge the gap left by Daniel and Holding, Garner sustained his promising form and maintained his place when Australia visited the Caribbean the following year. He collected another eight wickets in a match, this time in the second Test at Bridgetown, in front of his home crowd. But, afterwards, Garner joined the bulk of the rest of the team who opted to play World Series Cricket in Australia, where again he performed admirably.

Against England in the 1979 World Cup final, the Barbadian was instrumental in ensuring that Westindies retained the trophy, as he finished with five wickets for 38, including four batsmen bowled for four runs in 11 balls.

During the previous two years Garner had appeared for Somerset on a part-time basis and joined them on a full-time contract in 1979 where, together with Viv Richards, he turned them into one of the more successful counties of the late '70s and early '80s, as they won the Gillette Cup and the John Player League.

After 1979, Garner became a permanent member of the Westindies team. He helped them to win their first Test series in Australia in 1979-80 by heading the bowling averages, and did likewise in New Zealand, where his haul of wickets included six for 56 in the third Test at Auckland. He bowled well in Pakistan in 1980-81 and against Australia the following year he collected five for 56 in the concluding Test at Adelaide, to level the series for Westindies. In 1982-83 Garner played with great success for South Australia, taking 55 wickets at 17.74 apiece.

But the Barbadian ran out of steam when India visited the Caribbean in 1983, and his seven wickets cost him 43.3 runs each. Hampered by a shoulder injury and too much cricket, the "Big Bird" decided to opt out of the tour to India in late 1983 on the advice of his doctor.

So Garner spent his convalescent period swimming off the beach near his home at Enterprise in Christ Church. He returned to the Westindies side for the World Series one-day tournament in Australia in 1984, where he immediately experienced problems with his knees. The big Barbadian was forced to miss six matches, as he renewed his bowling muscles by weight-training, but returned in time for the three finals to capture 10 wickets for 89 runs in 29 overs.

Fully recovered by the time Australia visited the Caribbean later in 1984, the rejuvenated Garner opened the bowling in the absence of Holding and Malcolm Marshall who were both injured, and collected 31 wickets at 16.87 each. Garner's haul of wickets was 10 more than anyone else and set a new record for a series against Australia. He took six for 75 in the first Test at Georgetown and five for 63 in the fourth match at St. John's, but the Barbadian was at his best in the second match at Port-of-Spain. Australia had struggled to 16 for three, before Garner helped himself to a further four wickets, as he finished with six for 60.

Although Marshall and Winston Davis' speed grabbed the headlines on Westindies' tour of England later that year, it was Garner's awkward bounce which reaped the richest rewards as he finished as the leading wicket-taker with 29 victims from five Tests. He collected 19 wickets in the five-match series against Australia in 1984-85, including four for 67 in the second Test at Brisbane and three wickets in five balls in the fourth match at Melbourne. Garner played a key role in the record 11 successive Test wins Westindies achieved in this period.

A jovial, happy character with a smile once described by John Arlott as "like a slice of melon", Garner has aspirations to go into social work when he retires from cricket. A popular player, Garner further endears himself to the crowd with his cavalier approach to his batting which brought him a worthy 60 against Australia in the first Test at Brisbane in 1979, and a century against Gloucestershire when he toured with Westindies in 1980.

Awarded an MBE in 1985, Garner was released from Somerset in acrimonious circumstances in 1986, his benefit year. The sacking of Garner and Richards provoked unprecedented controversy and, although the two players had a popular following, neither was re-instated. After the furore died down, Garner returned to play in the Central Lancashire League, where he had begun his career in England.

Garner was appointed captain of Barbados in 1986, and was instrumental in lifting them to the Shell Shield after a disappointing year in 1985. He took 28 wickets at 13.5 apiece – the most by a Barbadian

Garner: one of ...ndies' most ...ssful and best-... bowlers

65

bowler in a Shield season – and skippered his side with authority and imagination. He carried his Shield form into the Test series against England when they visited the Caribbean in 1986, taking 27 wickets to equal the record for a Westindian in a home series against England. Garner also led Barbados to victory over England, and hit the winning runs to complete a thoroughly satisfying season, in which he took 57 first-class wickets altogether at a personal cost of just over 15 runs each.

On the tour to New Zealand in 1987, the irrepressible Barbadian topped the bowling averages in the three match series with 12 wickets at 18.08 each, including five for 51 in the first game at Wellington, before announcing his retirement from Test cricket.

In spite of his cosmopolitan lifestyle, Garner always enjoys going home to spend time with his friends in Barbados, where he still lives. After his retirement as a first-class player, Garner, whose heart seems proportionate to his body, is keen to stay involved with the game and impart his invaluable knowledge to a new generation of cricketers, who are doubtless as keen to learn from former Test players as he was.

Career details

Born: *16 December 1952*
Role: *Right-arm fast bowler*
Clubs: *Barbados, Somerset, South Australia, Central Lancashire League*
First-class record: *[1975-] 858 wickets (18.51) and 2,826 runs (16.82) including 1 century*
Tests: *58*
Test debut: *v Pakistan 1977*
Test wickets: *259 (20.97); BB: 6-56 v New Zealand, Auckland, 1980, 6-56 v Australia, Adelaide, 1982*
Test runs: *672 (12.44); HS: 60 v Australia, Brisbane, 1979*
Tours: *England (World Cup) 1979; Australia and New Zealand 1979-80; England 1980; Pakistan 1980-81; Australia 1981-82; England (World Cup) 1983; England 1984; Australia 1984-85; New Zealand 1987.*

Lancelot Richard Gibbs

Lance Gibbs was one of the finest off-spin bowlers the world has ever seen. The Guyanese was so talented that he broke the seeming stranglehold of Westindies' fast bowlers and, for a while, overshadowed them.

The young spinner had already built a strong reputation before he joined Demerara, one of the strongest clubs in Guyana. Gibbs started his career as a leg-spinner, but after a severe mauling from Robert Christiani during a trial in Guyana, he decided to become an off-spinner. Gibbs had an unorthodox chest-on action and delivered the ball from a great height through his long, supple fingers which enabled him to extract bounce and spin from most pitches. This, together with his variation of pace and flight, and impeccable control and accuracy, made him a formidable prospect for any batsman.

A tall, lean man, Gibbs made his first-class debut for Guyana against MCC in 1953-54 and his Test debut against Pakistan four years later. He enjoyed a superb series, heading the bowling averages with 17 wickets at 23.05 apiece, including five for 80 in front of his home crowd in the fourth Test at Georgetown and another four wicket haul in the next game at Port-of-Spain. His inclusion on the subsequent tour to India and Pakistan was virtually a formality, but the youngster was given little opportunity to prove himself in the wake of Wes Hall and Roy Gilchrist's success.

The Guyanese came of age as a bowler on the trip to Australia in 1960-61. In the third match at Sydney, after sitting the first two Tests out, the smooth Gibbs, bowling in tandem with Alf Valentine, almost collected a hat-trick as he took three wickets in four balls, and propelled the visitors to a comprehensive victory.

In the fourth Test at Adelaide, Gibbs was irrepressible as this time he completed a hat-trick, the first one in a Test in Australia since 1903-04. He dismissed Ken MacKay LBW, then Wally Grout fell for his third successive duck to Gibbs, before the latter clean bowled Frank Mission. Gibbs followed

this with four for 74 in Australia's first innings in the final match at Melbourne and, after playing in three Tests, he found himself heading the bowling averages with 19 victims at 20.78 each.

When India visited the Caribbean in 1962, Gibbs once again played second fiddle to the pace of Hall for the first two matches. But, ironically, the most comprehensive collapse came against the spin of Gibbs in the third Test at Bridgetown. The visitors made 258 on a docile wicket before Westindies crawled to 475. By lunch on the final day India were 158 for two and seemed content to settle for a draw, but Gibbs had other ideas. In 15.3 overs after the interval, the Guyanese entranced the batsmen and the crowd, as he bowled 14 maidens and collected eight wickets for six runs to bring Westindies an incredible victory. In one of the finest spells of bowling ever seen in Test cricket, Gibbs induced the visiting batsmen to snick catches to the waiting close fielders, as he finished with eight for 38.

For more than a decade after this triumph Gibbs was acknowledged as the finest off-spinner in the world and held his own in the Westindies team, despite the renewed emphasis on pace. On the tour of England in 1963, Gibbs bowled the visitors to victory in the first Test at Old Trafford as he took nine wickets for 157 in the match, and collected four in an innings in the third and fourth Tests at Edgbaston and Headingley.

Against Australia in 1965 the gifted spinner outshone Hall and Charlie Griffith, as the tourists were outplayed in every department. Gibbs saved some special magic for his home crowd in the third Test at Georgetown, where he took half his wickets for the series. In the visitors' first innings he took three for 51 and followed this up with six for 29 in their second innings, including the wicket of Bill Lawry who became the wily off-spinner's hundredth Test victim. Gibbs finished as Westindies' leading wicket-taker with 18 victims, and was instrumental in securing their first ever series victory over Australia.

As the pace duo of Hall and Griffith began to lose some of their zest, Gibbs was used increasingly as a stock bowler. In the 1966 series against England, he bowled almost one hundred overs more than Hall, and topped the averages again. His performance in

Lance Gibbs: one of the world's finest off-spinners and, for a while, the leading wicket-taker in Test history

the first Test at Old Trafford had uncanny parallels with his efforts on the same ground in 1963, as his calculating spin brought him 10 wickets in the match. He was instrumental in England's defeat in the fourth Test at Headingley as he took six for 39 in the home side's second innings, so it was with much relief that he failed to take a wicket in the final game at The Oval.

When Westindies toured India in 1966-67, Gibbs sewed up victory for the visitors in the first Test at Bombay, as he took four wickets for 67 in India's second innings and collected five for 51 in their first innings in the next match at Calcutta.

Gibbs was the centre of attention in the fifth Test against England at Georgetown the following year, when Westindies had to win to level the series. Gibbs took them to the edge of victory by snapping up six wickets for 60 but, in the end, he was thwarted by the fast bowler, Jeff Jones, who defended his wicket stoutly in Gibbs' last over to ensure that England clinched the rubber.

On Westindies' disappointing trip to Australia the following season, Gibbs was the only bowler to perform consistently, although even he lost some of his bite and, after an indifferent tour to England in 1969 as vice-captain, Gibbs took a well earned rest before returning for the second part of his illustrious career.

His temporary departure from the international scene left a noticeable void and the Guyanese was recalled to tackle the Australians in 1973. He immediately introduced a sense of urgency into the bowling by taking four wickets in the first match at Kingston and five and four in the two games played at Port-of-Spain.

Back in the groove, Gibbs spun England to defeat in the first Test at Port-of-Spain in 1974 and continued his match-winning ways in India, when he ran through the home side's batting in the second Test at New Delhi to finish with figures of six for 76. He completed a magnificent series by taking seven wickets for 98 in the first innings of the fifth match at Bombay.

After playing in the Lancashire and Durham Leagues, Gibbs qualified to play for Warwickshire in 1968, where he stayed for five years. He took a while to adapt to three-day county cricket and the variety of wickets he played on, but took his career-best figures and the season's best when he collected eight for 37 against Glamorgan in 1970, and enjoyed a vintage summer the following year, taking 131 wickets at 18.89 apiece.

Gibbs wore himself out on his third trip to Australia in 1975-76. He took five wickets in the first innings of the first Test at Brisbane, but had a lean spell after that and only retained his place in the hope that he would overhaul Fred Trueman's world record number of Test wickets. Gibbs reached that milestone when he had Ian Redpath caught on the first day of the final Test at Melbourne, and for a while remained the leading wicket-taker with 309 victims.

In the twilight of a remarkable career which saw him bowl 27,115 balls in Test cricket – more than the combined total of Hall and Griffith – it was disappointing that continual rain thwarted the possibility of Gibbs' enjoying his swansong on his home ground, as the third Test against India in 1976 was moved from Georgetown to Port-of-Spain.

No-one is better qualified than his cousin and long-time colleague, Clive Lloyd, to evaluate Gibbs' contribution to the game. He said: "There was never a more whole-hearted cricketer for the Westindies, nor an off-spinner in anything like his class...He was by no means a mechanical spinner, instead always thinking about the game, working an opponent out, assessing his strengths and weaknesses and laying the trap for him...He was a perfectionist and set high standards for himself and those who were playing with him. A fierce competitor, he would be giving total effort, no matter if the pitch was flat and docile, no matter if the total was 300 for two and the sun scorching, no matter if his finger had been rubbed raw."

Gibbs took five or more wickets 18 times in a Test innings and 10 or more on two occasions. As well as his fine bowling, Gibbs was also a superb close fielder, especially in the gully; although, without the demands of one-day cricket to cope with, he was a confirmed number 11 batsman. Even so, he added a record 74 for the eighth wicket with Gerry Alexander against Australia at Sydney in 1961.

Away from the cricket field, Gibbs had a keen interest in horses, and a remarkable knack of forecasting the results! He now lives and works in the United States.

Career details

Born: *29 September 1934*
Role: *Right-arm off-spinner*
Clubs: *Guyana, Warwickshire, Lancashire and Durham Leagues*
First-class record: *[1953-76] 1,024 wickets (27.22) and 1,729 runs (8.55)*
Tests: *79*
Test debut: *v Pakistan 1958*
Test wickets: *309 (29.09); BB: 8-38 v India, Bridgetown, 1962*
Test runs: *488 (6.97)*
Tours: *India and Pakistan 1958-59; Australia 1960-61; 1963; England 1966; India 1966-67; Australia and New Zealand 1968-69; England 1969; England 1973; India and Pakistan 1974-75; Australia 1975-76.*

Roy Gilchrist

Roy Gilchrist was born and brought up on a sugar plantation in Jamaica. A short, stocky figure, with unusually long arms and powerful shoulders, he developed his bowling technique without any formal coaching.

Gilchrist was selected for the tour to England in 1957, after an excellent season in Jamaica the previous year. The raw paceman was recruited along with another young bowler, Wes Hall, but everyone expected Sonny Ramadhin and Alf Valentine to entrance the Englishmen as they had in 1950. Indeed, Gilchrist's assets of devastating pace and bounce were not fully exploited.

He played under his compatriot, Gerry Alexander, during the subsequent series against Pakistan in the Caribbean, where his fearsome speed subdued the tourists and accounted for 21 wickets in the rubber.

Roy Gilchrist's splendid action captured here by Ken Kelly

'Gilly' was selected for Westindies' tour to India and Pakistan in 1958-59, again under the captaincy of Alexander, with whom he had never seen eye to eye. This manifested itself in their strained relations during the home series against Pakistan earlier in 1958.

Westindies met with early success on the tour of India, as Gilchrist and Hall swept all opposition aside. The Jamaican followed his four for 39 in the first Test at Bombay with six for 55 in the third, at Calcutta, clean bowling five of his six victims, three with the total on 131, to take Westindies to victory by an innings. That spell of bowling was as fast as anything ever seen in international cricket. In the fifth Test at New Delhi, Gilchrist's burst was decisive as he finished the Indian second innings by inducing Chandrakant Borde to hit his wicket four short of his second century of the match, and then bowled the two tail-enders as three wickets fell for one run. It turned out to be his last Test appearance as the simmering feud between him and Alexander, culminating in the excessive use of beamers,led to Gilchrist being sent home in disgrace.

The tragedy of the entire episode was that it deprived Westindies of their most gifted bowler since Manny Martindale. If Gilchrist had been able to partner Wes Hall in the series against England and Australia between 1959 and 1961, the narrow defeats would almost certainly have been pulled in favour of Westindies. Until Charlie Griffith made his impact in 1963, Gilchrist's ferocious pace was sorely missed by Westindies.

There was speculation that if Frank Worrell had been captain on the tour to the sub-continent, the trouble would not have occurred or, at least, would have been diffused more satisfactorily. Gilchrist himself believes that his ability would have been recognised earlier, and he would have been disciplined differently, if he had come from a higher social background.

Sadly then, the devastating paceman, whose pummelling power had induced the Indians to try four different captains and 24 players during their five match series, had his short and troubled Test career terminated.

Gilchrist played in the north of England leagues between 1958-86 as a professional, where his rapier speed brought him thousands of wickets, including many hat-tricks, as he carried his various clubs to success.

Over the years, Gilchrist's fiery character mellowed. After living in England for nearly 30 years, he recently returned to Jamaica to work for the merchandise company that gave him his first opportunities in cricket.

Career details

Born: *28 June 1934*
Role: *Right-arm fast bowler*
Clubs: *Jamaica, Hyderabad, North of England Leagues*
First-class record: *[1956-63] 167 wickets (26.00) and 255 runs (7.72)*
Tests: *13*
Test debut: *v England 1957*
Test wickets: *57 (26.68); BB: 6-55 v India, Calcutta, 1959*
Tours: *England 1957; India 1958-59.*

John Douglas Claude Goddard

John Goddard secured his name in the annals of Westindian cricket, after insisting on the inclusion of Sonny Ramadhin and Alf Valentine in his 1950 tour party to England. The two unknown spinners quickly became Goddard's secret weapons, as they helped the visitors to their historic 3-1 victory. It is perhaps reflective of the nature of cricket that, when Goddard was re-appointed as captain for the English tour seven years later, he was unable to rekindle that magic, as his side slid to a 3-0 defeat.

As a school-boy, Goddard was a sprint champion and a capable cricketer as he revealed when, at 17, he hit an unbeaten double century in a school match, and went on to make his first-class debut at the same age. He was one of the heaviest scorers in the War Goodwill Inter-Colonial series between 1941-46, making 1,362 runs, including five hundreds, at an average of 71.68. In the 1943-44 series of inter-colonial games, the Barbadian shared in an unbroken fourth wicket stand of 502 with Frank Worrell against Trinidad at Bridgetown. Goddard's contribution was 218 not out, and remained his career-best innings.

He made his Test debut in 1948 against the touring MCC side, and was promoted to the captaincy after two Tests. In one of the strongest batting line-ups ever fielded by Westindies, the resolute left-hander went in at number eight. In his first match as captain, Goddard spun out the English on a drying Georgetown pitch, to finish with five for 31. This swept Westindies to victory, and then he led them to

Westindies team vs Col. L. C. Stevens XI:
(l-r) John Goddard, Allan Rae, Robert Christiani, Cecil "Boogles" Williams (partially visible), Lance Pierre, Alf Valentine (partially visible), Gerry Gomez

success in the final Test at Kingston, chipping in with 46 not out in their second innings.

Goddard's success ensured that he retained the captaincy for Westindies' tour to India in 1948-49. He won the toss in all five Tests but the deadlock was only broken in the fourth match at Madras, when Westindies' handsome innings victory helped him keep the captaincy for the trip to England in 1950.

Although the 1950 tour was a triumph for the Westindies team, Goddard's only personal success came in the final Test at The Oval, where he hit an unbeaten half century and took four first innings wickets. It was widely felt that the pressures of the captaincy detracted from his individual performances, and Valentine replace him as the specialist spinner in the side.

Goddard retained the captaincy for the next series, this time for the disastrous tour to Australia in 1951-52. He stood up well to the bombardment from Ray Lindwall and Keith Miller in the first Test at Brisbane, top-scoring with 45 and, in the next match, in Sydney, moved himself up the order to try to protect the other batsmen in a ploy that failed.

Goddard's captaincy was criticised during the fourth Test at Melbourne when he was accused of losing control at crucial stages of the match, as lack of discipline allowed Australia's last pair, Doug Ring and Bill Johnston, to score the 38 runs needed for victory. Stollmeyer took over the captaincy for the final Test in Sydney, with the official reason for Goddard's absence being that he was unfit. Whatever the truth, Goddard retired from Test cricket after the tour to Australia.

He continued to represent Barbados and went as player-manager with a youthful team to New Zealand in 1956. After making an unbeaten 83 in the second Test at Christchurch, Goddard was recalled to the Test captaincy for Westindies tour to England in 1957, in keeping with the tradition of appointing a white amateur, with an upper-class background.

It proved an unwise choice, as the English took their revenge for their 1950 failure, subjecting Westindies to a 3-0 defeat. Goddard was unable to make an impression, apart from scoring an unbeaten 61 in three-and-three-quarter hours, in a match-saving stand of 174 with Collie Smith, in the third game at Trent Bridge. Overall, however, it was an unhappy return to Test cricket for Goddard, who seemed reluctant to bowl and ill at ease playing under the pressures of modern international competition.

A horse racing enthusiast, in later life, Goddard became an established breeder and owner in Barbados.

Goddard on the k against nd

Career details

Born: *24 April 1919*
Died: *27 August 1987*
Role: *Right-arm off spinner, left-hand batsman*
Club: *Barbados*
First-class record: *[1936-57] 146 wickets (26.33) and 3,769 runs (33.35) including 5 centuries*
Tests: *27*
Test debut: *v England 1948*
Test wickets: *33 (31.81); BB: 5-31 v England, Georgetown, 1948*
Test runs: *859 (30.67); HS: 83* v New Zealand, Christchurch, 1956*
Tours: *India 1948-49; England 1950; Australia and New Zealand 1951-52; New Zealand 1956; England 1957.*

John Goddard (left), calls correctly as the England captain, Norman Yardley, tosses before the start of the Lord's Test in 1950

Hilary Angelo "Larry" Gomes

"Larry" Gomes, a quiet, stylish left-hander, took a long time to establish himself in the Test team, often being overshadowed by the more flamboyant members of the side such as Viv Richards, Alvin Kallicharran and Clive Lloyd.

Gomes made his first-class debut for Trinidad & Tobago against New Zealand in 1972, three years after his brilliant, but erratic, elder brother, Sheldon. However, it was the less spectacular, more stable, Larry who was one of the key members of a weak Trinidadian batting side during the 1970s. Between 1973-75, Gomes was on the Middlesex staff and, although he was never quite able to establish himself as a regular first team member, it was probably his familiarity with English conditions that won him a place on the tour to England in 1976.

Fittingly, he made his Test debut at Lord's, but failed to command a regular place in the middle-order batting. Nonetheless, he scored prolifically against

Larry Gomes hits out during his 92 not out against England at Lord's in 1984.

the counties, hitting 1,393 runs, with five centuries, including 190 against Derbyshire. Ironically, however, Middlesex decided to release him in favour of Wayne Daniel in 1976.

The unassuming Gomes then spent two profitable years with Nelson in the Lancashire League. The left-hander hit nearly 1,100 runs in his first summer, surpassing Learie Constantine's record seasonal aggregate, and followed it with another 1,000 runs the next year.

But failure in the Tests saw the Trinidadian lose his place to Collis King and he had to wait two years, until the World Series contracted players withdrew from the Georgetown Test against Australia, for a second chance at the highest level. On his return to the Test match arena, having already made a hundred for Trinidad against the tourists, Gomes continued his assault by taking another century off the Australian bowlers. In the final match in Kingston, the left-hander showed his grit by scoring 115 out of a Westindies total of 280.

Gomes toured India in 1978-79, under Kallicharran, and got three fifties in the first two Tests at Bombay and Bangalore, and hit 91 out of a second innings score of 151 in the fourth match at Madras. He remembers: "That was the best innings I have ever played. It really was a fast pitch with plenty of grass and the scores were low. I just played shots and they came off."

His omission from the side to England in 1980 infuriated his supporters, but he was selected for the trip to Pakistan in 1980-81. Gomes finished second in the averages with 48.12 and staked his claim to a regular position in the side. Reward came when he was chosen for the series against England in the Caribbean later in 1981. He performed consistently, making fifty in the third Test at Bridgetown and a polished 90 in the fifth at Kingston.

Gomes underlined his advance by topping the batting averages in the subsequent three-match series against Australia, scoring centuries at Sydney and Adelaide, on the latter occasion helping Westindies to a five-wicket win to square the series. All this contrived to give him a tour average of 78.60, helped by an unbeaten double century against Queensland at Brisbane.

Gomes proved his worth again in 1983, this time against India, as he shared in a partnership of 237 with Lloyd in the second Test on his home ground at Port-of-Spain, after the first three wickets had fallen for one run.

Against England in the one-day series in 1984, prior to the Tests, Gomes was included as the fifth bowler and, although he made a useful contribution, there was some surprise when he was preferred to the more aggressive Richie Richardson for the first Test at Edgbaston.

It proved to be a sound decision as the thoughtful Gomes made 143, sharing in a partnership of 206 with Richards. In the next match at Lord's, Gomes put on 287 with Gordon Greenidge in a match-winning unbroken second-wicket stand, batting sensibly to give the Barbadian maestro as much of the strike as possible. And, in the third game at Headingley, the Trinidadian played a rearguard action after Westindies had collapsed from 201 for four to 206 for seven, helping Michael Holding in his hectic counter-attack, before finally reaching his own century.

Gomes developed a knack of rescuing Westindies when better known batsmen had failed. He excelled on the tour to Australia 1984-85, heading the batting averages with 64.42. He and Jeff Dujon both scored hundreds as they put on 146 for the sixth wicket in the first Test in Perth, after Lloyd and Richardson were both dismissed for ducks. In the third match at Adelaide, Gomes hit 60 in the first innings and was unbeaten on 120 in the second; before scoring a half century in his next innings in Melbourne to confirm his world-class ability. He thrived in Australia, scoring six Test hundreds there altogether, but was less prolific on his subsequent tours to Pakistan and New Zealand.

Gomes took longer than many players to realise his potential at Test level and was aided by unforeseen circumstances which affected the make-up of the Westindies team, such as the temporary loss of the World Series players and the permanent departure of those who went on the rebel tour to South Africa in 1983. But the personable left-hander took full advantage of his later opportunities to carve his own niche in the Test side and, with it, a reputation as an elegant and fluent batsman.

Career details

Born: *13 July 1953*
Role: *Left-hand batsman, right-arm medium pace bowler and off-spinner*
Clubs: *Trinidad, Middlesex, Lancashire League*
First-class record: *[1972-1987] 12,817 runs (40.94) including 32 centuries, and 107 wickets (39.20)*
Tests: *27*
Test debut: *v England 1976*
Test runs: *1,596 (42.00); HS: 126 v Australia, Sydney, 1982*
Tours: *England 1976; India 1978-79; England (World Cup) 1979; Pakistan 1980-81; Australia 1981-82; England (World Cup) 1983; India 1983; England 1984; Australia 1984-85; Pakisian 1986; New Zealand 1987.*

Gerald Ethridge Gomez

In 1939, Gerry Gomez made his Test debut against England, along with his school friend, Jeff Stollmeyer. The teenaged Gomez failed with the bat and it wasn't until 1948 that he bowled his first ball in Test cricket.

In 1946-47 Gomez and Stollmeyer, who had both been coached by the Australian, Arthur Richardson, failed by 11 runs to break the world record for a third wicket partnership, as they scored 434 for Trinidad against Guyana.

Gomez's experience showed during the following season in the first post-War Test, against England at Bridgetown, as he top-scored with 86 in the first innings. The Trinidadian was appointed captain for the second match at Port-of-Spain, when Stollmeyer pulled out through injury. He scored a solid 62 in the first innings and, after dismissing Billy Griffith, could have led his side to victory if it hadn't rained. John Goddard took over the captaincy for the Georgetown Test, and Gomez kept a low profile for the remainder of the series.

During the War and immediate post-War years, Gomez scored prolifically on his home territory in domestic cricket. The 1948-49 season was the only series in which he failed to make a hundred at Port-of-Spain. In successive matches in Trinidad between 1942-48, he made scores of 133 not out, 216 not out, 117, 58 and 108 not out, 190, 213 not out, 190, and finally 178 not out and 62 against England.

Selected for the 1948-49 tour to India, he immediately established his credentials in the opening Test in New Delhi, by scoring a hundred and sharing in a stand of 267 with Clyde Walcott, and then hit fifty in the fourth Test at Madras. On this tour Gomez's bowling came to the fore, and he emerged as a genuine all-rounder, finding himself opening the attack with Prior Jones. His movement through the air and off the pitch soon had the Indians in difficulties and, against the strong South Zone side at Madras, he took nine for 24: the first time a

A true all-rounder Gerry Gomez once acted as selector, umpire and radio commentator in on Test match

Westindian had taken nine wickets in a single innings of a first-class match. Altogeher on that trip he took 16 wickets (28.58) and scored 256 runs (36.57).

On the 1950 tour to England Gomez sometimes shared the new ball with Frank Worrell, although on that trip the bowling honours were monopolised by Sonny Ramadhin and Alf Valentine. Gomez also contributed with the bat during the famous 'calypso' Test at Lord's. He shared in a match-winning sixth wicket stand of 211 with Walcott, who thrashed his way to an unbeaten century, while Gomez defended stoutly for 70.

After their unprecedented 3-1 victory over England, Westindies confidently embarked on their tour to Australia the following year, only to face a 'barrage of bumpers' from Ray Lindwall and Keith Miller. During these trying times, Gomez showed outstanding courage to finish top of the batting averages, and shocked the Australians in the fifth Test at Sydney with his bowling, taking seven for 55 in their first innings to scuttle them out for 116.

C.L.R James wrote of Gomez's performances on that tour: "In Australia he surpassed himself. Alone among the Westindians who had been such successes in England in 1950, Gomez in match after match mastered the Australian bowling. In his own bowling, he was almost as successful. He increased his pace to fast-medium, moving the ball in the air, and in one innings took seven Australian wickets... Altogether, when one considers what odds he had to contend with, his all-round play in Australia was one of the most effective ever shown there by any visitor."

During that tour to Australia and New Zealand Gomez was at his peak, although he was selected for the home series against India in 1953 and England in 1954.

After his playing days were over, the capable all-rounder continued to serve Westindian cricket at the highest level, as a selector and as an active and capable administrator on the Board of Control. Indeed, on one memorable occasion, for the third Test between Westindies and Australia at Georgetown in 1965, Gomez was called upon to umpire, he after some disquiet over an earlier choice and transport difficulties with his replacement.

Although Gomez was a qualified umpire, he had never officiated in a first-class match before, but gave an admirable performance, including having the creases re-marked, as they had been incorrectly laid. All this after he had helped to select the Westindies side, and then had to make a hasty departure to summarise the day's play for radio!

Career details

Born: *10 October 1919*
Role: *Right-hand batsman, right-arm medium pace bowler*
Club: *Trinidad*
First-class record: *[1937-57] 6,794 runs (43.63) including 14 centuries, and 200 wickets (25.26)*
Tests: *29*
Test debut: *v England 1939*
Test runs: *1,243 (30.31); HS: 101 v India, New Delhi, 1948*
Test wickets: *58 (27.41); BB: 7-55 v Australia, Sydney, 1952*
Tours: *England 1939; India 1948-49; England 1950; Australia and New Zealand 1951-52; England 1957.*

George Copeland "Jackie" Grant

Having just left Cambridge University and being out of serious match practise, "Jackie" Grant was named as Westindies captain for their first tour to Australia in 1930-31. He was only 23 years old and remains the youngest man ever to lead Westindies. Indeed, he met his team mates for the first time when he joined them on the ship going to Australia at the Panama Canal.

Grant played cricket at Cambridge, taking part in the varsity matches at Lord's in 1929 and 1930 and was also an Association football blue, but he had no experience of captaincy. However, on the tour, Grant was one of the few players to enhance his reputation, hitting 124 runs without being dismissed in the first Test at Adelaide. This included his highest Test score of 71 not out, which helped him to head the batting averages with 42.50.

After the demoralising experience of losing the first four Tests, it was Grant's inspired and positive captaincy that secured the visitors a surprising win over the Sheffield Shield champions, New South Wales, and an even more surprising win in the fifth Test at Sydney.

Their success was all the more worthy when one realises that Australia fielded their strongest side in an attempt to complete a clean sweep of victories. There was widespread feeling in the Westindian camp that the pitches had been doctored to blunt their pace attack, but hundreds from Frank Martin and George Headley took Westindies to 350 for six, before Grant declared the innings closed, after overnight rain had affected the wicket.

Herman Griffith and George Francis bowled out Australia for 224 and, by the end of the third day, Westindies had a buffer of 250 runs. Rain washed out the fourth day's play, prompting Grant to make his second adventurous declaration of the match in bright sunshine on the fifth morning. Grant placed complete faith in his revitalised bowling duo of Francis and Griffith, who swept the visitors to victory

by 30 runs.

On his Test debut at Lord's in 1933, Grant top-scored in a Westindian first innings ravaged by the all-rounder, Walter Robins, and despite playing well in the second innings, it was not enough to stave off defeat. Apart from the first Test Grant had little personal batting success in the international matches, although he scored almost 2,000 first-class runs on the tour, including 115 against an England X1 at Folkestone, when he added 226 with Headley for the third wicket.

The 1934 *Wisden* was impressed with Grant's handling of his side, remarking: "In Grant, they were very fortunate to have not only a clever, but an enthusiastic captain. Astute in the management of his bowling and the placing of his field, he inspired the whole team by his own admirable example for very few men in England last summer fielded so brilliantly close to the wicket as he did…Grant played the game, and insisted on those under him doing so, in the most sporting spirit."

Grant was retained as captain for the whole series against MCC in 1935, in preference to the territorial fluidity which had existed in Westindies' leadership when England visited the Caribbean five years earlier.

On another rain-affected wicket in the first Test at Bridgetown, more enterprising captaincy from Grant nearly brought off another spectacular win, similar to that in Australia four years earlier. This time, however, the pitch was virtually unplayable and even imaginative captaincy could not overcome its awkwardness. Westindies had first strike and managed only 102, after which England stumbled to 81 for five. When, on the final day, another two wickets went down without addition to the overnight score, making it 81 for seven, Bob Wyatt, the England captain, declared the innings closed 21 runs behind to try and avoid the worst of the pitch.

Wyatt's sudden declaration prompted Grant to reverse his batting order in an effort to save his best batsmen until the pitch mellowed. The ploy might have worked had not another downpour delayed the start until after tea on the fourth day, allowing the English fast bowling giant, Jim Smith, to exploit the hazardous conditions by removing three batsmen with the score on four, before Cyril Christiani and Leslie Hylton steadied the innings, as the home side limped to 33 for three at the close.

Another deluge during the night and another delayed start, along with the subsequent removal of Headley for a duck, confirmed that the pitch was

getting worse. This induced Grant to chance his arm again as he declared on 51 for six at tea, with a miniscule lead of 72, even though Clifford Roach was not out at the wicket and there were still four frontline batsmen in the pavilion.

Wyatt imitated Grant by sending his fast bowlers in

Jackie Grant captained Westindies on their first overseas tour, to Australia in 1930-31. Here, he is seen with his tour party.
Standing: (l-r) George Headley, Clifford Roach, Errol Hunte, Frank de Caires, Tommy Scott, O.S. Wight, Ivan Barrow, Edwin St. Hill.
Sitting: (l-r) Herman Griffith, Learie Constantine, Joe Seheult (Asst. Manager), Jackie Grant (Capt.), R. H. Mallett (Manager), Lionel Birkett (Vice-Capt.), Frank Martin, Edward Bartlett, George Francis.
Sitting (at the front): Derek Sealy

first but, when the fiery Manny Martindale removed five English batsmen, it seemed that Westindies might repeat their dramatic performance in Sydney four years previously. But, with Martindale lacking any consistent support and Wally Hammond hitting a priceless 29 runs, after being held back until the last minute, England were the victors by four wickets in this remarkable cricket lottery.

In the deciding Test at Kingston, the home side rallied, thanks to a magnificent double century from Headley and a decisive spell of bowling by Martindale, which settled the series in Westindies' favour.

The irony of Grant's success was that he was called up from Cambridge University to lead Westindies in Australia without any previous experience of captaincy, not to mention sparse knowledge of the players he was to lead. Yet the gamble on Grant paid off in much the same way that Grant's own gambles as skipper invariably reaped rich rewards. The affluent Trinidadian became the first Westindian to hold on to the captaincy for more than one series.

The continuity in the leadership settled the team and was reflected in their results, as Grant became the first captain to lead Westindies to victory in a Test rubber, against England in 1935. Their success in the last match at Kingston not only clinched the series, but was also the first occasion that Westindies had scored over 500 runs in a Test (535 for seven declared) and the first time that they had won by an innings. It was unfortunate that Grant injured his ankle while fielding, and was not therefore able to share in the jubilation on the field as his team posted their victory in what was his last Test.

After Grant's retirement from the game his younger brother, Rolph, succeeded to the captaincy. The elder Grant is best remembered for his bold leadership demonstrated by his two declarations at Sydney, when others might have opted for the safety of a draw. Grant showed a stronger faith in his team than any previous Westindies captain, and laid the tentative groundwork in team morale which Frank Worrell, a generation later, would use as a vital ingredient in his success on the field.

At the early age of 28, having established himself as a major force in contemporary cricket, Grant decided to retire at his peak, and leave his family's flourishing business to take up missionary work in Africa. Grant worked in Zimbabwe (then Rhodesia) until 1976 when he was forced to leave because of government pressure, and died in England two years later.

Career details

Born: *9 May 1907*
Died: *26 October 1978*
Role: *Right-hand batsman*
Clubs: *Cambridge University, Trinidad, Rhodesia*
First-class record: *[1928-35] 3,831 runs (32.19) including 4 centuries, and 19 wickets (51.00)*
Tests: *12*
Test debut: *v Australia 1930*
Test runs: *413 (25.81); HS: 71* v Australia, Adelaide, 1930*
Tours: *Australia 1930-31; England 1933.*

Rolph Stewart Grant

Rolph Grant was the younger brother of Jackie, whom he succeeded as Westindies' captain. A tall, attractive player, the younger Grant enjoyed a remarkable all-round sporting career. He won blues at Cambridge for cricket and Association football, and a half-blue for boxing. His phenomenal athletic range allowed him to become England's amateur goal-keeper and Trinidad's heavyweight boxing champion.

On the cricket field, besides being a capable batsman and off-spinner, Grant was an outstanding fieldsman in any position and he and Learie Constantine lifted the standard of the entire team.

Grant's catching and bowling helped the home side to level the series against England in the second game at Port-of-Spain in 1935; while his best Test innings came in the fourth match at Kingston, when he hit 77, and shared in a record seventh wicket partnership of 147 with George Headley, as Westindies clinched their first-ever Test rubber.

Grant captained Westindies on their tour of England in 1939, and demonstrated his accommodating approach by opening the batting with the teenaged Jeff Stollmeyer, in an attempt to stabilize a vulnerable position for the visitors.

He enjoyed most success with the bat in the second Test at Old Trafford, when he scored nearly a third of Westindies' second innings total of 133, after England had declared on a deteriorating wicket. He played a captain's innings of 47 runs in 38 minutes, including three sixes off Tom Goddard, as 56 were scored while he was at the wicket. Grant's performance ensured his side a draw and kept the series alive.

The Second World War cut short what might otherwise have been a prolific career, and the younger Grant was never given the opportunity to emulate the feats of his brother as captain.

Career details

Born: *15 December 1909*
Died: *18 October 1977*
Role: *Right-hand batsman, off-spinner*
Clubs: *Cambridge University, Trinidad*
First-class record: *[1932-39] 1,883 runs (28.53) including 1 century, and 79 wickets (25.17)*
Tests: *7*
Test debut: *v England 1935*
Test runs: *220 (22.00); HS: 77 v England, Kingston, 1935*
Test wickets: *11 (32.09)*
Tour: *England 1939*

Anthony Hollis Gray

Alan Cozzi

At 6ft 6in tall and weighing 15 stone, Trinidadian Tony Gray seems tailor-made to take over Joel Garner's bowling mantle, now that the Barbadian has retired from Test cricket. After a successful domestic season in 1985, where his 23 wickets helped Trinidad & Tobago to win the Shell Shield, Gray was invited to Surrey as an emergency replacement for the injured Sylvester Clarke. He proceeded to top their bowling averages by taking 79 wickets at 22.98 apiece, before being catapulted into the Westindies team for their tours of Sharjah and Pakistan, to round off a successful, if hectic, year for the youngster.

Gray's early penchant for cricket was more the product of his own natural ability than any formal coaching. His father introduced him to the basics of the game but, as an able footballer himself, it seemed that the young Gray might opt for soccer instead. "I was goal-keeper for my school", he says, wistfully. But, at the age of 18, Gray won a scholarship to a different type of school: the Alf Gover Cricket School, thanks to the sponsorship of the Trinidad Cricket Board and Textel.

Before long the Board's investment in their first promising fast bowler since Prior Jones began to pay rich dividends as he made his first-class debut for North against South in 1984 and, later the same season, made his Shield debut against Barbados. Gray took seven wickets that year, as a prelude to his outstanding season in 1985, which included his best Shield bowling figures of six for 78 against Jamaica in Kingston.

His arrival at The Oval in May, saw his hunger for wickets continue unabated. He took more than five wickets in an innings six times, including eight for 40 against Yorkshire at Sheffield, which featured the only hat-trick of his career. Gray recalls: "It was a marvellous feeling to take that many wickets in one innings; I put 120 per cent effort into my hat-trick ball to dismiss Ian Swallow." Even so, the unassuming Trinidadian regrets that Geoffrey Boycott was not among his victims!

The gangling Gray had his path to Surrey

smoothed by Geoff Howarth, the New Zealand captain and Surrey stalwart. The paceman says: "I played well in a Shell Shield Award under-23 X1 and then for the President's X1 against New Zealand in 1985, when Geoff was the captain, and, after Sylvester Clarke sustained his back injury, he recommended me to Surrey."

Ironically, the inclusion of Gray in the side kept Howarth, their other overseas signing, out of the

Tony Gray

team as the young fast bowler went from strength to strength. Indeed, it was largely due to Gray that Surrey finished sixth in the county championship in 1985, after the early blow to morale with the loss of Clarke for the whole season, which heralded a succession of injuries to other players in the side.

His success in the championship and the Shield made it only a matter of time before Gray was elevated to the Westindies side and the illustrious bowling company of Michael Holding, Joel Garner and Malcolm Marshall. The Trinidadian says: "I enjoy bowling with them all, but I get particular inspiration from bowling with Malcolm: he whips up my enthusiasm because the pressure is always on the batsman and that tends to make things happen."

His inclusion in the Test side came for the tour to Pakistan in October 1986, after Garner and Holding had decided to opt out. It was a successful trip for Gray, who took 14 wickets at 16.21, including his best Test figures of four for 39 in the first match at Faisalabad, to finish second in the averages behind Marshall. He followed this up with a splendid display in the three-match series against New Zealand in 1987, collecting eight wickets at 18.75 apiece, and again finished second in the averages, this time to Garner. (His progress was halted temporarily when he broke his hand practising during the World Cup later that year.)

But there was a time when Gray might not have been striving to emulate Marshall and Garner at all. He says: "I used to be a wicket-keeper but, because I was getting so tall, my father suggested that I take up fast bowling. When I was about 15, I frightened a few guys and it gave me a real thrill to see those stumps flying."

To meet the demands of cricket in the 1980s, Gray keeps fit by running and working-out in the gym. "I like to swim, as well," he says, "especially at home in Trinidad." He also enjoys the tranquility of beaches and going for walks in parks. Gray says: "I'm a naturalist: I like the peace and quiet of the countryside and taking in the fresh air."

Indicative of his mature and generous personality is his desire to set up youth coaching programmes in Trinidad. He says: "I think that we have a lot of latent talent in Trinidad, and it is important that it is guided in the right way. After all, the youth are the future."

And, it would appear that the youthful and level-headed Gray, with continued application and fitness, has a glowing future to look forward to himself.

Career details

Born: *23 May 1963*
Role: *Right-arm fast bowler*
Clubs: *Trinidad & Tobago, Surrey*
First-class record: *[1984-] 286 wickets (20.49) and 617 runs (13.41)*
Tests: 5
Test debut: *v Pakistan 1986*
Test wickets: *22 (17.13); BB: 4-39 v Pakistan, Faisalabad, 1986*
Tours: *Pakistan 1986; New Zealand 1987; India and Pakistan (World Cup) 1987.*

Cuthbert Gordon Greenidge

Gordon Greenidge spent his formative cricketing years in England, yet still bats with the flamboyant brilliance associated with Westindians. A strong man, who hits the ball incredibly hard, Greenidge is merciless on anything on a poor line or length as he drives the ball between cover and mid-wicket. The power of his shots – he has a peerless hook and square-cut – together with his superb footwork and impeccable temperament have combined to make him one of the most accomplished of contemporary batsmen.

Greenidge was born at Black Bess, St. Peter, and brought up by his grandmother after his mother left to work in England. He joined his mother at the age of 14 and the family settled in Reading, where he played cricket and was soon selected for the South of England's school-boys' team.

The Barbdian came to the attention of Ray Robinson, the Wantage chairman, in a school match in Reading and then impressed the Hampshire coach, Arthur Holt, while playing for the Berkshire Bantams. Knowing that Warwickshire were also interested in him, Holt quickly arranged for the young right-hander to have a trial at the county ground. Indeed, John Arlott was apparently so moved by his ability that he paid his £4 fare to the ground.

Greenidge was taken onto the ground staff and made his Second X1 debut in 1967, the same season as he made 95 in 55 minutes playing for Holt's Colts against the Hampshire Hoggets. This performance earned him a two-year contract, but his impetuous approach to his batting and his apathetic attitude to fielding which, by his own admission, he did not enjoy, nearly meant that his contract wasn't renewed.

In the winter of 1969-70 Greenidge resolved to commit himself to a career in cricket, and tuned up for the coming season by road-running (he was once stopped by a police car and asked why he was running around the streets of Southampton with such zest at midnight!) and visiting the gym regularly.

In August 1970 Greenidge opened the batting with the South African, Barry Richards. Their first five opening partnerships realised stands of 40, 88, 201, 57 and 43, and so began one of the finest post-war opening partnerships and certainly the best one confined to domestic competition.

The Barbadian learned much from batting with Richards, including the philosophy of going on the attack from the start of his innings. In 1974 Greenidge matched the Springbok stroke for stroke, as he scored 273 runs in just over four hours, with 13 sixes and 31 fours, for Derrick Robins' X1 against Pakistan at Eastbourne. Afterwards Richards remarked that his

Gordon Greenidg square-cuts durin his 85 not out aga England at The C in 1976

partner's performance was "probably as near to a perfect innings as I have ever seen – every bad ball was hit to the boundary."

His penchant for hitting sixes soon became one of his hallmarks: he has hit 13 on two occasions in a first-class innings. Greenidge said: "To me, hitting sixes is the easiest thing in the world. I would not know how to hit the ball any other way and I have always felt that if other people put their mind to it, they too could hit more sixes. You do not have to be massively strong...and it's a quick way to make runs." Greenidge seems to have patented a shot that often brings him six runs: the one where he pulls the ball between mid-wicket and square-leg, balanced on his right leg, with his left one in the air.

Towards the end of 1972 Greenidge was invited to play for Barbados in the Shell Shield and made his Test debut against India in 1974, as Roy Fredericks' latest opening partner. In the first Test at Bangalore Greenidge was run out seven short of a century in his first Test innings. But he made early amends in his second, hitting 107, to give him a match aggregate of 200, as he joined the illustrious band of players who have made a century on their Test debut.

The following tour to Australia in 1975-76 was a disaster for Greenidge and the team as a whole. He began with a pair in the first Test at Brisbane and was dropped, failing to reach double figures in any of the four Test innings he played. When India visited the Westindies in 1976, Greenidge was troubled by the Caribbean glare, and his most significant role in the series was when he appeared as 12th man at Bridgetown. But he came of age as an international batsman on the tour to England later that year.

The Barbadian was perhaps fortunate to be picked in front of the illustrious Lawrence Rowe, but he soon confirmed his standing by hitting a splendid 84 in the second Test at Lord's. He then performed at his majestic best, scoring 134 runs out of 211 in poor batting conditions in the first innings of the third Test at Old Trafford. Greenidge followed this up with another century in the second innings, to become the second Westindian batsman after George Headley to score a hundred in each innings of a Test in England. Altogether, his match aggregate was 38 more than the whole England team.

In the next match at Headingley Greenidge and Fredericks put on 192 runs for the first wicket, with 147 coming off 27 overs before lunch. The Barbadian hit 115, including two sixes and 14 fours, in the first innings, as he became only the third player to score three successive centuries in Tests against England. He ended the series with a duck and an unbeaten 85 in the final Test at The Oval, putting on an undefeated 182 with Fredericks in 32 overs in the second innings.

Greenidge finished the tour with nearly 2,000 first-class runs to his name including 123 out of a total of 222 against Middlesex, 130 off Glamorgan and a century in 69 minutes off Nottinghamshire.

Against Pakistan in 1977 Greenidge excelled on his native soil for the first time at Test level, paving the way for Westindies' victory with 70 in the second Test at Port-of-Spain. He hit a more attacking 91 in the first innings of the third game at Georgetown, and followed this up with 96 before he was out to the last delivery of the match.

The fifth Test at Kingston was the decider and the right-hander scored a hundred in the face of fine bowling from Imran Khan, sharing in a first wicket stand of 182 with Fredericks, who was playing his last Test. Pakistan were overwhelmed by 140 runs, as Greenidge totalled 500 runs for the second consecutive series. The best feature of the pairing between Fredericks and Greenidge was that, in their own way, each was as brilliant as the other and no-one had to play second fiddle.

Before he signed for World Series Cricket, Greenidge and his new partner, Desmond Haynes, had time to share one century stand against the touring Australians in the second Test at Bridgetown in 1978. After that, the Barbadians were out of official Test cricket for one-and-a-half series.

Back in the official fold for the World Cup in 1979, Greenidge played well in the preliminary rounds of the competition, although he was dismissed early in the final.

He had a disappointing tour to Australia later that year, being hampered by a knee injury (although he is often at his most savage when disabled) but hit 80 and 98 not out against England in the finals of the one-day triangular tournament. He perked up in

New Zealand averaging 45.66, including two nineties in the second Test at Christchurch.

When England visited the Westindies in 1981, Greenidge and Haynes greeted them with their customary century partnership, before Greenidge went on to collect further fifties at St. John's and Kingston.

Greenidge and Haynes have formed the longest and most successful opening partnership in the history of Westindies Test cricket, which has been a key factor in the team's remarkable success in recent years. They complement each other splendidly, with Greenidge being the more serious and introverted of the two; while their understanding between the wickets is exemplified by their record partnership against all countries, when they added 296 against India in the fifth Test at St. John's in 1983. It was Greenidge's fiftieth first-class century but, sadly, he had to finish his innings on 154 to join his daughter who was fatally ill. In the return series, Greenidge hit his then highest score of 194, in the first Test at Kanpur.

Against Australia in the first Test at Georgetown in 1984, Greenidge and Haynes shared in an unbeaten opening stand of 250, with Greenidge making 120. The openers added 132 in front of their home crowd in the third Test at Bridgetown, before Greenidge scored the only century of the match in the fifth game at Kingston, as the pair put on 162 and the visitors were trounced by 10 wickets.

In spite of his outstanding success, after an indifferent start to the tour of England in 1984 and his failure in the first innings of the second Test at Lord's, Greenidge was under pressure. On the fifth day, Greenidge and Haynes went out with Westindies needing 342 runs to win. It seemed an unlikely target, especially after Haynes was run out. But Greenidge found a steady partner in the unassuming Larry Gomes, who gave the Barbadian as much of the strike as possible. The opener romped to an unbeaten double century, as the pair shared in an unbroken stand of 287. In the end the target became a canter, as Greenidge's 214 came off 242 balls, with two sixes and 29 fours.

In the fourth Test at Old Trafford, Greenidge found himself battling against rain and bad light, as well as

the English bowling attack. But he defended his wicket stoutly, sharing in partnerships of 197 and 170 for the fifth and sixth wickets with Jeff Dujon and Winston Davis. The Barbadian eventually fell for 223 after batting for 10 hours, as he rescued his side and finished the series with an average far in front of any of his team-mates.

Greenidge has always thrived in English conditions and in 1986 he topped the national averages with 2,035 runs at 67.85, including four consecutive centuries.

Over the years Greenidge has been a loyal servant of Hampshire, and it was the county's good fortune that they were able to enjoy the fruits of an illustrious opening partnership between Barry Richards and the Barbadian, which would have been at home in any Test side in any era. Greenidge hit 259 runs for Hampshire against Sussex in 1975, including 13 sixes – a record for the county championship – and 136 and 120 (in 91 minutes) against Kent in 1978.

At one time Greenidge was the remarkable owner of the highest individual score in each of the three English limited-overs tournaments: 177 in a 60 over Gillette Cup match against Glamorgan in 1975, 173 not out in 55 overs in a Benson & Hedges Cup match against the Minor Counties South in 1973 and 163 not out in 40 overs in the John Player League in 1979, an innings which included 10 sixes. He was awarded a benefit by Hampshire in 1983.

Greenidge took over as captain of Barbados in 1982-83, in the wake of the defection of many of the island's leading players to South Africa. He celebrated his promotion in typical style by hitting 237, his highest score in the Westindies, against the touring Indians.

Australia remains the only country where the Barbadian has struggled. He came within five runs of his first Test century in that country in the third match at Adelaide in 1984. Back in the Westindies he found his form again making a hundred in the first Test against New Zealand at Port-of-Spain in 1985, adding 185 for the third wicket with Richie Richardson.

Greenidge had a quieter tour to Pakistan at the end of 1986; but enjoyed a prolific series in New Zealand in 1987, as he scored more than twice as many runs as anyone else to head the batting averages. In the second Test at Auckland, the Barbadian hit a masterful double century – an eventful innings which included three missed chances, seven sixes and 20 fours – as he laid the platform for a decisive victory by the tourists. He then returned to the Westindies, and hit a masterful double century for Barbados against Trinidad & Tobago in his mandatory Shield appearance.

Greenidge's prolific run scoring has already secured his name indelibly in the annals of cricket history but, perhaps, what makes his contribution even more phenomenal, is the way that he has forged several invincible opening partnerships, notably with Fredericks and Haynes for Westindies and with Richards for Hampshire.

One of the outstanding cricketers of his generation, Greenidge is married to Anita, who is the cousin of the Westindian fast bowler, Andy Roberts. The illustrious opener was awarded an MBE in 1985.

Career details

Born: *1 May 1951*
Role: *Right-hand batsman*
Clubs: *Hampshire, Barbados*
First-class record: *[1970-] 32,799 runs (46.00) including 78 centuries, and 17 wickets (27.52)*
Tests: *77*
Test runs: *5,509 (48.32); HS: 223 v England, Old Trafford, 1984*
Tours: *India and Pakistan (missed Pakistan leg through injury) 1974-75; England (World Cup) 1975; Australia 1975-76; England 1976; England (World Cup) 1979; Australia and New Zealand 1970-80; England 1980; Pakistan 1980-81; Australia 1981-82; England (World Cup) 1983; India 1983; England 1984; Australia 1984-85; Pakistan 1986; New Zealand 1987.*

Charles Christopher Griffith

Charlie Griffith was one of the most feared fast bowlers of all time, but like his partner and friend, Wes Hall, he did not begin his career as a pace bowler. He played for his club as a right-arm spinner when, one Saturday, he was invited to take the new ball. He promptly snapped up seven wickets for one run and quickly became one of the most talked of bowlers in Barbados.

Griffith made his debut for Barbados against MCC in 1959-60, at the age of 21, and during that match accounted for some of England's most illustrious post-War batsmen. However, after playing in the final Test of the home series against England, he was left out of the side to Australia in 1960-61.

When India visited the Caribbean in 1962 the big fast bowler then endured the sickening experience of felling a batsman, as the touring captain, Nariman Contractor, ducked into a bouncer from Griffith in the visitors' game against Barbados. Contractor suffered a fractured skull, and only a substantial blood transfusion saved his life. In that game, the unfortunate Griffith was also no-balled for "throwing", and despite being exonerated by yards of film of his action, the accusation that he was a "chucker" marred the rest of his career.

When Griffith was selected for the tour of England in 1963, his partner, Hall, had already established himself in international circles, but it was the former who was the overwhelming success of the summer. Griffith captured 32 wickets in the Tests (16.21) and finished the tour with a tally of 119 (12.83) as he headed the bowling averages, and lived up to the enthusiastic publicity accorded to him and Hall during the warm-up weeks of the tour.

Griffith fondly recalls his relationship with Hall, which is as strong as ever today. He says: "We were like brothers, we roomed together and spent a lot of time discussing how to get different batsmen out. We learned by asking questions. Everton Weekes was my captain in Barbados and he was also a tremendous source of strength to me."

In the second Test at Lord's, coming in from the unfavoured Nursery End, Griffith helped Westindies to a slender first innings lead as he captured five wickets for 91. In the second innings Brian Close went on the attack against the Westindian pace bowlers, and nearly brought off an unlikely win for the home side, before Griffith induced him to snick a catch behind down the leg-side.

Westindies were beaten by Yorkshire at Headingley, but Griffith had been paying close attention to Fred Trueman's action, remarking: "...what especially struck me about Freddie was the way in which he used the crease and how he controlled his speed. He used to come in close to the stumps to bowl the out-swinger and he had these subtle variations of pace that troubled all of us."

The Barbadian paceman had clearly picked up some valuable tips as, in the fourth Test on the same ground, he was at his supreme best. He took six for 36 in England's first innings to give Westindies an unassailable lead in the series. It was during this game, however, that his action was publicly queried for the first time, although many, including Norman Yardley and Keith Miller, jumped to his defence.

Griffith had also been "called" in a county match which prompted several unpleasant letters and further Press comment, and deeply hurt the player himself. Yet, Griffith always gave his best on the field and, in the fifth and final Test at The Oval, he completed a splendid series by capturing six first innings wickets for 71 as the visitors won the series in style.

The 6ft 2in Barbadian firebrand was a superb athlete who bowled off a 20 yard run, with a full-frontal action; batsmen were often so wary of his savage bouncer that they fell victim to his equally lethal yorker, as he could bowl both deliveries with no appreciable difference in his action.

Even though he was not the central figure in the defeat of the Australians when they visited the Caribbean in 1965, taking 15 wickets at 32.00 apiece, Griffith was again attacked as a "chucker" – an accusation which seemed to affect his performance.

In the second Test at Port-of-Spain, Griffith removed Bill Lawry and Bobby Simpson, the

Australian captain, and brought about Norman O'Neill's second retirement in the series, after striking him with a bouncer; but Westindies failed to capitalise on Griffith's early work and the match was drawn. In the fourth game at Bridgetown, Griffith hit his highest Test score of 54, and rallied with the ball in the final match at Port-of-Spain, taking six for 46.

By the time of Westindies' 1966 tour to England both Griffith and Hall had lost some of their zest. Yet when Griffith was called for throwing in the match against Lancashire at Old Trafford, the unhappy saga renewed as Griffith was condemned as the "big bad boy of cricket". The criticism made the fast bowler brood and he achieved little in the series. By the third Test at Trent Bridge, he had dropped down to become the first-change bowler, but bounced back in the closing stages of the game to take four for 34, his best figures of the series.

Gary Sobers, perhaps, summed up Griffith's situation most aptly when he said in *King Cricket:* "I don't think any cricketer has been pushed so deep in to the freeze since Harold Larwood invented bodyline bowling...These suggestions came at him sideways, like so many angry crabs, never straight so that he could face up to them."

Griffith seemed to enjoy a new lease of life in the next series against India in 1966-67. In the first innings of the first Test at Bombay he and Hall reduced the home side to 14 for three on a docile pitch, before Lance Gibbs eventually spun the visitors to victory. In the third Test at Madras, Griffith took four for 61 in India's second innings, before sharing in an unbroken partnership with Sobers, as the paceman enjoyed unusual success with the bat. Griffith made 40 not out to help the tourists to a draw, after Westindies had slumped to 193 for seven with an hour-and-a-half remaining, chasing 322 to win.

Earlier in the tour, in the second Test at Calcutta, the game had been stopped because of rioting, and the Westindies team had to improvise their passage back to their hotel, with most of them returning by car. But Clive Lloyd remembers Griffith's unconventional route home as he "somehow ran all the way from the ground to the hotel through what must have seemed unfamiliar streets, a distance of almost three miles."

After the trip to the subcontinent, it was clear that the magnificent bowling partnership of Griffith and Hall was coming to an end. Nonetheless, their prestige and reputation carried them through another two series: against England in 1968 and against Australia and New Zealand later that year.

In the drawn first Test against England at Port-of-Spain, Griffith took five for 69 in the visitors' only innings, but a muscle injury restricted him to three overs in the fourth match at Port-of-Spain and ruled him out of the last game at Georgetown altogether. The tired fast bowling duo of Griffith and Hall took only 19 wickets in that series against England compared to 48 in 1963, and they finally exhausted themselves on the subsequent tour of Australia and New Zealand, when they were rarely fit together.

Yet Griffith and Hall are acknowledged as one of the greatest fast bowling partnerships ever, and they attracted a huge turnout when they appeared together in a match at The Oval in 1982; while Griffith's personal popularity was emphasised by the large number of spectators who went to Blackheath to watch the Barbadian bowling for Desmond Haynes' Cavaliers on the day that Westindies completed their 5-0 trouncing of England in 1984.

After his retirement from first-class cricket, Griffith became a national coach. In 1973 he joined a timber company where he now works as sales manager. He says of his job: "It was a change and I like change. Many people think once you are a cricketer you cannot do anything else, but it is easy to make a meaningful contribution to society in a different sphere."

Still an active cricketer and a regular face at over-40 matches, Griffith also has a keen interest in horses and spends many hours watching them at the Garrison.

Career details

Born: *14 December 1938*
Role: *Right-arm fast bowler*
Clubs: *Barbados, Lancashire League*
First-class record: *[1959-69] 332 wickets (21.60) and 1,502 runs (17.26)*
Tests: *28*
Test debut: *v England 1960*
Test wickets: *94 (28.54); BB: 6-36 v England, Headingley, 1963*
Test runs: *530 (16.56); HS: 54 v Australia, Bridgetown, 1965*
Tours: *England 1963; England 1966; India 1966-67; Australia and New Zealand 1968-69.*

Herman Clarence Griffith

As one of the first in a long line of distinguished Barbadian fast bowlers, it seemed inevitable that Herman Griffith, after his devastasting exploits in the Caribbean, exemplified by his seven for 38 against Trinidad in the 1921-22 inter-territorial series, would be selected for Westindies' tour to England in 1923. But he failed to make the trip: there was talk that his explosive fast bowling was sometimes reflected in his behaviour, as he barracked people on the field and acquired a reputation of being difficult to handle.

Yet Griffith was instrumental in the only defeat of the Hon F.S.G. Calthorpe's touring MCC side in 1925-26. With fellow opening fast bowler, George Francis, they took nine wickets each as Barbados romped to victory by 73 runs. After this performance it seemed unlikely that he would be omitted from the touring side to England in 1928, when Test match status was finally granted.

Duly selected as a first-change bowler, as if to make up for his earlier absence, he finished second in the averages to Learie Constantine. In the third and final Test at The Oval, he took six for 103. In an hour of extremely hostile bowling with the second new ball, he dismissed four batsmen as the home side added just 44. Unfortunately for Westindies, when Griffith tired, no one else seemed able to maintain his momentum and the tourists' advantage evaporated.

The Barbadian was similarly frustrated in the second match against England at Port-of-Spain in 1930, when, after taking five for 63 in the first innings, and dismissing Andy Sandham and Greville Stevens in the second, no one capitalised on his efforts as Westindies slid to defeat. Ironically, Griffith did not play in the third Test at Georgetown, where the elusive first victory finally came.

By the time Westindies embarked on their first tour to Australia in 1930-31, the stocky Griffith, whose confidence bordered on arrogance, was approaching 40. Even so, he still managed to dismiss Don Bradman for his first duck in Test cricket in the fifth

man Griffith es the ball. Karl es is the wicket- er and Ernest lesley the man.

game at Sydney. In the second innings he took four for fifty to help Westindies to their first win over Australia.

Constantine recalled Bradman's famous dismissal at Sydney in his book *Cricket and I*, after Griffith had bowled him a maiden: "...Then Griffith resumed to Bradman, who was averaging 89 in the series. Another leg-side delivery was allowed past, as was a widish off-side ball, before a straight ball impelled the batsman to come out, swing with an almighty cross-bat swipe, to be bowled neck and crop."

Sweet revenge for Griffith, who suffered at the hands of Bradman during his double century in the third match at Brisbane. Indeed, having dismissed "The Don" for four in an earlier Test, Griffith delighted in referring to the great batsman as "his rabbit".

Griffith made his last tour to England in 1933. However, with age creeping up on him, he finally made way for his younger prodigy, Manny Martindale. The penalty of being a pioneer of Westindian cricket was that, like many of his colleagues, the early part of Griffith's career was not spent in Test cricket. Inevitably, therefore, his Test record is not as impressive as one would expect from a bowler of his calibre, who cleverly varied his pace and maintained a good line and length during a first-class career spanning 13 years.

Career details

Born: *1 December 1893*
Died: *18 March 1980*
Role: *Right-arm fast bowler*
Club: *Barbados*
First-class record: *[1922-1935] 256 wickets (28.49) and 1,214 runs (15.17)*
Tests: *13*
Tests debut: *v England 1928*
Test wickets: *44 (28.25); BB: 6-103 v England, The Oval, 1928*
Test runs: *91 (5.05)*
Tours: *England 1928; Australia 1930-31; England 1933.*

Wesley Winfield Hall

It is ironic that Wes Hall, one of the greatest fast bowlers of all time, should have come into bowling by accident. Like all youngsters, Hall played cricket at his school, Combermere, which Frank Worrell and Clyde Walcott had attended before him, but, by the age of 18, he had still not bowled a ball in competition. When he left school the young Barbadian played as an opening batsman and wicket-keeper for his office side, Cable & Wireless.

His 6ft 2in frame and muscular build put paid to his aspirations of becoming a jockey and despite being thrown from a horse at Garrison Savannah, which resulted in two broken ankles and left him flat-footed, his love of horses was undiminished. It must have been of some consolation to Hall that, if he had all the ingredients of a natural fast bowler, then at least his son was of a more suitable stature to become one of Bridgetown's most popular riders.

Hall's rise to fast bowling fame was rapid, if not quite meteoric. One Saturday afternoon he was invited to open Cable's attack against Wanderers, after the regular opener had failed to appear. In his typically obliging manner Hall took the ball and six wickets, to herald the start of a spectacular career.

Still in his teens, Hall was the surprise choice for the tour to England in 1957. Without a first-class wicket to his name, the selectors gambled on him being a success, as he was picked on much the same basis as George Francis had been for the tour to England in 1923. Initially, the gamble seemed to have failed, as the youngster's enthusiasm could not make up for the problems he was having with his run-up and his line and length. On a dismal trip, which saw Westindies trounced 3-0, Hall failed to make his Test debut, even when the tourists had several injuries to contend with.

After this indifferent start, Hall was cast aside for the subsequent home series against Pakistan and overlooked for the trip to the Indian subcontinent in 1958-59. His international career seemed to have reached an early impasse, but it was given an unexpected lift thanks to the withdrawal of Worrell from the squad, and the selection of Hall as the late replacement and deputy for Jaswick Taylor.

The trip to India and Pakistan marked the unfolding of Hall's magnificent career, as his speed surprised his team-mates and probably Hall himself. He bowled with such ferocity in the game against Baroda state, the domestic champions, that he replaced Taylor as Roy Gilchrist's regular opening partner. Gilchrist was deadly in short bursts, but Hall seemed to possess unlimited stamina even under blistering sun.

Hall's second overseas trip, to India and Pakistan, was as successful as his earlier one to England had been dismal. During the series he took a fifth of all his Test wickets, collecting 46 at an average of 17.76 in eight Tests and 87 (15.08) on the whole tour.

In the first Test at Bombay, Hall had Nariman Contractor caught for duck and then took another two wickets with the score on 37, before Gilchrist completed the damage with four for 39. Hall dominated the second Test at Kanpur as he bagged 11 wickets for 126, to set up Westindies' victory by 203 runs.

By the third Test at Calcutta, the Indians' overwhelming priority was to survive and, after the visitors had romped to 614 for five declared, their innings succumbed to Hall and Gilchrist. Following on 490 behind, the duo scythed through the side again, as the Indians collapsed to an innings defeat. Indeed, the home side seemed relieved to return to the safety of their dressing room.

By the Pakistan leg of the trip Hall was irrepressible. In the second Test at Dacca, his movement through the air reduced the home side to 22 for five. The Barbadian finished with four for 49 in the first innings, and wrapped up Pakistan's tail in the second, taking the last four wickets in the course of 14 runs. But this could not prevent the tourists from sliding to defeat as they struggled against the accurate medium-pacer, Fazal Mahmood.

In the third and final game at Lahore, Hall was able to propel his team to success as he took the only hat-trick of his Test career, dismissing Mushtaq Mohammad, Nasimul Ghani, and Fazal Mahmood. Hall finished the innings with five for 87, as Westindies avenged their earlier defeats with victory by an innings.

This splendid looking athlete, whose trademark was a golden crucifix dangling in his open-necked shirt, was the complete fast bowler. Over his easy 25 yard run-up he would lengthen his stride so that, when he arrived at the wicket, his feet and left shoulder were perfectly positioned for his thunderous delivery and if, by chance, the batsman had survived the delivery he would soon be confronted by the jovial face of Hall, as he completed his follow-through.

Hall's classical action served him especially well against England in the third Test at Kingston in 1960, when he took seven for 69, as only Colin Cowdrey's excellent innings of 114 kept England in the game. Hall took a further six wickets for 90 in the next match at Georgetown, but the advantage he had secured was whittled away by some slow scoring from the home batsmen.

It was during the Australian series that Hall first demonstrated his superb temperament, when he found himself the central figure in one of the closest matches in Test history. It occurred in the opening game at Brisbane in 1960 as Australia were chasing 233 to win, a target boosted by Hall's first Test fifty, which he had scored in just 69 minutes.

By the time of the last (eight-ball) over – to be bowled by Hall, who had been on the field all day and already taken four wickets – six runs were required. Richie Benaud, who had shared in what appeared to be a match-winning stand of 134 for the seventh wicket with Alan Davidson, was caught behind off the second ball of the over. Wally Grout should have been out off the fifth ball, as he skied a catch to square-leg which the bowler ought to have left to Rohan Kanhai. In Hall's anxiety, the catch was dropped and the home side scrambled two more singles. Ian Meckiff crashed the sixth ball to backward square-leg and, attempting a third run, Grout was run out by Conrad Hunte, whose sizzling throw from the boundary landed right over the top of the stumps, as the scores drew level.

Then, Lindsay Kline, the last man in, strode to the wicket, as Worrell whispered to Hall: "Whatever you do don't bowl a no-ball Wes, or they won't let you back in Barbados." With his foot well behind the line,

Hall bowled a blistering delivery which Kline somehow managed to lay a bat on and raced towards the bowler's end. Joe Solomon who had run out Davidson a few minutes earlier, picked up the ball and threw down the stumps to run out Meckiff and bring off the most famous result in the history of the game: the first tied Test.

In the second Test at Melbourne, Hall removed both openers and the famed duo from Brisbane, Davidson and Benaud, to give him figures of four for 51. But poor batting from Westindies left Australia requiring just 67 to win, and although Hall dismissed Colin McDonald and Neil Harvey at the same score, it was in vain, as the tourists lost by seven wickets.

For the remaining matches in the series, the pitches were more conducive to slower bowling and Hall was able to share his workload with Lance Gibbs and Alf Valentine. Nonetheless, Hall, a favourite with the crowd, had already made such a good impression that he was invited to play for Queensland in the Sheffield Shield, and became a major influence on the development of Australia's great fast bowler of the 1970s, Dennis Lillee.

Hall was at his most lethal against India in 1962 when he collected 27 wickets (15.74). In the second match at Kingston, the Indians must have felt sure of a draw as they scored 395 in their first innings and then watched Westindies labour over 631 for eight declared; but Hall had different ideas as he took six for 49 in the tourists' second innings, sweeping the home side to a comprehensive victory.

By this stage of the tour, the Indians' confidence was at a low ebb. Hall added to their problems again in the fourth Test at Port-of-Spain when, after helping himself to an unbeaten fifty, he whipped through the Indian first innings with five for 20, to leave the tourists even more bewildered.

On Westindies' tour of England in 1963, the pace duo of Hall and Charlie Griffith attracted the same degree of intense publicity previously accorded to the likes of Ray Lindwall and Keith Miller, as the two men had their actions minutely analysed and photographed in the build-up to the Test series.

Hall lived up to his reputation as a magnificent athlete when, in the second game at Lord's, he bowled unchanged for three hours and twenty

minutes in an unprecedented demonstration of stamina. A gallant innings of 70 by Brian Close brought England to the verge of victory, but more splendid bowling from Hall, who finished with four for 93, secured a draw, even though the result could have gone either way in his tense last over.

Hall and Griffith had a majestic series and, even at The Oval, which is renowned for being helpful to spinners, the pair bowled well, with Hall collecting four for 39 in the second innings. That Phil Sharpe's unbeaten 85 at Edgbaston was the top English score of the series, is indicative of their dominance, which was not emulated until 1976 by Andy Roberts and Michael Holding.

In the first Test against Australia at Kingston in 1965, Hall collected five wickets for 60, including the top three batsmen, to secure Westindies a lead of 22 despite their own inpoverished first innings batting display. They eventually set Australia 400 for victory and, once again, the visitors were routed by the speed of Hall who took four for 45, to secure Westindies' first win over Australia in the Caribbean and set them on the path to clinching the rubber.

By the time of Westindies next series, in England in 1966, Hall and Griffith had lost some of their energy, and on the tour of India in 1966-67, nearly a decade after he had blown through the subcontinent, Hall was unable to find his best form on some unhelpful pitches.

He was below par for England's visit to the Caribbean in 1968, having lost some of his pace and was not fully recovered from a car accident the previous August, being several pounds over his optimum weight; and finally exhausted himself on the subsequent tour of Australia and New Zealand.

After his playing days were over, Hall entered the political fray of his native Barbados, where he became a senator in the lower house and is now an MP in the House of Assembly. He once remarked: "If you think my run-up was long, you should see my speeches!" He has been active in coaching programmes to promote grass-roots cricket in Barbados, and has also managed several Westindian teams abroad. As the Minister of Tourism and Sport, Hall presided over the first Sir Garfield Sobers International Schools Tournament, held in Barbados in 1987, and is hoping to develop the event into a World Cup competition for schools.

In his heyday Hall's bowling was described as "pace like fire", which later became the title of his autobiography. Although he didn't reach his top speed of 91 mph, he and Griffith rekindled old memories of their glorious summer almost two decades previously when, in the autumn of 1982, they played in a match at The Oval, organised by the Barbados Tourist Board, in front of thousands of enthusiastic spectators.

Career details

Born: *12 September 1937*
Role: *Right-arm fast bowler*
Clubs: *Barbados, Trinidad, Queensland, North of England Leagues*
First-class record: *[1955-71] 546 wickets (26.14) and 2,673 runs (15.10) including 1 century.*
Tests: *48*
Test debut: *v India 1958*
Test wickets: *192 (26.38); BB: 7-69 v England, Kingston, 1960*
Test runs: *818 (15.73); HS: 50* v India, Port-of-Spain, 1962*
Tours: *England 1957; India and Pakistan 1958-59; Australia 1960-61; England 1963; England 1966; Australia and New Zealand 1968-69.*

Roger Andrew Harper

Roger Harper's exclusion from the Westindies tour party to New Zealand in 1987 was, perhaps, one of the most surprising selection decisions of recent times. The first specialist slow bowler to penetrate the prevailing preference for speed since 1974, when his compatriot, Lance Gibbs, held sway, it seemed strange that Harper, widely believed to be being groomed for the captaincy, should have been dropped.

Having been elevated to the captaincy of Guyana and the vice-captaincy of Northamptonshire in 1986, after impressing with his astute handling of the Young Westindies side in England in 1982, it seemed that Harper was set to become the first specialist spinner since John Goddard, in 1948, to lead his country. Yet, as Clayton Goodwin asks in his book *West Indians at the Wicket*: "…(can) any slow bowler, however good, be sure of selection on merit for every Test match the captain is required to play(?)" In Harper's case, though, it seems fair to say that his all-round cricketing ability would very likely gain him selection.

The towering Harper stresses the influence of his elder brother, Mark, who has played for Guyana since 1976, on the development of his cricket. He says: "Because the age gap between us is six years, and he was playing youth cricket at 14, I came under his influence at an impressionable age." Roger played cricket at school, being selected for the First X1 at the age of 12, but he didn't allow his studies to suffer and passed seven 'O' levels. He remembers: "I went to Queen's College High School, Georgetown, which was supposed to be the best school in the country, and where sport was a secondary consideration to your studies. By nature, I'm an outdoor person, but I am sure that my qualifications will stand me in good stead in years to come." One of the most difficult decisions that the youngster subsequently had to make was when he abandoned his 'A' levels in favour of playing league cricket with Woodville in Northern Ireland in 1981.

A splendid all-round sportsman, the Guyanese

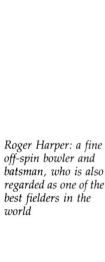

Roger Harper: a fine off-spin bowler and batsman, who is also regarded as one of the best fielders in the world

excelled at athletics and basketball. Even so, he was seen at his best in the school cricket team, where he batted at number three, but had little opportunity to bowl. Soon the lanky youngster set a precedent by gaining permission to play for his club, Demerara, which had an illustrious pedigree as the former home of Lance Gibbs, Roy Fredericks and Clive Lloyd. "Normally," says Harper, "you weren't allowed to play for your club in preference to your school, but I got a special exemption." With their strong batting line-up, Demerara's latest recruit was fitted in at number eight, although Harper played mainly as an off-spinner.

It was an inspirational experience for Harper to be playing in the same team as his cricketing idol, Fredericks. He says: "I don't ever remember having a specific conversation with him about my cricket, but I learned so much from just observing him." At 16, Harper was playing national youth cricket, before he graduated to the Westindies youth team at the age of 17 years and three days. Then, in 1980, he was selected for Guyana under the captaincy of Fredericks. Harper failed to take a wicket on his Shell Shield debut against Barbados, but collected 17 in the last three games of the season.

In 1982 he was appointed captain of the Young Westindies team to England, and made a good impression, leading them to a 2-0 victory in the Test series, although they lost the one-day internationals. After an impressive year in the Shield in 1983, which saw him take 24 wickets, the young Harper was caught in an upward spiral which culminated in his selection for the full Westindies side to India later that year. "From that time on," recalls Harper, "Clive Lloyd has been the greatest influence on my cricket; in fact, he is more of a mentor. I admire his outlook on life: as a cricketer and as a person he has been a great example to me."

Good performances against Australia in the Caribbean secured Harper's place in the tour party to England in 1984. He enjoyed considerable success, finishing the series with 13 wickets at 21.23 apiece, including his best Test figures of six for 57 in the fourth match at Old Trafford.

His encouraging performance, which saw him take 37 wickets on the tour, prompted Ken Turner, then Northamptonshire's secretary, to sign Harper before anyone else had an opportunity to make him an offer.

After playing well in Australia in 1984-85, the Guyanese then visited Pakistan and Sharjah with Westindies and, on his return to the Caribbean, enjoyed a splendid Shield series in 1986, taking 23 wickets and scoring 270 runs. He played in two Tests against the English tourists that year and, in the game at St John's, hit his best Test score of 60 and took four wickets, including three for 10, in England's second innings.

The young all-rounder had a vintage season at Northamptonshire in 1986 and embarrassed those who doubted the wisdom of signing an overseas slow bowler, by topping the county's averages with 62 wickets at 26.93 apiece, while his spectacular fielding lifted the whole team. He proved himself time and again with the bat and, perhaps, one of the most brilliant innings ever seen in county cricket, came as he stepped off the 'plane on a chilly May morning that year and made his way to the county ground to smash a career-best 234 runs off Gloucestershire's front-line bowlers. His innings, which included 12 sixes and 25 fours, set a new record for a number seven batsman in England.

However, the Guyanese was brought back to earth by a disappointing end to the year, when he took just two expensive wickets and scored hardly any runs on Westindies' tour of Pakistan. Similarly poor form in the extended series of one-day internationals in Australia the following year, led to him being dropped from the Test side for the tour of New Zealand. This was a severe blow for the youngster who has the best Test average of any contemporary spin bowler.

Yet, in spite of these set-backs, the philosophical Harper returned home to lead Guyana to success in the Shield, and bounced back with one of his most successful seasons ever. In his first two club matches he scored 244 runs and took 11 wickets and, captaining Guyana against Barbados in a pre-Shield game, returned his best ever all-round performance when he hit a century and took 10 wickets.

This was the prelude to a magnificent Shield season in which he played a key role in all of Guyana's victories. He bowled tidily and lived up to his reputation as the finest fielder in the world. But, once again, it was his batting which featured most prominently. He said: "I thought our prospects were good, if our batting became more reliable, and it was in this department that I felt I could be of value. I made 277 in three innings for once out, including a century in the final against the Leeward Islands. We also played some good team cricket and were systematic in our approach, which contributed to our success."

These performances reveal Harper's steely resolve and have strengthened his claim to be a regular member of the Test team and, perhaps, one day, its captain. The young Guyanese has already made a move in that direction, with his appointment as Westindies' vice-captain for their World Cup campaign last year.

Away from the pressures of cricket, Harper enjoys going to the cinema, relaxing to music and visiting his family, most of whom live in America. His parents and sister live in New York while his oldest brother, Michael, works as a chemical technologist in California. The likeable Harper explains: "We're all quite scattered, so it's not often that we have family reunions, but I drop in to see my parents whenever I can."

Career details

Born: *17 March 1963*
Role: *Right-arm off-break bowler, right-hand batsman*
Clubs: *Guyana, Northamptonshire*
First-class record: *[1979-] 380 wickets (28.13) and 4,226 (29.34) including 7 centuries*
Tests: *19*
Test debut: *v India 1983*
Test wickets: *40 (27.25); BB: 6-57 v England, Old Trafford, 1984*
Test runs: *352 (16.00); HS: 60 v England, St. John's, 1986*
Tours: *England (WIYC) 1982; India 1983; England 1984; Australia 1984-85; Pakistan 1986; India and Pakistan (World Cup) 1987.*

Desmond Leo Haynes

A very good timer of the ball, Desmond Haynes has also timed some of his best innings to perfection. He was drafted into the Barbados team in 1977 and, after some disappointing scores, he was dropped for the game against the touring Pakistanis. But, when Gordon Greenidge withdrew from the match at the last minute, Haynes was recalled to the side and capitalised on his good fortune by scoring a century. His 136 contained 20 fours and booked his place as Barbados' permanent opener.

Born in St. James, Haynes was weaned in the prolific nursery at Holder's Hill and was greatly influenced by Seymour Nurse. At the age of nine, Haynes watched Nurse hit a double-hundred against Australia at Bridgetown in 1965 and it was he who later coached Haynes at the Federal High School. Nurse kept a watchful eye over the youngster when he played in the Barbados youth team in the annual Westindies championships in the mid-1970s, as a middle order batsman and wicket-keeper, and the two have maintained their friendship ever since.

Haynes played in the Barbados League, but it was when he moved to play for Carlton in Barbados, Division One, that he won wider recognition and got his first opportunity in the Shell Shield. After two indifferent matches for Barbados he might well have faded from the scene but for Greenidge's absence in the Pakistan game.

A happy character, who lives by the motto on the chain round his neck of "Live, love, laugh", Haynes quickly secured the succession as Westindies' regular opener after the retirement of Roy Fredericks in 1977. In the first one-day international against the touring Australians the following year, he confirmed his promise by scoring 148 glorious runs off 136 balls, and won the vacant opener's place.

In the first Test at Port-of-Spain, the Barbadian hit a solid 61, and top-scored with 66 in the first innings of the second match at Bridgetown, reviving memories of Conrad Hunte with his positive approach. When Haynes and Greenidge added 131 in the second innings to set up victory for the home side, it seemed

Desmond Haynes celebrates his century against England at the Oval in 1984

that Westindies had found a reliable new opening partnership with relative ease. But, when the World Series crisis evolved and Haynes was dropped from the side because he could not guarantee his availability for the imminent trip to India, his pairing with Greenidge was lost to official Test cricket for several months.

When diplomatic relations were restored, Haynes, along with the other WSC players, returned to the official fold. He had a disappointing comeback tour to Australia in 1979-80, averaging just 27.80. But, he found his form on the New Zealand leg of the trip and established himself as a world class batsman. The right-hander hit a century in the first Test at Dunedin and 122 in the second at Christchurch, adding 225 for the first wicket with Greenidge.

Haynes was at his best against England in the second Test at Lord's in 1980, when he smashed 184 runs off the home attack in 490 minutes. He said afterwards: "To tell the truth, I was beginning to wonder whether I had it in me to bat that long without losing concentration, without making some silly strokes to get out. Those centuries in New Zealand and then at Lord's convinced me that I could. It was a breakthrough, I suppose."

Haynes toured Zimbabwe with Westindies Young Cricketers in 1981, as vice-captain to Faoud Bacchus, and, with the latter's defection to South Africa, the Barbadian replaced him in the official Test side as opener and short-leg, where his brilliant reflexes are called upon regularly.

The muscular Haynes hits the ball hard and plays strokes all round the wicket with great confidence. Even so, he struggles against spin bowling and had difficulties in Pakistan in 1980-81, and could not get into his groove against the Indians when they visited the Caribbean in 1983; although on a placid pitch in the final Test at St. John's, he and Greenidge finally overcame the wiliness of the spinners to share in a record breaking partnership of 296. Their stand was unbroken and remains the Westindian record for the first wicket against all countries.

Haynes fared better when England visited the Caribbean in 1981, falling four short of his century as he added 168 with Greenidge in the first Test at Port-of-Spain, and then made a sound 84 in the fifth game in Kingston.

Many of Haynes' finest innings have come in one-day matches. He hit three successive centuries for once out off the Australians in limited-overs competitions in early 1984, when he also enjoyed his most successful Test series. He scored 468 runs (93.66) including an unbeaten century in the first Test at Georgetown and 145 in the third at Bridgetown, his first Test century in his home ground. Haynes has particularly fond memories of his hundred at Kensington Oval. He said: "You always want to do well at home…You get your cricket friends telling you it's all very well to make runs but you haven't proved yourself until you've made them in a Test at Kensington."

The Barbadian struggled against England in the first four Tests of the 1984 series but came good in the last match at The Oval, as he hit a century on a difficult pitch; and had a consistent, if not prolific, series against Australia towards the end of that year.

Haynes has enjoyed an outstandingly successful partnership with Greenidge for Barbados and Westindies. The two complement each other well: the former is a cheerful fellow, with a ready smile, and often plays a supportive role to the more studious Greenidge. Nonetheless, with a Test average of over 40, Haynes compares with Westindies' most illustrious openers. Besides their brilliant individual batting ability, Haynes and Greenidge have a good understanding between the wickets. This has helped them to 10 century stands – the highest number for any Westindian opening pair – and their overall record partnership of 296. The solid starts that these two have given Westindies for the last 10 years have been invaluable in keeping their side at the top of world cricket.

When England visited the Caribbean in 1986 Haynes returned to his best form, averaging 78.16 for the series. This included a splendid 131 in the fifth Test at St. John's, as he scored 117 out of 228 for four on a difficult opening day, to set up victory for the home side. The Barbadian visited Pakistan in 1986, hitting an unbeaten 88 in the third Test at Karachi, which helped him to head the batting averages. His success continued in the series against New Zealand in 1987, as he collected his ninth Test century in the

first match at Wellington.

Haynes has an insatiable appetite for cricket and, immediately after Westindies' tour of England in 1984, this lively character led his Cavaliers side on another tour of the "old country". Even so, Haynes has not played county cricket in England, although he has appeared for Scotland and in the Durham League, and had a season of district cricket in Australia. Instead he is heavily involved with the development of cricket in Barbados, and has set up the Desmond Haynes Cavaliers team at senior and junior level in the Holder's Hill area.

Desmond Haynes in pensive mood during the Trent Bridge Test against England in 1980

Career details

Born: *15 February 1956*
Role: *Right-hand batsman*
clubs: *Barbados, Scotland, Durham League*
First-class record: *[1977-] 9,843 runs (43.55) including 18 centuries, and 2 wickets (27.00)*
Tests: 65
Test debut: *v Australia 1978*
Test runs: *4,012 (41.79); HS: 184 v England, Lord's, 1980*
Tours: *England (World Cup) 1979; Australia and New Zealand 1979-80; England 1980; Pakistan 1980-81; Zimbabwe (under-26 side) 1981; Australia 1981-82; England (World Cup) 1983; India 1983; England 1984; Australia 1984-85; Pakistan 1986; New Zealand 1987; India and Pakistan (World Cup) 1987*

George Alphonso Headley

Born in Panama of a Jamaican mother and Barbadian father, George Headley grew up in a sporting environment in Cuba. There, he developed an early panache for baseball and met Clarence Passailaigue, a capable baseball player, who was to partner Headley in some of his most memorable innings.

Headley was taken to Jamaica as a boy of 10, and less than 10 years later, in 1927, he played his maiden first-class game for St. Catherine Cricket Club. The following season, still in his teens, he hit 71, 211 and 71 for Jamaica in matches against Lord Tennyson's MCC touring team, as he exploited his cricketing skills in preference to pursuing a career in dentistry in America.

His outstanding ability caused a great stir, and it came as a surprise when he was omitted from the tour party to England in 1928. Headley had to wait for the first Test ever played in the Westindies, against England at Bridgetown in 1930, to make his first international appearance, and what a debut it was. He scored 21 and 176, to join the elite band of players who had made centuries on their Test debut, as he shared in big partnerships with Clifford Roach and Frank de Caires, in his maiden first-class match outside Jamaica.

In the early days of Westindian cricket, transportation difficulties, not least the economics of the situation, influenced selectorial policy. But, Headley soon became such an indispensable member of the side that an exception was made for him, even though, as a Jamaican, he came from the most northerly island. He played in the first three games of the series against England in 1930, before he was joined by another seven Jamaicans for the fourth Test at Kingston.

He failed to leave his mark in the second Test at Port-of-Spain, but returned to his more splendid form for the third game at Georgetown. He savaged the English attack for 114 in the first innings and 112 in the second, to become the first Westindian to score

The first black man ever to lead Westindies, George Headley also shouldered his side's batting for most of his Test career

two centuries in the same Test and, with it, secure Westindies their first victory in Test cricket. By scoring two separate hundreds in a Test match, Headley became one of cricket's "immortals".

He saved his best magic for his home crowd in the final game at Kingston, where he scored a magnificent 223, with 28 fours, in six-and-a-half hours, adding 228 with Karl Nunes. The home side were chasing 836 for victory and were reasonably placed on 408 for five before the rains came and washed out the match.

So, in just four Tests, this slightly built man, whose appearance reflected some of his Latin upbringing with his matching ties and hankerchiefs, had four hundreds under his belt, and a record aggregate of 703 runs for his first series, as he finished with an average of 87.87.

When Headley toured Australia the following year and scored another two Test hundreds, people were already saying that he was impossible to bowl to. The visitors went into the first Test at Adelaide, having suffered three defeats against state sides. Only Headley had shown his calibre with two accomplished innings in the opening game against New South Wales. Learie Constantine considered his first innings 25 to be one of the best performances of the tour; and it was left to Headley to salvage some pride for his side as he hit 131 out of 212 in their match against Victoria at Melbourne.

But his true ability was revealed as, over a period of several weeks, he adapted his technique after failing to score more than 20 in eight successive innings in the early part of the tour. Headley arrived in Australia as a strong off-side player, and countered his initial failure against the leg-break bowling of Charlie Grimmett by changing his stance and grip.

He had perfected this revised style by the third Test at Brisbane, to become the first Westindian to score a hundred in Australia. His unbeaten 102 proved that he had overcome his difficulties against Grimmett, who had dismissed him for a duck in his first Test innings of the series, and, by the end of it, Grimmett was saying that Headley was the best on-side player he had ever bowled to.

The Jamaican's century was a lone show of resistance as the tourists were forced to follow-on 365

runs behind, although it must have consoled him that the two outstanding batsmen in the Australian side, Don Bradman and Stan McCabe, came into the Westindian dressing room to congratulate him on his performance. Headley top-scored in the tourists' second innings, but with Grimmett collecting nine for 144 in the match, he could not prevent a comprehensive defeat by the Australians.

In the fourth game at Melbourne, Headley scored exactly a third of Westindies' first innings total of 99 as Australia set up another decisive victory.

By the time of the fifth match at Sydney the tourists were predictably demoralized, but a brilliant 105 in two-and-a-quarter hours from Headley who at last found support in the shape of his compatriot, Frank Martin, who carried his bat for 123, laid the foundations of an unexpected and morale-boosting win. The two Jamaicans shared in a partnership of 152, giving the visitors an early advantage so that, by the start of the last day, Jackie Grant was able to declare on 350 for six to give his bowlers enough time dismiss the Australians on a rain-affected wicket.

After Headley's return from Australia, Lord Tennyson's side visited the Caribbean and, once again, the Jamaican treated him to some marvellous batting displays, including 344 not out, as he shared in a world record undefeated partnership of 487 for the sixth wicket with his friend, Passailaigue, who finished unbeaten on 261. Headley followed this up with 84, 155 not out and 140 in the space of a month. His Lordship said of Headley's performances in 1932: "I cannot recollect such perfection of timing nor variety of shots, and the delight of it all was that he himself was, I am sure, unconscious that he was doing anything out of the ordinary..."

Headley was irrepressible when he finally toured England in 1933, scoring 2,320 first-class runs, including seven superb centuries, most notably an unbeaten innings of 224, with 31 boundaries, out of a total of 440 against Somerset. Predictably, he headed both the tour and Test averages, but it was the gulf between him and the next man, as he scored nearly twice as many runs as anyone else, that marked him out as a player of rare quality.

His standard of play prompted the English public to dub him the "Black Bradman", which stemmed

George Headley with Jeff Stollmeyer

from the parallels in his batting with Bradman's outstanding performances in England in 1930, while Jamaicans referred to Bradman as the "White Headley".

In the Tests he made fifty at Lord's and an unbeaten 169, including 18 fours, out of a total of 375 at Old Trafford, as he and Ivan Barrow added 200 for the second wicket; with Barrow just pipping the maestro to being the first Westindian to score a century in England, as the pair thwarted "Nobby" Clarke's attempt at body-line bowling.

The impact of Headley's batting in that long, hot summer is perhaps best revealed in the 1934 *Wisden* which said: "From what we had been told by English players who had been in the West Indies we were fully prepared for Headley's success, but even so he astonished most of us..."

Headley had an enviable technique, keeping his head perfectly still as he played the ball remarkably late, watching its movement until the very last moment. He was similarly alert in the field, observing: "You always know when a man is going to be in form with the bat: the ball comes easily to his hands in the field." Headley had marvellous balance, and the secret of his batting lay in his impeccable timing as he cut or drove with equal power on both sides of the wicket. Primarily a back-foot player, Headley also possessed a sound defence and was widely regarded as the best bad wicket player since the celebrated Victor Trumper.

When England sent an understrength team to the Caribbean in 1935, they lost the series 2-1, due, in the main, to the Jamaican's performances. In the infamous first Test at Bridgetown, where the wicket bore more resemblance to a marsh, Headley lived up to his reputation by top-scoring in Westindies' first innings, as only one other player reached double figures. The worsening nature of the pitch was revealed as the great man was dismissed for a duck in the home side's second innings, which prompted Jackie Grant to declare in an effort to avoid further trouble but, in the end, England scampered home by four wickets.

Headley played a restrained innings of 93 in the victory at Port-of-Spain and hit a solid 53 at Georgetown but, as so often, he seemed to save his

George Headley: one of cricket's "immortals"

vintage performance for his home crowd: he registered Westindies' only century of the series in the last game in Kingston, thrashing an unbeaten 270, with 30 fours, in 500 minutes. In that historic game, which secured Westindies their first-ever rubber, the Jamaican's innings was, at the time, the highest score by a Westindian in Test cricket, as he dominated record stands of 202 with Derek Sealy for the third wicket and 147 with Rolph Grant for the seventh, setting the scene for Manny Martindale to wrap up the victory over the tourists with a superb display of fast bowling. The visitors might have guessed that Headley was warming up for a big Test innings as, a few days prior to the match, he had scored 127 for Jamaica against them.

There was a four year gap before Westindies played any more Test cricket, then they toured England in 1939. Again, the magnificent Headley was dominant, so much so that the Press soon nicknamed him "Atlas", as once more he shouldered the burden of Westindies' batting virtually on his own.

Perhaps the pinnacle of his career came in the first Test at Lord's, as he scored two memorable centuries at the headquarters of cricket. He opened his account with 106, adding 118 for the second wicket with Jeff Stollmeyer, to take the tourists to 226 for three, whereupon the rest of the side collapsed to 277 all out! An excellent partnership of 248 between Len Hutton and Denis Compton then swung the match decisively in England's favour but, nonetheless, could not detract from Headley's chanceless second innings 107, as he became only the second man in the history of Test cricket to score two centuries in the same Test on two separate occasions.

The Second World War deprived the world of some of Headley's best years, but with the resumption of Test cricket in the Caribbean, his experience was called upon as he became the first black player to lead Westindies when MCC toured in 1948. Even so, his appointment was restricted to the first Test in Barbados and the fourth in Jamaica, as other players were nominated for the remaining matches.

Even if this did cause Headley some private consternation, a strained muscle hampered his performance in the first match and ruled him out of the rest of the tour. But, if his own captaincy was short-lived, the advice he offered to others was highly valued, as Stollmeyer revealed in a letter to him written from Santa Cruz, Trinidad, in October 1956: "...I have realised for some time now that ever since I was of an age to appreciate the finer points of our game I learned more of cricket strategy and tactics from you than from anyone else...I want to thank you for your help over the years..."

Nonetheless, his appointment as captain, how ever fleeting the tenure, was a major advance in social and political progress; indeed, during his career, Headley went from sharing a bed with Constantine in Barbados and Guyana in 1928-29 to sharing a room with the white captain, Grant, on Westindies' tour to Australia two years later.

Headley was the oldest man ever to play for Westindies, when he appeared in the first Test against England at Kingston in 1954. At the age of almost 45, his adoring Jamaican public raised £1,183 0s 2d to bring him back from England, where he played league cricket for Haslingden, for one final Test performance at his beloved Sabina Park. It was an ordeal that Headley should not have been subjected to, but public pressure forced his inclusion in the side, and he made 16 and 1, in an unfortunate end to a peerlessly successful career.

One of his sons, Ron, born two days after his father's second century at Lord's in 1939, played in the Shell Shield in 1966 and 1967. He also played for Worcestershire and Derbyshire in the English county championship, and captained the former to the Sunday League title. He graduated to Test honours in 1973, partnering Roy Fredericks against England. Another of his sons, Lindy, was an international sprinter, who represented Jamaica at the Olympic games.

But it was Headley Senior whose standards of batsmanship set the tone for the new generation of players. He carried the pre-War Westindian batting, like Martindale did the bowling, but even his genius could not always bridge the gap, as reckless stroke-play from others squandered any advantage the bowlers might have gained. Even so, in Tests he scored 10 centuries, two of which he converted into double hundreds and, at his peak, in the 1930s, he scored a century every other Test, while the

remaining Westindian batsmen could only manufacture five hundreds between them. The most remarkable fact about Headley's batting was that, almost uniquely in the history of the game, he invariably had to stand alone: in 15 out of 35 Westindian innings he was the top-scorer, in 11 of those he made at least a third of the runs and in three it was over half of the total.

Perhaps the most fitting epitaph on Headley's career came from Berkeley Gaskin, who played under him at Bridgetown in 1948. When asked, several years later, how he would compare the great Jamaican with the then outstanding players, headed by the three "W"s and Gary Sobers, he replied: "They could sit in the same cathedral as George, but not in the same pew."

Career details

Born: *30 May 1909*
Died: *30 November 1983*
Role: *Right-hand batsman*
Clubs: *Jamaica, Birmingham and Lancashire Leagues*
First-class record: *[1927-54] 9,921 runs (69.86) including 33 centuries, and 51 wickets (36.11)*
Tests: *22*
Test debut: *v England 1930*
Test runs: *2,190 (60.83); HS: 270* v England, Kingston, 1935*
Tours: *Australia 1930-31; England 1933; England 1939; India 1948-49.*

John Leslie "Jackie" Hendriks

Jackie Hendriks, one of Westindies' finest wicket-keepers who, nonetheless, was prone to injury

For someone widely acclaimed as the best wicket-keeper ever produced by Westindies, "Jackie" Hendriks made remarkably few Test appearances in a career punctuated by injuries and exacerbated by playing in the shadow of Gerry Alexander.

With Alexander's appointment as captain for the tours of Pakistan and India in 1958-59, Hendriks' fate as the second-string wicket-keeper was sealed, even though the latter was technically the superior of the two. It is interesting to muse on how Hendriks' career might have developed if Frank Worrell had been available as captain.

In the end, Hendriks had to wait until Alexander's retirement after the 1960-61 tour to Australia, before taking over the gloves, having been the best wicket-keeper in the Caribbean for five years prior to his elevation to Test honours.

Tragically, after his long apprenticeship, Hendriks broke his finger during India's first innings on his Test debut in the opening game at Port-of-Spain in 1962 and, despite bravely top-scoring with 64 in the home side's reply, the Jamaican took no further part in the series. He had to wait another two years to regain his place, as a youngster from Trinidad, named Deryck Murray, made his mark on the subsequent tour to England, after Hendriks had

Catching practise for (l-r) Rudy Cohen, Peter Lashley, David Holford and Jackie Hendriks on Westindies' 1966 tour of England

missed selection by being employed temporarily in the United States.

When Murray stayed in England to study, Hendriks was recalled and, for nearly 10 years, the identity of Westindies' wicket-keeper was largely determined by Murray's availability and Hendriks' injuries. Indeed, had it not been so serious, the injury Hendriks sustained on his return to the side would have been farcical. He was hit on the side of the head by a ball from Graham McKenzie in the fourth Test against Australia at Bridgetown in 1965, and only narrowly avoided brain damage, but recovered to tour England in 1966.

The series against Australia in the Caribbean was the setting for Lance Gibbs' splendid 18-wicket haul, with half of them coming in the third game at Georgetown, thanks largely to some magnificent wicket-keeping by Hendriks. On the last day, the Jamaican stumped Bob Cowper and caught Brian Booth for a duck off Gibbs' bowling, and then snapped up another two catches off other bowlers, before his ill-fated appearance at Bridgetown.

Hendriks made the trips to India in 1966-67 and Australia and New Zealand in 1968-69, although a back injury and his job kept him out of the intervening series against England in the Caribbean.

Yet, through all his disappointments, Hendriks played in the knowledge that his contemporaries rated him as the finest and most consistent 'keeper of his age. He was as competent to the speed of Charlie Griffith and Wes Hall as he was to the spin of Gibbs, not to mention the varied range of Gary Sobers, and his catching could turn matches. Clive Lloyd commented: "The thing with Jackie was that he never seemed to have a bad day with a standard which was always consistently high." This remark is confirmed by the fact that Hendriks is the only Westindian to have kept wicket in three innings which have passed 500 runs without conceding a bye: Barbados' 521 for seven declared at Bridgetown in 1967 and Australia's 510 at Melbourne and 619 at Sydney in 1968-69.

A product of Wolmer's Boys' School, Hendriks, although lacking the fluency of Alexander and Murray, was an able middle-order batsman and a powerful driver, who registered two Test fifties. He was a stout defender and gained a reputation of being difficult to dislodge.

After he retired, Hendriks followed the path of previous Westindian wicket-keepers and became involved with the administration of the game. Hendriks has served as a selector and managed the victorious side which trounced England 5-0 in 1984, shielding his team from the stress and traumas of modern competition in a firm, yet diplomatic, fashion.

It was fitting that a man whose own career at the highest level seemed to be fated, even allowing for the uncertainty of tenure invariably experienced by Westindian wicket-keepers, should have had the opportunity to impart his knowledge and experience to an admiring band of modern players.

Career details

Born: *21 December 1933*
Role: *Wicket-keeper, right-hand batsman*
Clubs: *Jamaica*
First-class record: *[1953-69] 140 catches and 50 stumpings, and 1,568 runs (17.42)*
Tests: *20*
Test debut: *v India 1962*
Test catches: *42;* Test stumpings: *5*
Test runs: *447 (18.62); HS: 64 v India, Port-of-Spain, 1962*
Tours: *India and Pakistan 1958-59; Australia 1960-61; England 1966; India 1966-67; Australia and New Zealand 1968-69; England 1969.*

Vanburn Alonza Holder

Vanburn Holder came into the limelight of Test cricket for the series against England in 1969, as a successor to Wes Hall and Charlie Griffith. Holder was never as fast as Hall and Griffith, and the quiet, reliable Barbadian was far more effective when Andy Roberts and Michael Holding made their entrance into the Test arena, and Holder became the third seamer.

With Gary Sobers and John Shepherd, Holder used the new ball with moderate success on the 1969 tour, taking four for 48 at Headingley. He bowled consistently, without much luck, in the next rubber against India in 1971, and topped the bowling averages against New Zealand the following season in a series where all the Tests were drawn, as Westindies lacked the firepower to bowl out the tourists twice.

Holder was selected for the tour to England in 1973, as part of a three-pronged pace attack consisting of himself, Keith Boyce and Bernard Julien. In the third Test at Lord's, Holder took four for 56 to help Westindies to one of their most comprehensive victories.

Holder, was familiar with English conditions, having joined Worcestershire in 1968, and often caused havoc on deteriorating pitches. He was one of the main contributors to their championship-winning side of 1974 – a year which saw him return his best championship bowling figures of seven for 40 against Glamorgan. It was also a profitable year for him with the bat, as he later hit a career-best 122 for Barbados against Trinidad in the Shell Shield.

He toured India and Pakistan in 1974-75 and produced one of his best bowling performances during the fifth and deciding Test at Bombay. Extracting bounce and movement from a wearing pitch, the Barbadian finished with six for 39 to clinch the series for Westindies.

Holder was included in the successful 1975 World Cup squad; and, with the selection of Roberts and Holding, was taken as a first-change bowler for the subsequent trip to Australia. On a generally

Vanburn Holder

disappointing tour, Holder's best figures were five for 108 in the fifth Test at Adelaide.

On his third tour to England in 1976, Holder was used mainly as a stock bowler, and kept the Englishmen quiet while the frontline bowlers were rested.

Thereafter, Holder's Test career appeared to be over. But, after the Packer crisis of 1978, the Barbadian made an unexpected return to the team as vice-captain to Alvin Kallicharran. The surprise revival of his international career seemed to inspire Holder, who recorded his best Test performance, taking six for 28 with the new ball against Australia in the fourth Test at Port-of-Spain, to help clinch the series for Westindies.

Although he was selected for the tour to India in 1978-79, the self-effacing Holder was on the wrong side of 30 for a fast-medium bowler to make a sustained comeback and, once the Packer defectors returned to the side, the hard-working Barbadian was sidelined for good.

When he left first-class cricket, Holder played minor county cricket and in the Central Lancashire League, and has played in South Africa.

Career details

Born: *8 October 1945*
Role: *Right-arm fast-medium bowler, right-hand batsman.*
Clubs: *Barbados, Worcestershire, Orange Free State, Central Lancashire League*
First-class record: *[1966-   ] 948 wickets (24.57) and 3,393 runs (12.24) including 1 century.*
Tests: *40*
Test debut: *v England 1969*
Test wickets: *109 (33.27); BB: 6-28 v Australia, Port-of-Spain, 1978*
Test runs: *682 (14.21); HS: 42 v New Zealand, Port-of-Spain, 1972*
Tours: *England 1969; England 1973; India and Pakistan 1974-5; England (World Cup) 1975; Australia 1975-76; England 1976; India 1978-79.*

Michael Anthony Holding

Regarded by many as the finest fast bowler of his generation, Michael Holding is best remembered for a remarkable display of sustained quick bowling against England in the final Test at The Oval in 1976. He alone, out of seven fast or medium-fast bowlers, was able to coax some pace out of a lifeless pitch, as he collected 14 wickets for 149, while the others shared six scalps between them. In the whole game 28 wickets fell at a cost of 53.8 runs each, while the Jamaican's 14 victims cost him 10.90 apiece. Nine of his 14 victims were clean bowled, as he wrote himself into the record books by collecting the most wickets in a Test by a Westindian.

Holding only started playing cricket seriously in 1971 and might well have taken an athletics scholarship to the United States instead. A 400-metre runner and a university graduate, he could easily have been lost to cricket but, perhaps influenced by his family's cricketing connections – his father, Ralph, was president of one of the strongest cricket clubs in Kingston, Melbourne – and his sports teacher, Trevor Parchment, he stayed and became one of the greatest fast bowlers of all time.

Holding enjoyed a meteoric rise, moving smoothly from his debut in the Westindies youth tournament in 1972 to his maiden first-class appearance the next year. With only a few first-class games to his name and having just turned 21, the shy Jamaican was taken to Australia in 1975-76, to partner Andy Roberts.

He began the tour by scoring two fifties in the first two state games, before he bowled out a state team at Sydney taking six for 60, to secure his place in the Test side for the first match at Brisbane. He had an inauspicious beginning, returning figures of nought for 127; but, in the second match at Perth, he collected four for 88, including three wickets in his second over on the second day. Then, later in the game, the youngster pulled a muscle which ruled him out of the next Test at Melbourne, and seemed to

Michael Holding, whose graceful action brought him record bowling figures of 14 for 149 against England at The Oval in 1976

unsettle him for the rest of the series, as his 10 wickets cost 61.40 each.

Holding was involved in a much publicised incident in the fourth game at Sydney. Ian Chappell deflected the Jamaican's first delivery into Deryck Murray's gloves and, after the umpire turned down the appeal, the batsman refused to walk and it was a while before the distraught Holding could be persuaded to bowl again.

In the series against India at home later that year, Holding bounced back from his disappointments in Australia to head the bowling averages with 19 wickets (19.89), including his best bowling figures of six for 65 in the third Test at Port-of-Spain. In the fourth game at Kingston, Holding exploited a ridge at the northern end of the ground, as his venemous deliveries accounted for four wickets for 82 runs in front of his home crowd. After two Indian batsmen were injured by rising balls, the visitors declared. Then Westindies went into the lead due, in the main, to a whirlwind 55 from Holding. When India batted again they lost three wickets on 95, prompting five batsmen to withdraw from the contest "absent hurt", after complaints from the tourists about intimidatory bowling, which only enhanced the Jamaican's reputation further.

Writing in *The Cricketer* in 1985, Holding said: "I do not agree with excessive use of the bouncer, but it would be naive and misleading of me to claim that I never bowl bouncers without trying to intimidate the batsman. On the contrary, I want him to be aware that if he gets onto the front foot against me he might find himself in trouble – in other words he might get hurt. But that is quite a different thing from actually *wanting* or intending to hurt him...it is human nature for a fast bowler in an important match to do what he can within the law to take as many wickets as he can in as short a time as possible."

A natural athlete, Holding has one of the most beautiful bowling actions ever to grace a cricket field: his perfect balance, impeccable rhythm and flowing run engender phenomenal speed and bounce. Someone once said of the lithe Jamaican that even at the culmination of his run-up he could run on soft snow without leaving the imprint of his foot, which led to him being dubbed "whispering death"; a view

confirmed by many umpires who say they cannot hear him as he approaches the wicket.

His most memorable season came in 1976 when, between them, Holding and Roberts pulverised the English batting as they shared 28 wickets apiece in the series, with 14 of Holding's coming at The Oval. After mesmerizing the cream of England's batting in an early game on the tour against MCC at Lord's, the Jamaican missed the opening Test with mild glandular fever and was struggling for fitness in the second. But in the third at Old Trafford, Holding gave the home batsmen a taste of things to come, as he collected five wickets for nine runs in 7.5 overs in England's second innings to send them crashing to defeat.

This was merely the *hors-d'oeuvre* for his performance at The Oval, where his second innings bowling figures of eight for 92 were then the best Test figures by a Westindian.

Holding was the only member of the 1976 Westindies team not to have played county cricket, although he has since had short-term contracts with Lancashire and Derbyshire and has also played for Tasmania and in the Lancashire League.

After his vintage summer in England, Holding was troubled by injury, and his involvement in World Series Cricket delayed his return to official Test cricket further. But he was back at full throttle to face England again in 1980. He took six for 67 in the second Test at Lord's and, in an inspired spell at the start of England's second innings in the fourth Test at The Oval, he reduced the home side to 10 for two, by removing Graham Gooch and Wayne Larkins.

When England visited the Caribbean in 1981, Geoff Boycott had to endure a sustained assault by the Jamaican during the third Test at Bridgetown. He subjected the England opener to an over of terrifying pace before breaking through his defences. Holding maintained his momentum into the three-match series against Australia in 1981-82 when he captured 24 wickets at 14.33 each, including five or more wickets in four innings out of six.

Even when he cut down his run, the thoughtful Jamaican, who worked as a computer programmer for the government, remained one of the most formidable bowlers in the world, as the Indians found out in late 1983 after they had wrested the World Cup from the Westindians earlier in the year. Holding took the new ball again, this time with Malcolm Marshall, as the pair evoked memories of Wes Hall and Roy Gilchrist a generation earlier, with the Jamaican taking 30 wickets at 22.10 apiece.

By the 1984 series against Australia, Holding was regarded as the veteran of Westindies' speed machine. Yet, in the first Test at Perth, he ran through the home side's batting to dismiss them for their lowest total of 76 against Westindies, collecting his six wickets in 35 blistering deliveries at a cost of 21 runs.

Because of the endless batting talent at Westindies' disposal, Holding only occasionally had a chance to shine with the willow. In the series against England in 1984 he demonstrated a sound technique that brought him 69 runs in the first Test at Edgbaston, as he shared in a record ninth wicket stand of 150 with Eldine Baptiste. In the third match at Headingley, with Westindies still 64 behind, he crashed 59 runs in a stand of 82 with Larry Gomes, including five sixes off Bob Willis, and finished the series with a commendable batting average of 31.60.

In the last Test at The Oval, returning to the scene of his historic performance in 1976, Holding marked out his long run one more time. In a few overs of unprecedented pace he accounted for Chris Broad, David Gower and the in-form Allan Lamb.

It was a suitable swansong in England for a man who always saved his best performances for the highest level. His slender frame often failed him at crucial times in his career but, like Dennis Lillee, the other great fast bowler of his generation, Holding

always returned with even more success.

When Westindies entertained England at home in 1986, Holding was vice-captain and collected 16 wickets at 24.06 each in the series. He ran riot with the bat in the third game at St. John's, thrashing 73 including four sixes and six fours.

Holding toured New Zealand in 1987, and after that series, with a long and illustrious career behind him, the Rolls-Royce of fast bowling as he was once described, announced his retirement from Test cricket. The Jamaican played at the highest level for over a decade and was a key figure in the unprecedented success enjoyed by Westindies during those years.

Career details

Born: *16 February 1954*
Role: *Right-arm fast bowler*
Clubs: *Jamaica, Lancashire, Derbyshire, Tasmania, Lancashire League*
First-class record: *[1973-] 668 wickets (23.18) and 3,214 runs (15.75)*
Tests: *60*
Test debut: *v Australia 1975*
Test wickets: *249 (23.68); BB: 8-92 v England, The Oval, 1976*
Test runs: *910 (13.78); HS: 73 v England, St. John's, 1986*
Tours: *Australia 1975-76; England 1976; England (World Cup) 1979; Australia and New Zealand 1979-80; England 1980; Pakistan 1980-81; Australia 1981-82; England (World Cup) 1983; India 1983; England 1984; Australia 1984-85; New Zealand 1987.*

David Anthony Jerome Holford

As a young man David Holford was a consistently outstanding performer in the Barbados Cricket Association's senior competitions. He played for Spartan and captained Barbados, being picked for his island while studying at the University of the Westindies. Widely recognised as a player of exceptional talent he seemed to have a glowing international future ahead of him.

When the all-rounder, Joe Solomon, left the Test scene in 1966, Holford, an excellent leg-break bowler and capable middle-order batsman, seemed the obvious choice to fill the void. In the first Test against England at Old Trafford, he shared in a century stand with his cousin, Gary Sobers; and, during that match, he, Sobers and Lance Gibbs frustrated England with their accurate spin bowling.

Holford shared his finest hour, again with his cousin, when they added 274 runs for a record unbroken sixth wicket partnership, almost snatching an unlikely win from the jaws of defeat, in the second drawn Test at Lord's. When Holford arrived at the wicket, Westindies had already lost five men for a paltry lead of nine runs. Despite knowing that he was an uncertain starter, Sobers made no effort to shield him from the bowling. Holford's growing confidence eventually dispersed the close fielders, allowing Sobers to take some easy singles as the English concentrated their efforts on the less recognised batsman. Holford went on to complete the only hundred of his Test career.

His efforts at Old Trafford and Lord's seemed to add weight to the prediction that he was on the verge of a stunning Test future, and he was included in the tour party to India later the same year. In the opening Test at Bombay he made a resolute 80 and took five wickets in the match. Sadly, Holford then contracted a severe bout of pleurisy which kept him out of the rest of the tour; and thereafter seemed to arrest his hold on a regular place in the side, even though he played against England in 1968 and went to Australia

*id Holford, a
ble leg-spinner
useful batsman*

and New Zealand for the subsequent series. Indeed, when New Zealand visited the Caribbean in 1972, the Barbadian bowled so well that he was seen as a possible captain for the tour to England the following year. In the event, he was not selected for the trip at all.

Just as it seemed that he had disappeared from the Test scene for good, the enigmatic Holford took a match-winning five wickets for 23 against India in the first game at Bridgetown in 1976. He later became a recruit to Kerry Packer's World Series Cricket.

An outstanding all-rounder, Holford perhaps did not realise his early promise at the highest level, preferring to devote his energies to his career as an agronomist instead.

Career details

Born: *16 April 1940*
Role: *Right-hand batsman, right-arm leg-spinner.*
Club: *Barbados*
First-class record: *[1960-79] 3,821 runs (31.31) including 3 centuries, and 253 wickets (32.00)*
Tests: *24*
Test debut: *v England 1966*
Test wickets: *51 (39.39); BB: 5-23 v India, Bridgetown, 1976*
Tours: *England 1966; India 1966-67; Australia and New Zealand 1968-69.*

John Kenneth Holt (Junior)

If John Holt Junior's Test career was shorter than many others, it was also more controversial. On the verge of selection for several years, the Jamaican finally got his chance in the first Test against England on his home ground in 1954. When Holt was dismissed six short of his century, LBW to Brian Statham, having put on 135 for the second wicket, the partisan crowd reacted vociferously.

In the next match at Bridgetown, Holt opened the batting and scored his maiden Test century – an innings acknowledged as one of the most brilliant ever played at Kensington Oval. His 166 contained one six and 26 impeccable fours, as he added 222 for the second wicket with Frank Worrell.

Holt completed his hat-trick of excitement during the third Test at Georgetown. Clifford McWatt, the home batsman, was run out attempting a second run, after a partnership of 99 with Holt, who was batting at number nine with a runner because of a pulled leg muscle. Crowd trouble ensued, with disgruntled spectators throwing bottles onto the outfield. Despite his injury, Holt top-scored in the second innings with 64 and hit 40 in a losing cause in the fourth game at Port-of-Spain.

In the series against England 1954, Holt averaged 54, ensuring that he retained his place when Australia visited the Caribbean the following year. In the first Test in Kingston, he made 60 but, like most of the other batsmen, succumbed to the pace of Ray Lindwall and Keith Miller later in the rubber.

Holt toured India and Pakistan in 1958-59, and scored over 1,000 runs, including three hundreds. In the fourth Test at Madras, he made 63 in the first innings and was unbeaten on 81 in the second. He

union in ...ston in 1983 to ...ur Jamaicans ...played Test ...et before ...pendence: Back ...(l-r) Chester ...son, Alf ...ntine, Esmond ...ish, Roy Miller, ...s Johnson, Reg ...ett, Allan Rae. ...dle row (l-r) Ken ...ards, John Holt ...ior), Ken ...kes, George ...ie, Dickie ...r. Front row ...Alfie Binns, ...e Hendriks, ...r King, Howard ...ilton (Regional ...ager of Shell)

scored a century in the fifth match at New Delhi, before he and his partner, Conrad Hunte, were dropped after poor performances in the opening games of the second leg on the tour against Pakistan. While Hunte later enjoyed greater recognition at international level, it proved to be the end of the road for Holt.

The attacking right-hander never came to England, unlike his father, who toured with Harold Austin's team in 1923. Holt (Junior) was omitted from the tours to New Zealand in 1956 and England in 1957, after an indifferent time with the bat against Australia's fast bowlers.

On the edge of Test selection for so many years, Holt initially found success when he finally supplanted fellow Jamaican, Allan Rae, as the other opener with Jeff Stollmeyer. But, in a career dogged by controversy, this fluent stroke-maker, was seen at his best only occasionally at the highest level.

For many years a national coach, Holt toured India with the Commonwealth XI, and was also an international footballer.

Career details

Born: *12 August 1923*
Role: *Right-hand batsman*
Club: *Jamaica*
First-class record: *[1946-62] 4,256 runs (41.32) including 9 centuries.*
Tests: *17*
Test debut: *v England 1954*
Test runs: *1,066 (36.75); HS: 166 v England, Bridgetown, 1954*
Tours: *India and Pakistan 1958-59.*

Conrad Cleophas Hunte

Conrad Hunte began his career as a delightfully free-scoring batsman, building a formidable reputation in his native Barbados in the early 1950s. However, when he achieved Test status he tailored his batting to the needs of the team adopting a more defensive posture, especially in the later stages of his career, when his name became synonymous with reliability.

It was unfortunate for Hunte, and even more so for Westindies, that he was not able to find anyone else as consistent and, in his 44 Tests, he opened with 12 different partners, and enjoyed just five century opening stands in 78 innings.

Hunte made his first-class debut in 1950, but had to wait eight years for Test recognition, during which time he played for Enfield in the Lancashire League. He seemed an automatic choice for the tour to England in 1957, underlining his ability with 151 for Barbados against an E.W. Swanton XI, which included Frank Tyson, in 1956, but was overlooked, apparently because the selectors could not locate him.

When he eventually made his debut in the first Test against Pakistan at Bridgetown in 1958, he scored 142 in front of his home crowd, to emphasise the error of his earlier omission. In only his fourth Test innings, in the third match at Kingston, he scored 260 before he was run out, after sharing in a record second-wicket partnership of 446 with Gary Sobers. Indeed, Hunte seemed to be threatening Len Hutton's record score of 364, before Sobers went on to overhaul it later in the innings. Hunte scored yet another century in the Georgetown game to help him to a run aggregate of 622 and an average of 75.55 in his first Test series.

On the subsequent tour to India and Pakistan, Hunte made an indifferent start, although he shared in a partnership of 159 with John Holt in the fifth Test at New Delhi, but was dropped when he failed to sustain this form in Pakistan.

Nonetheless, the unassuming Barbadian played in

d Hunte: one of dies' most e opening n

117

the series against England in 1960, and his unbeaten 72, after being injured by a bumper from Fred Trueman in the fifth Test at Port-of-Spain, secured his passage to Australia the following season.

Hunte made his mark as a batsman of outstanding quality when he scored 110 in difficult conditions in the second innings of the second Test at Melbourne, as Westindies followed on 167 runs behind. It was during this series that Hunte swapped his aggressive stroke-play for a more defensive role. Even so, in the fourth Test at Adelaide he shared in a splendid partnership of 163 with Rohan Kanhai, before the latter ran him out, after Hunte had suggested some short singles because of poor fielding by the Australians. Typically, Hunte proceeded to comfort the mournful Kanhai, before amusing the crowd as he lost his way looking for the gate to the pavilion.

Hunte restricted himself to two fifties in the 5-0 defeat of India in the Caribbean in 1962, seeming to prefer to save himself for stiffer opposition. He was appointed vice-captain to Frank Worrell for the tour to England in 1963, and celebrated by topping the batting averages with 58.87. He excelled in the first Test at Old Trafford, with an eight hour innings of 182, and then hit Trueman's first three balls to the boundary in the next game at Lord's, before reverting to a more restrained role. He made a decisive contribution to Westindies' victory in the final match at The Oval, making 80 and 108.

Hunte had been an able vice-captain, and it must have been a bitter blow to him when, following Worrell's retirement at the end of the series against England, the captaincy passed to Sobers. But, in keeping with his generous character, Hunte accepted the decision and supported the new skipper.

In the series against Australia in 1965, Hunte headed the batting averages once again, as he hit six successive half centuries, top-scoring with 81 in the important win in the first match at Kingston; and finishing unbeaten on 60, out of a total of 131, in the final Test at Port-of-Spain, to become the first Westindian to carry his bat in a Test in the Caribbean. During this series Hunte was ably supported by the Trinidadian, Bryan Davis, as they shared in four successive stands of over fifty.

On his return to England in 1966, Hunte's 135 on the first day of the first Test at Old Trafford, after the tourists has lost two early wickets, rekindled memories of his performance on the same ground three years earlier. But, this time, he was unable to maintain his momentum and failed to make a half century in any of his following seven Test innings.

Hunte recovered his form in the subsequent three-match series against India, being the only Westindian to make a hundred, which he scored in the first Test at Bombay, and passed 40 in his next three innings. He was at the peak of his career and it seemed that he was assured of playing cricket at the highest level for several more years. But, after watching the film *The Crowning Experience* in Australia, Hunte was moved to devote his life to the Moral Re-armament Movement.

In a sense, it was not surprising that this quiet, thoughtful man, who scored Test centuries on four continents, should have been lost to cricket through such a cause. His unfailing loyalty and selfless behaviour, combined with his outstanding cricket ability, made his premature departure doubly regrettable.

Career details

Born: *8 May 1932*
Role: *Right-hand batsman*
Clubs: *Barbados, Lancashire League*
First-class record: *[1950-67] 8,916 runs (43.92) including 16 centuries, and 17 wickets (37.88).*
Tests: 44
Test debut: *v Pakistan 1958*
Test runs: *3,245 (45.06); HS: 260 v Pakistan, Kingston, 1958*
Tours: *India and Pakistan 1958-59; Australia 1960-61; England 1963; England 1966; India 1966-67.*

Hophnie Horace Hines Johnson

After making his debut for Jamaica in 1934-35, Hines Johnson quickly built a reputation as a formidable fast bowler, but had to wait over 10 years for his first Test appearance. When it finally arrived, at the age of 37, in the last game against England at Kingston in 1948, the paceman bowled his side to victory in the rubber, returning the remarkable match figures of 10 wickets for 96 runs. Spurred on by his home crowd, the 6ft 3in Jamaican took five for 41 in England's first innings, including the two openers, and five for 55 in their second.

It seemed that Westindies had found a successor to Manny Martindale, with *Wisden* commenting that "he looked a truly great bowler"; but he was unavailable for the subsequent tour to India, and failed to recover his magical form when he played in two Tests on Westindies' tour of England in 1950. In the third match at Trent Bridge, he took three for 59 in the home side's first innings and is also remembered for sheltering under the covers protecting the wicket, rather than in the pavilion, during a storm at that game.

Several of the best years of Johnson's bowling career were lost to the Second World War and when he was eventually elevated to Test status, apart from his astonishing debut, he was too old to establish himself. However, it must have been of some consolation to him that, in the two series in which he played, Westindies were decisive victors.

Hines Johnson watches the play at Fenners with Allan Rae during Westindies tour of England in 1950

119

Career details

Born: *17 July 1910*
Died: *24 June 1987*
Role: *Right-arm fast bowler*
Club: *Jamaica*
First class-record: *[1934-51] 68 wickets (23.36) and 316 runs (17.52)*
Tests: *3*
Test debut: *v England 1948*
Test wickets: *13 (18.30); BB: 5-41 v England, Kingston, 1948*
Tour: *England 1950*

Hines Johnson bowling against Cambridge University during Westindies tour of England in 1950

Prior Erskine Jones

A powerful right-arm medium-fast bowler, Prior Jones had the unfortunate and, for a Westindian, unusual experience of playing second fiddle to an illustrious spin bowling partnership, namely that of Sonny Ramadhin and Alf Valentine. Jones was selected as one of the main strike bowlers, along with his Trinidadian compatriot, Lance Pierre, and the Jamaican, Hines Johnson, for the tour to England in 1950, but became somewhat redundant after the remarkable success enjoyed by the spin twins.

The hostile Jones, who had the ability to move the ball, first encountered England when they toured the Caribbean in 1948. In the opening match at Bridgetown, he bowled impressively to finish with four for 54, but didn't make another appearance that year.

The following season Jones was selected to open the bowling on the tour to India, and despite being hampered by the slower pitches he finished with an admirable 51 wickets (18.54) including 17 Test victims. The tall Trinidadian gave the visitors an encouraging start by dismissing Vinoo Mankad cheaply in the first Test in New Delhi. Jones returned decisive figures of four for 30 in the fourth match at Madras, which won the Test and the series for the tourists, as he and John Trim retaliated in kind after Dattu Phadkar had bowled an excessive number of bouncers in Westindies' only innings of the game.

Jones maintained his momentum into the final match at Bombay, worrying the Indians, who were set 361 to win in 395 minutes. He removed the prodigious Mushtaq Ali, and then thwarted the home side's advance by dismissing Vijay Hazare for 122. Jones almost engineered an unlikely win for Westindies in a bizarre end to an entertaining match: having sent Mankad and Shute Banerjee back to the pavilion, six runs were required off Jones' last ball, with eight Indian wickets down and the wicket-keeper, Probir Sen, injured. But, as the big fast bowler walked back to the start of his run, the umpire removed the bails and called time, realising that he had miscounted the over admist the excitement.

The Trinidadian was taken to Australia in 1951-52

or Jones in action inst Cambridge iversity during stindies tour of gland in 1950

as a veteran at the age of 34 and, although he played in only one Test, he was used extensively in the games against the states. In his sole Test appearance in the second match at Sydney, the result might have been different if a difficult chance offered by Lindsay Hassett off Jones, when he was on nine, had been accepted. It was dropped and the diminutive Hassett went on to make 132, to steer Australia to victory by seven wickets.

Jones was a strongly-built man who, besides being an excellent bowler, was a superb fielder with an enviable throw and outstanding in the slips. A perennial trier, he was unlucky to be at his peak when the spinners were enjoying a fleeting pre-eminence and when the overseas wickets on which he operated did not always suit his style of bowling.

Career details

Born: *6 June 1917*
Role: *Right-arm medium-fast bowler*
Club: *Trinidad*
First-class record: *[1940-52] 169 wickets (26.81) and 775 runs (14.09)*
Tests: *9*
Test debut: v *England 1948*
Test wickets: 25 (30.04); BB: 5-85 v India, Bombay, 1949
Tours: *India 1948-49; England 1950; Australia and New Zealand 1951-52.*

Bernard Denis Julien

Bernard Julien's early comparisons with Gary Sobers, prompted by his outstanding all-round cricketing ability, clouded his career and, perhaps, explains why the boisterous Trinidadian never lived up to his early potential.

As a 13-year-old, Julien represented Trinidad primary schools on a two-week tour of Barbados, scoring a swashbuckling 78 in one of the matches and being among the wickets in the others. By the age of 16, he had scored a double century for St. Mary's College and, by 17, had played for North against South in Trinidad. In one game he got a hat-trick, and eventually finished with eight for 58, opening with the new ball and later switching to his left-arm spin. He was also an unorthodox chinaman and googly bowler, as well as being a good fielder close to the wicket.

Indeed, this was part of Julien's problem: he excelled at many aspects of the game, yet he was unable to concentrate and develop one or two facets. His initial successes had come early and quite easily which, perhaps, made him a little complacent. The parallels with Sobers and Julien's liking for the good life also hampered his progress.

Yet, of his ability there was no doubt, and he was spotted by Colin Cowdrey when he visited Trinidad with the Duke of Norfolk's team. Cowdrey promptly signed the youngster for Kent, for whom Julien played between 1970-77. As with his Test career, his performances varied from the amazing to the abysmal; while his early games with Kent were overshadowed by personal problems. His father had died just before he left Trinidad and he worried about his mother coping on her own.

By the time he made his Test debut, on Westindies' 1973 tour to England, like Keith Boyce at Essex, Julien had become a familiar figure on the English county scene. In the second match at Edgbaston, he recorded his first Test fifty as a prelude to his scintillating 121 off 127 balls, mostly in partnership with Sobers, during the third Test at Lord's, which earned him an extended run in the team.

Bernard Julien hits out during his memorable innings against England at Lord's in 1973. His 121 came off just 127 balls

The following season he played against England in the Caribbean and was the only batsman to support Alvin Kallicharran, by making an unbeaten 86, to help Westindies to a seven-wicket win in the first Test at Port-of-Spain. He followed this with a hard-hit 66 in the next game at Kingston, and produced his best Test bowling figures of five for 57 in the third match at Bridgetown. Altogether it was a successful series for Julien, who took 16 wickets and made some useful contributions with the bat, given that he did not come in until number seven.

Julien had a modest tour to India and Pakistan in 1974-75, shining briefly in the final drawn Test at Karachi, where he hit the second hundred of his career against a strong Pakistani attack.

He was included in the World Cup side to England in 1975, and got Westindies off to a good start in their opening fixture by taking four for 20 against Sri Lanka, as they crumbled to 86 all out, and took four important wickets for 27 against New Zealand in the semi-finals.

Julien was selected for the disastrous tour to Australia the following year and, as the temporary opener with Roy Fredericks, added 92 runs at more than nine runs an over in the second Test at Perth, to usher Westindies to their solitary victory of the series.

After the overwhelming defeat in Australia, the balance of the Westindies side altered with the emergence of Andy Roberts and Michael Holding and, after poor performances with both bat and ball in 1976, Julien disappeared from the Test scene. With his best days behind him, the gregarious Trinidadian was contracted to play World Series Cricket and subsequently toured South Africa with Lawrence Rowe's rebel side in 1983.

However, Julien later renounced the system of apartheid and came off the UN blacklist. He returned to play for Trinidad, but without any notable success.

Career details

Born: *13 March 1950*
Role: *Right-hand batsman, left-arm fast medium bowler, orthodox left-arm spinner, left-arm chinaman and googly bowler*
Clubs: *Trinidad, Kent*
First-class record: *[1967-84] 5,792 runs (24.44), including 3 centuries, and 483 wickets (28.72)*
Tests: *24*
Test debut: *v England 1973*
Test runs: *866 (30.92); HS: 121 v England, Lord's, 1973*
Test wickets: *50 (37.36); BB 5-57 v England, Bridgetown, 1974*
Tours: *England 1973; India and Pakistan 1974-75; England (World Cup) 1975; Australia 1975-76; England 1976.*

Alvin Isaac Kallicharran

Alvin Kallicharran was one of the finest batsmen of his generation and also one of the most controversial. Born at Port Mourant in Berbice County, the diminutive left-hander learned his cricket at Paidama and appeared in the Guyana schools team in the Westindies championships in 1966. The following year, at the age of 16½, he became the youngest player to appear for Guyana in the Shell Shield.

Like his mentor, Rohan Kanhai, the tiny Kallicharran is a touch player and derives his power from his tremendous sense of timing. The wristy left-hander has all the strokes at his command and is acknowledged as one of the best post-War players of spin bowling. His compatriot and captain, Clive Lloyd, said of Kallicharran: "(He) is one of the best players of spin bowling I have seen, and one only needs to glance at his scores at Queen's Park Oval…a traditional spinners' paradise to be convinced of this. This is not to say that he was inadequate against pace and, at his best, is the complete player."

Kallicharran made his international debut against New Zealand in the fourth Test at Georgetown in 1972. There, in front of his home crowd, he joined the distinguished band of players who have made a century on their Test debut. The Guyanese finished unbeaten on a hundred on a placid pitch, scoring his last 41 runs in an hour after his innings had been interrupted by a bottle-throwing incident. In his second Test innings in the final match at Port-of-Spain, Kallicharran scored another splendid century to secure his place in the side against the touring Australians the following year.

The left-hander opened his account with fifty at Kingston and confirmed his promise with 53 and 91 in the third match at Port-of-Spain, as he nearly brought off victory for the home side, demonstrating a sound technique on a treacherous pitch.

Kallicharran's continuing good form earned his passage to England later that year and he hit 80 in each innings in the first Test at The Oval, sharing in a double century partnership with Lloyd in the first. He hit three centuries against county sides and

Alvin Kallicharran: one of Westindies' most accomplished batsmen

124

finished the tour with an average of 64.78. In the return rubber the little man consolidated his international reputation by hitting 158 in the first Test at Port-of-Spain, and followed that up with 93 in the second match at Kingston. In the third game at Bridgetown Kallicharran scored 119, sharing in a record second wicket partnership of 249 with Lawrence Rowe.

His stream of runs continued to flow unabated on Westindies' tour to India and Pakistan in 1974-75, as he passed fifty in six of the seven Tests. In the first match at Bangalore he hit a masterful hundred on a difficult wicket and, in the deciding game at Bombay, he made 98, sharing in century partnerships with Roy Fredericks and Lloyd, to clinch the series for Westindies. Kallicharran top-scored with an unbeaten 92 in the first Test on the Pakistan leg of the tour, at Lahore, and in the final match at Karachi he scored 115, sharing in a three figure stand with Lloyd.

When Westindies visited Australia later that year Kallicharran stood up to the blistering pace of Dennis Lillee and Jeff Thomson admirably. In the first Test at Brisbane he scored a century, adding 198 with Rowe for the fourth wicket, and a brave 57 in the second match at Perth, despite a broken nose. He collected another two half centuries in the fifth game at Adelaide.

Kallicharran had a consistent series against the Indians when they visited the Caribbean in 1976, finishing second in the averages to Viv Richards. After the pair had shared in a double century third wicket stand in the first Test at Bridgetown, the Guyanese hit an unbeaten hundred in the third game on his favourite Port-of-Spain ground.

Soon afterwards Kallicharran was afflicted with fibrositis in his shoulder, a painful condition which seriously affected his performance against England later that year. Even so, the Guyanese worked hard for 97, sharing in a triple century partnership with Richards, in the first Test at Trent Bridge, but a pair at Lord's and further problems at Old Trafford ruled him out of the rest of the tour.

The left-handed lightweight continued to struggle when Pakistan visited Westindies in 1977, with his only notable innings being 72 in the third match at

Georgetown. Apart from his injury, Kallicharran was doubtless tired from playing continuous cricket but, within a few months, he was plunged into the biggest responsibility of his career after the Kerry Packer crisis erupted.

Even though his batting invariably captured the headlines, Kallicharran was often in the news over various controversial incidents that punctuated his career. The left-hander was one of the first players to sign for Packer's World Series tournament. But, he later withdrew from his contract, which conflicted with an earlier one he had signed with a radio station in Queensland, and returned to lead the official Westindies side.

Kallicharran's world class ability merely underlined the short-comings of his patched up official team. The gifted Guyanese had already top-scored in the opening Test against the Australians with his customary century at Port-of-Spain, before the walk-out by the Packer players on the eve of the third game at Georgetown. Installed as the new captain, Kallicharran guided his inexperienced colleagues to victory in the fourth Test at Port-of-Spain with 92 and 69, and hit a splendid hundred in the final match at Kingston.

The Guyanese maintained his momentum into the series against India in 1978-79. In the first Test at Bombay he hit 187, then 71 at Bangalore, 55 at Calcutta, 98 at Madras, and 45 at New Delhi, confirming that he would maintain his place in the official Test side even when the Packer players returned. But, after becoming the first Westindian skipper to lose a rubber in India, Kallicharran could not expect to retain the captaincy. Despite being hampered without the World Series players, Dicky Rutnagur reported in *Wisden* that "Kallicharran's captaincy was one of the major weaknesses of the touring team".

Picked for the tours to Australia and New Zealand in 1979-80, he made a century in the third match at Adelaide and 75 and and 46 in the second and third Tests in New Zealand. However, he struggled on the subsequent tours to England and Pakistan.

Controversy was never far from Kallicharran and he caused uproar by becoming the first Westindian player to appear in South Africa's Currie Cup competition when he joined Transvaal in 1981-82.

The Guyanese was also involved in a famous drama on the field. In the opening Test against England at Port-of-Spain in 1974, Kallicharran was run out by Tony Greig with the last ball of the first day. Bernard Julien played the delivery to Greig at short-leg, whereupon Kallicharran began walking to the pavilion without first grounding his bat in the usual way. Greig threw down Kallicharran's wicket, and upon Greig's appeal, the umpire was obliged to give the astounded batsman out. The ensuing furore was diffused only after the appeal was withdrawn overnight. Kallicharran, clearly unsettled, returned the next morning to add 16 runs to his score before he was finally dismissed for 158.

But it is probably his remarkable batting prowess for which Kallicharran will be remembered best. One of the most memorable batting assaults of the 1970s came when the Guyanese savaged Lillee in a preliminary round match of the 1975 World Cup against Australia at The Oval. Described by Gordon Ross as batting "like a firecracker, exploding all round" Kallicharran hooked the great bowler indiscriminately. In the space of 10 balls he thrashed one six and seven fours, as he raced to 78 and brought his team to the edge of their win, and then top-scored in the semi-final confrontation with New Zealand.

His brilliant run-scoring attracted worldwide recognition and the prodigious Guyanese signed contracts with Warwickshire and Queensland. He thrived at Warwickshire and, in the early 1980s, if he had not gone to South Africa, Kallicharran's sparkling form would have certainly demanded a Test recall. Indeed, after his banning, Kallicharran said he looked on county cricket as his Test cricket. In 1982 he scored over 2,000 runs, featuring three championship double centuries – including 230 not

out as he shared in a record fourth wicket stand of 470 with Geoff Humpage against Lancashire at Southport, which remains the highest partnership in English county cricket – and five single hundreds. In 1982 and 1983 Kallicharran topped Warwickshire's batting averages while, in five of his first seven seasons with the club, he hit 1,000 first-class runs. Altogether in the championship he has scored 46 centuries – including a record nine in 1984 – and six double hundreds.

A happy character with an enviable temperament, the Guyanese is a good fielder, with a strong throw from the deep and a reliable catcher, as well as a great talker in the slips.

Kallicharran has made his home in Birmingham, and is hoping to persuade the TCCB that he can play for Warwickshire and, indeed, England as a qualified Englishman. Whatever happens, it is not beyond the realms of possibility that another Kallicharran will force himself into the official Test arena as his young son, Rohan, has shown a lot of early promise.

Career details

Born: *21 March 1949*
Role: *Left-hand batsman*
Clubs: *Guyana, Warwickshire, Queensland, Transvaal, Orange Free State*
First-class record: *[1966-] 31,331 runs (45.20) including 84 centuries, and 81 wickets (48.22)*
Tests: *66*
Test debut: *v New Zealand 1972*
Test runs: *4,399 (44.43); HS: 187 v India, Bombay, 1978*
Tours: *England 1973; India and Pakistan 1974-75; England (World Cup) 1975; Australia 1975-76; England 1976; India 1978-79; England (World Cup) 1979; Australia and New Zealand 1979-80; England 1980; Pakistan 1980-81.*

Rohan Babulal Kanhai

Rohan Kanhai was arguably the finest of a crop of young batsmen to emerge from Guyana, after Clyde Walcott went there as national coach in the 1950s. Walcott guided the prodigious Kanhai through his first tentative steps at Berbice Cricket Club and onto the world stage, where he became a leading player.

Like Walcott, Kanhai began his career as a capable wicket-keeper and on his first tour, to England in 1957, the Guyanese kept in three Tests. The youngster was surrounded by fiery pacemen from all angles: as wicket-keeper he had to take Roy Gilchrist and Wes Hall and, when opening the innings, he had to face Fred Trueman and Brian Statham.

Of Guyanese Indian ancestry, the young Kanhai stood up to the ordeal admirably, despite being used as a makeshift opener in the first two Tests, before he returned to the middle order where he was most at home. He made three solid forties, and top-scored with 34 out of a total of 127 in the first innings of the second Test at Lord's.

Kanhai impressed sufficiently to keep his place against the Pakistanis when they visited the Caribbean the following year. The right-hander fell four short of his century in the second Test at Port-of-Spain and hit a sparkling 62 in front of his home crowd in the fourth match at Georgetown, which won his passage on the tour to India and Pakistan in 1958-59.

Once more Kanhai found himself opening the innings in an experiment which failed again, even though he top-scored with 66 opening in the first Test at Bombay. The Guyanese showed his true class in the third match at Calcutta, batting at number three, when he scored a magnificent 256 runs out of a Westindies total of 614 for five declared, including a partnership of 217 with his compatriot, Basil Butcher.

This was a turning point for Kanhai, who booked a permanent place in the Test side, as his extravagant hooking and sweeping brought comparisons with Everton Weekes. Having proved to himself that he had the ability to make a huge score at the highest level, Kanhai went from strength to strength. Indeed,

n Kanhai

after his position became settled, Kanhai was as lethal with the bat as Gilchrist and Wes Hall were with the ball and established himself as a world class batsman, scoring more runs than anyone else on the tour. He seemed set for another big hundred in the fourth match at Madras, before he was run out for 99 – which was not the first or the last occasion that Kanhai's impetuosity cost him his wicket.

On the Pakistan leg of the tour, Westindies' fortunes took a downturn which was reflected in Kanhai being juggled about the batting order again. But he ended the tour on a high note, when he returned to the number three position in the third match at Lahore, and helped himself to 217 – an innings which, incidentally, was more than the combined total of any other player on that part of the tour. He added 162 runs with Gary Sobers to guide the tourists to victory by an innings.

When England visited the Westindies the following year, Kanhai began the series with a restrained 40 in the first Test at Bridgetown. But he was back to his flowing best when he hit 110 in just over six hours in the defeat in the next game at Port-of-Spain. In the third match at Kingston, set 230 runs to win in slightly over four hours, Westindies looked to Kanhai for inspiration. But the Guyanese was hampered by a muscle injury and when he was refused a runner – a decision later found to be wrong – the game fizzled out into a draw.

Kanhai seemed to reserve his best form for the visit to Australia in 1960-61. Early in the tour he hit a splendid hundred against an Australian X1, and followed this with a double century against Victoria. He scored 54 in the first Test at Brisbane, and 84 out of a total of 181 in the next match at Melbourne. He top-scored with centuries in both innings of the fourth Test at Adelaide, beginning with 117, as he shared in a three figure stand with Frank Worrell, and then hit 115, adding 163 for the second wicket with Conrad Hunte.

A small man, Kanhai was sometimes accused of sacrificing his wicket in his haste to make runs. Walcott explained that this reflected his desire not to disappoint people who had faith in him, while his fetish for keeping the scoreboard moving brought back memories of Clifford Roach.

Kanhai excelled against the weak Indian side that visited the Caribbean in 1962, collecting centuries in the second Test at Kingston, as he added 255 with Sobers, and in the fourth match at Port-of-Spain.

By the time Westindies visited England in 1963, Kanhai was regarded as a veteran of the side. Although he did not get a century in the series, his contributions were often decisive to the outcome of the match. He hit a splendid 90 in the first Test at Old Trafford before, typically, he was run out. He top-scored in the first innings of the next game at Lord's with a more restrained 73, before falling eight short of his century in the first innings of the fourth match at Headingley. England had to win at The Oval to level the series, but Kanhai's scintillating 77 – scored in less than even time – put the match out of England's reach. Once again Kanhai's unexpected burst of scoring had decided the outcome of a match and, in this case, the rubber.

By now Kanhai had established his international credentials and was a household name in sporting circles. Eagle eye-sight, sharp reflexes, good footwork and impeccable timing all contrived to make him a formidable opponent; although part of his genius was his unpredictability, and he was never as reliable as someone like Sobers. Even so, his prodigious talents were in great demand and he played for Western Australia in 1961 and later appeared for Warwickshire – for whom he scored 1,000 first-class runs in each of his 10 years with them – and Tasmania. Kanhai also played in several English and Scottish leagues and married a Lancastrian.

Kanhai confirmed his liking for the Australian attack when they visited the Caribbean in 1965. In difficult batting conditions in the third Test at Georgetown he was the only batsman to reach a half-century, as his 89 set up the home side's victory. The Guyanese hit 129, sharing in a double century stand with Seymour Nurse, on a docile pitch in the next match at Bridgetown. He rounded off the series with 121 runs out of 224 at Port-of-Spain, demonstrating a more resolute approach, which evolved as he matured and which complemented his more aggressive style when circumstances were in his side's favour.

In the 1966 series against England, Kanhai collected an unusually dour 63 in the third match at Trent Bridge, undeterred by the difficult situation in which he found himself after England had secured a first innings lead or by the crowd's barracking, as his efforts gave Westindies an invincible lead in the series. The Guyanese finished the series with 104 in the last match at The Oval – his first century in 15 Tests in England – as he shared in a three figure partnership with Sobers.

Against India later that year, Kanhai top-scored with a solid 90 in the second match at Calcutta, to usher the tourists to an innings victory and an unassailable lead in the series. He helped himself to 77 in the final drawn match at Madras, before enjoying a year's break from international competition which rejuvenated him for the visit by England to the Caribbean in 1968.

He began with an impressive 85 in the first Test at Port-of-Spain, but saved his best form for the final two games in the series. He made an exhilarating 153 in the fourth match, again at Port-of-Spain, which was his fourth century in as many series on that ground, as he shared in a huge third-wicket stand of 273 with Nurse. He followed this up with another big hundred in the last Test at Georgetown, sharing in another double century partnership, this time with Sobers.

Kanhai failed to score with his usual fluency in Australia in 1968-69. His best effort came in the opening match at Brisbane when he made 94 and, after a modest series by his standards, he asked to be left out of the trip to England in 1969.

Kanhai's rest from Test cricket seemed to give him the tonic he needed, and he returned to the international fold for the home series against India in 1971 full of his old sparkle. He top-scored with 56 in the first innings of the first Test at Kingston and, following on, smashed an unbeaten 158 off the Indian bowlers, to prevent the tourists from gaining an early initiative in the rubber. However, after that gallant effort, Kanhai only reached fifty once more that year and didn't play against New Zealand when they visited the Caribbean the following season.

Given his own fluctuating fortunes, it was something of a surprise when Kanhai was elevated to

the captaincy in 1973, and he began his reign with a difficult baptism against a confident Australian touring side. Nonetheless, his own performances seemed to rise to the occasion, and he became the first Guyanese to captain Westindies for a sustained

One of the Westindies' most prolific batsmen, Rohan Kanhai, also took part in the world record second wicket stand of 465 with John Jameson for Warwickshire against Gloucestershire in 1974

length of time. He hit 84 in the first Test at Kingston and top-scored with a century in the second innings of the second match at Bridgetown, while further half centuries in the matches at Port-of-Spain and Georgetown ensured that he retained the captaincy for the tour to England, even though Westindies lost the series.

After an unfortunate *contretemps* with the umpire, Arther Fagg, in the second Test at Edgbaston, when the official refused to uphold an appeal against Geoff Boycott, Kanhai erased any memories of bad feeling by cracking a masterly 157 in the final match at Lord's to take his team to a decisive victory. It was fitting that a man who was always at home in England – he enjoyed an illustrious career with Warwickshire, scoring 31 county championship centuries, including 213 in a world record undefeated second wicket stand of 465 with John Jameson against Gloucestershire at Edgbaston in 1974 – should have led his side to victory in the rubber and their first series win since 1967.

Sometimes criticised for his defensive approach as skipper, which contrasted sharply with his attacking style of batting, Kanhai nonetheless played an important role during the transition years from Sobers to Clive Lloyd. In his 13 Tests as captain, Kanhai instilled the killer instinct in the side which Lloyd was to use to transform Westindies into a world-beating combination.

When England visited the Caribbean in the return rubber, Kanhai failed to distinguish himself and, after England squared the series, he lost the captaincy. Of his 79 Tests, Kanhai appeared in 61 of them consecutively and his run was only broken when he had to go to England for a cartilage operation. But Kanhai proved he was far from a spent force when he hit a careful half century, in a match-winning stand of 149 with Lloyd in the 1975 World Cup final, as the Guyanese pair gave their bowlers a reasonable score to defend.

An athletic fielder anywhere, Kanhai also had a habit of falling flat on his back when he swept the ball ferociously to the boundary – a stroke which became his hallmark.

After his retirement, Kanhai moved to Jamaica where he is currently coaching the national team.

Career details

Born: *26 December 1935*
Role: *Right-hand batsman, wicket-keeper.*
Clubs: *Guyana, Trinidad, Warwickshire, Western Australia, Tasmania, English and Scottish Leagues*
First-class career: *[1955-77] 28,639 runs (49.29) including 83 centuries, 315 catches and 7 stumpings*
Tests: *79*
Test debut: *v England 1957*
Test runs: *6,227 (47.53); HS: 256 v India, Calcutta, 1959*
Tours: *England 1957; India and Pakistan 1958-59; Australia 1960-61; England 1963; England 1966; India 1966-67; Australia and New Zealand 1968-69; England 1973; England (World Cup) 1975.*

Esmond Seymour Maurice Kentish

Esmond Kentish was a sturdy right-arm fast bowler who, above all else, had plenty of stamina. His two Test appearances were separated by an interval of six years, and he became the oldest cricketer to appear in a varsity match when he played for Oxford against Cambridge at Lord's in 1956, at the age of 39.

Both his Tests were at home against England, the first being in 1948, when he opened the bowling with his compatriot, Hines Johnson, his regular partner for Jamaica, in the fourth match at Kingston; and the second, also on his home ground, in the opening Test of the 1954 series.

On the second occasion the powerful Jamaican distinguished himself by bowling at the leg-stump to an on-side field of seven men, which brought him rich rewards. He finished with five for 49 in the tourists' second innings, inducing an unexpected collapse after some solid batting from Willie Watson, Peter May and Len Hutton. Kentish began the rot by having May and Tom Graveney caught and then bowled Godfrey Evans, Tony Lock and Fred Trueman as seven English wickets fell for a remarkable six runs, allowing Westindies to post victory by 140 runs. This kept the visitors under pressure for the remainder of the series.

Kentish subsequently played a key role in the administration of Westindies cricket, serving on the Board of Control and managing several overseas tours.

He later became Governor of the Bank of Jamaica.

Career details

Born: *21 November 1916*
Role: *Right-arm fast bowler*
Clubs: *Jamaica, Oxford University*
First-class record: *[1947-57] 78 wickets (26.17) and 109 runs (13.62)*
Tests: *2*
Test debut: *v England 1948*
Test wickets: *8 (22.25); BB: 5-49 v England, Kingston, 1954*

Collis Llewellyn King

Even though he had already appeared in four Tests, Collis King's explosive batting ability only received worldwide recognition after he blasted the English bowling attack into submission during the 1979 World Cup final. Westindies found themselves in the unusually shaky position of 99 for four, but King changed the course of the match as he thrashed 86 runs off 66 balls. In 21 stupendous overs of power hitting, the extravagant Barbadian and, for once, more conservative Viv Richards, added 139 runs and effectively put the game out of England's reach.

A batsman who is always on the attack from the start of his innings, King is also a competent medium pace bowler and a gregarious fielder. He made his debut for Barbados in 1973 and was a specially registered player for Glamorgan in 1977.

The tall Barbadian toured England in 1976, and shone brightly even among the glittering array of batting talent that Westindies had at their disposal in that vintage summer. He hit 1,320 runs (55.00) including six glorious hundreds, the highest of which was 163 against Northamptonshire, and also took 27

Collis King on the move during his innings of 63 against England at The Oval in 1976

wickets. In three Tests King helped himself to 167 runs, including fifty off 39 balls in the second match at Headingley. He didn't miss out in the run riot in the fifth Test at The Oval either, as he made 63 sizzling runs.

The touring Pakistanis were fortunate to avoid the boisterous Bardadian when they visited the Caribbean in 1977, as he was sidelined for most of their trip due to injury.

Besides the acclaim and recognition that his World Cup innings brought him, there were penalties to be paid too. That summer King was banned from playing for Ponthlyddyn in the North Wales League because he was too good! The exuberant Barbadian had scored 283 in an afternoon game in 1978. Nonetheless, he was permitted to play in the Lancashire League.

Yet, his remarkable panache for whirlwind innings continued unabated, and he entertained the New Zealanders in 1980 with an unbeaten hundred in the second Test at Christchurch, in a drawn game that featured four other centuries.

Later on King was banned from cricket again, this time from the Westindies' Test team, after he had opted to go on the two tours to South Africa between 1982-84. It was an abrupt end to a peerlessly entertaining career in official Test cricket, but wherever he went King could not curb his prolific scoring, and on both trips to South Africa he topped the batting in the first-class matches with 518 runs at an average of 51.80 and 450 at 40.90 respectively.

Career details

Born: *11 June 1951*
Role: *Right-hand batsman, medium-pace bowler*
Clubs: *Barbados, Glamorgan, Worcestershire, Natal, English and Welsh leagues*
First-class record: *[1972-] 6,770 runs (38.24) including 14 centuries, and 128 wickets (34.21)*
Tests: *9*
Test debut: *v England 1976*
Test runs: *418 (32.15); HS: 100* v New Zealand, Christchurch, 1980*
Tours: *England (World Cup) 1975; England 1976; England (World Cup) 1979; Australia and New Zealand 1979-80; England 1980.*

Collis King hitting one of his three sixes during his innings of 86 in the 1979 World Cup Final

Frank McDonald King

The introduction of the Barbadian paceman, Frank King, into the Test arena in the early 1950s seemed to signal a revival in Westindies' fast bowling. He harangued the visiting Indians in 1953 and tried to emulate Fred Trueman's hostility in the subsequent series against strong English and Australian batting sides. However, as the only genuine fast bowler at the time, King was probably over-used and this, together with fitness problems, contrived to shorten his Test career after he broke down on the trip to New Zealand in 1956.

King was at his most effective in his first series against India when he took 17 wickets (28.23). He bowled particularly well in the third Test at Port-of-Spain, collecting five for 74 in the visitors' first innings but, in the end, the Indian opener, Madhav Apte, saved his side with an unbeaten 163 in the second. Even so, King had created a favourable impression in his first series, although the spinning partnership of Sonny Ramadhin and Alf Valentine was still shouldering a disproportionate amount of the bowling attack.

He performed moderately against England in 1954; but, a year later, the touring Australians provided King with stiffer opposition. In the fifth game at Kingston in 1955, although the Barbadian removed Les Favell before a run had been scored, the batsmen soon regained the initiative as they totalled 758 for eight declared.

When he went to New Zealand in 1956, King was approaching 30 and the burden of Test cricket proved too much for his vulnerable physique, which often failed to cope with the enthusiasm that he put into his bowling.

Career details

Born: *14 December 1926*
Role: *Right-arm fast bowler*
Clubs: *Barbados, Trinidad*
First-class record: *[1947-57] 90 wickets (28.75) and 237 runs (9.11)*
Tests: *14*
Test debut: *v India 1962*
Test wickets: *29 (39.96); BB: 5-74 v India, Port-of-Spain, 1953*
Test runs: *116 (8.28)*
Tour: *New Zealand 1956*

Patrick Douglas "Peter" Lashley

A magnificent double century for Barbados against Guyana at Bridgetown in 1959-60, secured "Peter" Lashley's passage on the tour to Australia in 1960-61. But the left-handed Barbadian was not the success that many had hoped for, as he averaged just 19.40. Nonetheless, he scored an invaluable 41 in the fifth Test at Melbourne, buttressing the middle-order batting with Joe Solomon. But despite their gallant efforts, Westindies trailed on the first innings and eventually lost the game, and with it the series, by two wickets.

Lashley was selected for the tour to England in 1966 but again struggled in the Tests, although he made 49 – an innings which took over three hours – in the third match at Trent Bridge, when he was promoted to open the innings with Conrad Hunte.

A slim, amiable man as well as being a fluent batsman, he was an occasional medium-pace bowler and an outstanding fieldsman. He is the leading run-scorer for Barbados in the Shell Shield with 2,763 at an average of 55.83 and shares the record for the most Shield centuries for his island with Carlisle Best: they have scored six each.

Lashley has had a major influence on the development of grass roots cricket in Barbados, and is a key figure behind the lottery run on behalf of the Barbados Cricket Association in support of the game on the island.

Like most Westindians of his era, Lashley played in the leagues in the north of England for several years.

Career details

Born: *11 February 1937*
Role: *Left-hand batsman*
Clubs: *Barbados, North of England leagues*
First-class record: *[1957-75] 4,932 runs (41.44) including 8 centuries, and 27 wickets (35.48)*
Tests: *4*
Test debut: *v Australia 1960*
Test runs: *159 (22.71); HS: 49 v England, Trent Bridge, 1966;*
Tours: *Australia 1960-61; England 1966.*

Peter Lashley

134

Ralph Archibald Legall

A capable wicket-keeper, Ralph Legall's services were called upon for the home Test series against India in 1953, as the Westindian selectors searched in vain for a successor to Clyde Walcott, whose back injury had terminated his career behind the stumps.

Legall was one of several distinguished wicket-keepers, including Alfie Binns and Clairmonte Depeiza, who filled the role fleetingly at Test level in the mid-1950s, before the selectors finally settled on Gerry Alexander. Against the Indians, Binns was chosen for the first Test at Port-of-Spain, before Legall took over the gloves for the four remaining matches of the series – the only ones of his Test career.

Born in Barbados, Legall settled in Trinidad after he was stationed there with the Southern Caribbean Forces just after the War. He soon revealed his remarkable all-round sporting aptitude, winning national recognition from his adopted island for basketball, soccer, and table tennis, as well as cricket. He also represented Westindies at Davis Cup tennis, making him arguably the finest sportsman ever to emerge from the Caribbean.

After the Test series against India, Legall, who besides being a competent wicket-keeper was also a useful right-hand batsman, came to England to play league cricket.

Career details

Born: *1 December 1925*
Deceased
Role: *Wicket-keeper, right-hand batsman*
Clubs: *Barbados, Trinidad, North of England Leagues*
First-class record: *[1946-58] 32 catches and 10 stumpings, and 485 runs (22.04)*
Tests: *4*
Test debut: *v India 1953*
Test catches: *8; Test stumpings: 1*

Clive Hubert Lloyd

The longest serving and most successful Test captain of all time, Clive Lloyd rose rapidly through the ranks of junior cricket to become one of the world's best known and most respected sportsmen.

At the age of 14, he was captain of Chatham High School in the Chin Cup inter-school tournament and was soon appearing regularly for one of the best known Georgetown clubs, Demerara, in the Wight Cup and Case Cup competitions.

Born in Georgetown, Lloyd is a cousin of Lance Gibbs, and like the great off-spinner he has a Barbadian mother and a Guyanese father. Brought up in a cricketing environment, the youngster seemed destined to make his career in the sport and never appears to have been handicapped by his glasses which he has worn since childhood, after being injured breaking up a fight.

Lloyd had no basic coaching as a young man but, by his late teens, "supercat" as he was known for his feline prowess in the covers, was a permanent member of Demerara's first team batting line-up. He was elevated to the national side in 1964, but after an indifferent game against Jamaica, Lloyd was dropped and failed to make an impression against the touring Australians the following year.

Lloyd made his Shell Shield dedut in 1966 and had a disappointing first innings against Barbados, when he was dismissed for a duck by Gary Sobers. In the second innings Lloyd went into bat with his side in the precarious position of 86 for four. After a shaky start, the youngster grew in confidence against the bowling of Sobers and Charlie Griffith and went on to an impressive century. The Guyanese made a splendid 194 against Jamaica at Kingston in the next match to confirm his outstanding promise, and was selected for the tour to India at the end of that year.

Lloyd had an auspicious start to his Test career. In the opening match at Bombay he hit a sparkling 82 in the first innings and finished unbeaten on 78 in the second, as he and Sobers ushered the tourists to victory with a century stand on a turning wicket. Described as "looking scholarly behind thick-rimmed

The most successful Test captain of all-time, Clive Lloyd was also one of the most gifted batsmen of his generation

136

spectacles", Lloyd went from strength to strength scoring hundreds against the Prime Minister's XI at New Delhi and against Sri Lanka at Colombo.

After that tour Lloyd began his illustrious association with Lancashire cricket. He played for Haslingden in the Lancashire League and appeared for the county's first team in 1969.

By this time Lloyd had established his international credentials and, as Westindies' general fortunes took a downturn, their latest batting star hit timely centuries against England in the first Test at Port-of-Spain in 1968 and in the third game at Bridgetown, finishing the series with an average of over fifty.

An automatic choice for the subsequent trip to Australia and New Zealand, Lloyd began the series with a decisive 129 in the first match at Brisbane. Then he started to struggle along with the rest of the team before finding his form in the final match at Sydney, as he hit a sound half-century. In the short series against England in 1969, the Guyanese hit a quickfire 70 in the second match at Lord's and an unbeaten double century against Glamorgan at Swansea.

With the retirement of Basil Butcher and Seymour Nurse, Lloyd became one of the senior batsmen in the side, but he struggled to repeat his overseas successes in three consecutive rubbers at home. He began moderately with three half centuries against India in 1971, but an undistinguished series against the visiting New Zealanders the following year meant that his inclusion to meet the touring Australians in 1973 did not meet with universal approval.

But Lloyd answered his critics in the middle by scoring a brilliant 178, including one six and 24 fours, in front of his home crowd in the fourth Test at Georgetown, adding a record 187 for the fourth wicket with his compatriot, Rohan Kanhai. He seemed more at ease batting in his glasses and had abandoned the contact lenses he had worn in the previous game at Port-of-Spain.

A big man for the big occasion, Lloyd confirmed his renaissance with a scintillating hundred in the first Test against England at The Oval later in 1973, sharing in a double century partnership with Alvin Kallicharran. He scored a solid 94 in the second match at Edgbaston and finished the series with an average of 63.60.

Always at home in England, Lloyd played a leading role in Lancashire's revival in the early Seventies and was instrumental in helping the county to win the Gillette Cup four times between 1970-75, as he collected a record eight Man of the Match awards. He was appointed captain of Lancashire in 1981.

He did not have much success when England visited the Caribbean in 1974; but was made captain for the tour to India and Pakistan later that year. He opened his account as skipper with a stupendous 163 in the first Test at Bangalore, in almost even time, adding 207 for the fourth wicket with Gordon Greenidge. The Guyanese made his career-best score of 242 not out – after he had been dropped on eight – adding 250 for the sixth wicket with Deryck Murray in the last game at Bombay. Lloyd's final run aggregate of 636 (79.50) was his highest in any series, and decisive in Westindies winning the rubber as, in the two Tests that they lost, Lloyd failed with the bat.

The captaincy seemed to add consistency to his batting: he made 14 of his 19 Test centuries as skipper. However, one of the best examples of Lloyd leading from the front as a batsman came in the first World Cup in 1975, when he hit a match-winning century in the final. This came after he had helped to retrieve his side in their game against Pakistan at Edgbaston by hitting 53, as Westindies scraped home by one wicket.

Lloyd's opening months as captain were very successful, but facing the Australians on their own territory was an altogether different proposition. Before the start of the series in 1975-76, Lloyd wrote: "There is not much between the two teams where talent and skills are involved and you don't need a crystal ball to predict the outcome could hang on a slender thread."

However, the outcome was far more decisive than that, as Westindies were overwhelmed by Dennis Lillee and Jeff Thomson. But, in spite of his team's traumas, Lloyd excelled with the bat himself. He crashed 149, with a six and 22 fours, in the second match at Perth; and followed this with splendid innings of 102 and 91 not out respectively in the two matches played at Melbourne, as he collected more

runs than any other visiting batsman.

Clive Lloyd

By the time India visited the Caribbean in 1976, Westindies' rehabilitation was underway as Lloyd put complete faith in an all-out pace attack. The Guyanese was again in fine form with the bat, scoring a century in the first Test at Bridgetown – his 10th Test hundred in his 50th Test – and saved the second game at Port-of-Spain with a determined 70, after being dropped on 27. He misjudged the declaration in the third match, also at Port-of-Spain, which gave the tourists an unexpected win, before Westindies clinched the rubber in the final Test at Kingston, admist accusations from the Indians of intimidatory bowling by the home team.

Westindies enjoyed overwhelming success in England later that summer as Lloyd unleashed his four-pronged bowling attack. On the only occasion that his team's batting faltered, in the first innings of the second Test at Lord's, Lloyd scored a half-century and then smashed 84 runs off the demoralised English bowlers in the final match at The Oval, sharing in a splendid partnership of 174 with Viv Richards.

Lloyd scored over 1,000 first-class runs on that tour, including another unbeaten double century off the unfortunate Welsh club, this time in 120 minutes, as he equalled the record for the quickest double hundred in first-class cricket.

As a batsman Lloyd hit the ball ferociously, while the sight of his languid physique pouncing on the ball in the covers is perhaps his most memorable legacy. In his youth, he compared with the best cover fielders in the history of the game, although as he got older his fragile knees forced him into slips where he remained a formidable prospect. Lloyd was dogged by injury for most of his career; indeed a nasty fall in Australia while he was on a Rest of the World tour once paralysed him for two weeks.

He was irrepressible in the first match against Pakistan at Bridgetown in 1977. He hit a sparkling 157, with three sixes and 21 fours, sharing in a stand of over a hundred runs with Deryck Murray. Lloyd began the subsequent rubber against Australia confidently with a hard hit 86 in the first Test at Port-of-Spain, adding 170 with Alvin Kallicharran for the fourth wicket, to give Westindies an early lead in the series. However, the official Test side lost its momentum when Lloyd and other prominent players defected to World Series cricket for 18 months midway through the rubber.

Lloyd's resignation was the first occasion that a Westindian captain had withdrawn from the leadership while in office and, at the time, there was no guarantee that the Guyanese would return to official cricket, far less the captaincy.

It is indicative of the loyalty to Lloyd that the bulk of his colleagues followed his example. Indeed, just before he retired from the captaincy, nearly a decade later, Lloyd wrote: "The most important requirement for a successful captain is respect. I have been fortunate that my players have respected me as a man and a cricketer and consequently as a skipper."

The high esteem in which Lloyd was held was also influential in stemming the tide of Westindians going to South Africa, as their allegiance to his values outweighed the lure of the Rand.

However, the rift between the Packer players and the Westindies Board healed in time for the 1979 World Cup. Lloyd returned to the helm of Westindian cricket and was instrumental in retaining the Cup, playing as if he had never been away, as he top-scored with 73 against New Zealand in Westindies' closest match.

On the short tour to Australia after the World Cup, Lloyd hit a magnificent 121 in the final game at Adelaide to clinch Westindies' first ever rubber in Australia. The triumphant trip was made even happier for Lloyd after he underwent a knee operation that allowed him to move more freely. Then the Guyanese led his side to success against England in 1980, holding his team together with a splendid century in front of his adopted "home" crowd in the third match at Old Trafford.

Lloyd continued his good form against England in the return rubber in 1981: he never scored less than fifty in the whole series. He hit a century in the third match at Bridgetown and fell five short of three figures in the final game at Kingston. The Westindian skipper finished the Test series with an average of 76, almost one hundred short of his Shell Shield average for that year, which stood at 172.50 runs per innings.

In the three-match series against Australia in 1981-

82 Lloyd hit a match-winning 77 not out in the third Test at Adelaide to level the series, ending premature talk of the eclipse of Westindies' domination of world cricket. Indeed, in acknowledgement of his remarkable contribution to Westindies' run of success, Lloyd was carried off the field by his team-mates.

In 1983 Lloyd led Guyana to a unique double success in the Shell Shield and the Geddes Grant-Harrison Line Trophy. The delighted Lloyd said: "I can't remember gaining as much satisfaction out of the game as I did in seeing Guyana do so well this year. We had some very talented young players but they lacked self-confidence. They needed motivation, to be convinced that we were as good as the next team, no, even better."

His domestic success spilled over to the Tests, as the Indians were beaten 2-0 when they visited the Caribbean that year. In the second Test at Port-of-Spain, Lloyd hit a scinitillating 143, after his team had lost three wickets for one run, sharing in a huge partnership of 237 with Larry Gomes. The big Guyanese ended the series with another memorable hundred at St. John's, as he shared in another double century partnership, this time with Jeff Dujon.

After the shock of losing the World Cup to India in mid-1983, which Lloyd rates as his biggest disappointment, Westindies exacted their revenge when they visited the subcontinent later in the year. The tourists won the one-day series 5-0 and, leading by example, Lloyd topped the batting averages in the Tests with 82.66. He hit two splendid centuries, including an unbeaten 161 in the fifth Test at Calcutta, steering the tourists to a decisive 3-0 victory in the rubber.

When Australia visited Westindies in 1984, Lloyd's team defeated them by the same margin as the Indians. Yet, for Lloyd, true vengeance for his team's humiliation almost a decade earlier had to be on Australian soil over a full five match series – and that happened at the end of 1984.

Meanwhile, Lloyd completed a hat-trick of success against England on their home territory. He led Westindies to victory in the summer of 1984, in an unprecedented 5-0 trouncing of the home country. The scoreline contributed to the remarkable record of

11 consecutive wins that Westindies secured at this time, and was the crowning glory of Lloyd's captaincy. Once again, on the few occasions that the batting machine faltered, Lloyd could be relied on to lead them out of a temporary impasse, as he did when he scored with 60 not out in the last Test at The Oval.

So came retribution in Australia in 1984-85, Lloyd's last Test series. In the second match at Brisbane the Westindies captain thrashed 114 runs from as many balls to give his side an unassailable lead in the series. He hit 78 in the third game at Adelaide, and finished the campaign with a masterful display in the last match at Sydney, when he scored 72 on a difficult pitch. In recognition of his services to cricket, he was awarded the Order of Australia at the end of the tour, and also received the second highest honour in his native Guyana, the Order of Roirama.

Lloyd's performance as a Test captain is unrivalled: he led Westindies in a record 74 matches, including 26 successive games without defeat. He skippered them to a record 36 victories and, on his retirement, Lloyd's run aggregate was second only to Sobers. The Guyanese also held 89 catches, more than any other Westindian apart from Sobers and wicket-keepers, Deryck Murray and Jeff Dujon.

In his retirement speech to the Westindies Board in Georgetown in April 1985, Lloyd said he regarded his career as "the continuation of the revolution started by Sir Frank Worrell", while, according to Garner, one of the perpetual trump cards in Lloyd's pack: "Worrell inspired his men, Sobers led mainly by example and Lloyd combined the best features of both."

Yet, perhaps, the most distinctive aspect of Lloyd's captaincy was the rapport he enjoyed with the Westindian public at large. Less detached than some previous captains, he recognised the importance that winning had on the morale of the Caribbean as a whole. In his book *Caribbean Cricketers from the Pioneers to Packer*, Clayton Goodwin wrote that Lloyd "has apparently stepped straight from the crowds on the terraces onto the field of play and shares the public's hopes, their fears and their sentiments. He opened up the game when they would and has made mistakes when they would."

In 1985 Westindies competed in the Rothman's Challenge Cup, a tournament held in Sharjah principally in honour of Lloyd's recent retirement. Lloyd arrived in time to see the Westindies win the Cup after receiving an honorary degree from the University of the Westindies in Jamaica. He also has honorary degrees from Manchester and Hull universities.

Since his playing days, Lloyd has had an even fuller diary. Last year he was appointed as a part-time member of the Commission for Racial Equality, and is also a patron of Help the Aged and the Sickle Cell Anaemia Foundation. In addition, Lloyd is an executive of the charity Project Fullemploy which helps to finance training and find work for people from ethnic backgrounds.

Recently he and his wife bought a 23-bedroom house in Wilmslow, Cheshire, which they have converted into a home for old people. Now a British citizen, Lloyd seems well suited to the tempo of life in the north, and is as inspirational a figure in his new surroundings off the field as he was for his team-mates on it.

Career details

Born: *31 August 1944*
Role: *Left-hand batsman*
Clubs: *Guyana, Lancashire, Lancashire League*
First-class record: *[1964-86] 31,232 runs (49.26) including 79 centuries, and 114 wickets (36.00)*
Tests: *110*
Test debut: *v India 1966*
Test runs: *7,515 (46.67); HS: 242* v India, Bombay, 1975*
Tours: *India 1966-67; Australia and New Zealand 1968-69; England 1969; England 1973; India and Pakistan 1974-75; England (World Cup) 1975; Australia 1975-76; England 1976; England (World Cup) 1979; Australia and New Zealand 1979-80; England 1980; Pakistan 1980-81; Australia 1981-82; England (World Cup) 1983; India 1983; England 1984; Australia 1984-85.*

Augustine Lawrence Logie

The diminutive cricketer *par excellence,* Gus Logie's prolific scoring for Trinidad & Tobago in the Shell Shield elevated him into the Test side for the series against India in the Caribbean in 1983. The 5ft 4in and 120lbs lightweight had had some experience of international cricket when he toured Zimbabwe in 1981 with the under-26 Westindies side, but his first taste of Test cricket seemed to unsettle him and he had an inauspicious start with a succession of low scores.

But, the selectors' faith in him paid off when Logie registered his first Test hundred in the fourth match at Bridgetown, as he capitalised on a simple missed slip chance early in his innings to reach his maiden century in splendid fashion.

In 1983 the Trinidadian became the first player for eight years to score over 500 runs in the Shield, when he averaged 60, with two centuries. But he couldn't maintain his momentum on Westindies' tour of India later in 1983 and faded from contention after collecting a pair in the third Test at Ahmedabad. His position was made even more vulnerable with the emergence of Richie Richardson and the renaissance of Larry Gomes.

Logie has all the hallmarks of a quality batsman: his quick eye allows him to play the ball unusually late and, on his day, he can subdue any bowling attack. Nonetheless, at the moment, his inconsistency prevents him from commanding a regular spot in the Test side.

Logie was back in favour against the Australians in 1984 when, in the second Test at Port-of-Spain, he fell just three short of his hundred, after enjoying splendid three figure partnerships with Viv Richards and Jeff Dujon.

The affable Trinidadian was included on the subsequent tours to Australia and England, although he failed to establish a regular place in the batting line-up. Even so, Logie impressed in England in 1984, scoring 585 first-class runs at an average of 73; and

Logie

thrilled the crowds with his magnificent fielding, particularly in the covers.

The last child in a family of 10 – almost a cricket team in itself – Logie was introduced to the game with impromptu matches in the backyard. His coach, Willie Guadaloupe, nurtured the youngster's talent while he was at school, easing his path into the Trinidad & Tobago team for the Westindies youth championships at the age of 15. Logie made his first-class debut in 1979 and underlined his ability by hitting 163 for Young Westindies against Young England in St. Lucia in 1980.

The right-hander has not played county cricket in England, but has appeared in the northern leagues and also had a brief spell with a South Australian club in Adelaide in 1982-83. He continues to play for his Third Division Trinidadian side, Texaco-Brighton, even though his game would doubtless benefit from a more rigorous standard of competition. But Logie's loyalty lies with the club that gave him his early opportunities. He says: "When you're a nobody no one wants to know you, but when you make it all the bigger clubs wants to grab you. I've always had this policy that if I start here, I finish here. I've made the Trinidad team and now the Westindies team and I have no reason to change."

Logie didn't play in any of the three Tests against Pakistan in 1986 and had a disappointing tour to New Zealand the following year, but remains one of Westindies' brightest prospects. To book a permanent place in the side, however, he must turn his occasional big scores into regular features of his batting.

Career details

Born: *28 September 1960*
Role: *Right-hand batsman*
Clubs: *Trinidad, North of England Leagues.*
First-class record: *[1978-] 3,736 runs (33.06) including 9 centuries, and 3 wickets (42.66)*
Tests: *16*
Test debut: *v India 1983*
Test runs: *555 (27.75); HS: 130 v India, Bridgetown, 1983*
Tours: *England (WIYC) 1980; Zimbabwe (under-26 side) 1981; Australia 1981-82; England (World Cup) 1983; India 1983; England 1984; Australia 1984-85; Pakistan 1986; New Zealand 1987; India and Pakistan (World Cup) 1987.*

Easton Dudley Ashton St. John McMorris

Easton McMorris must be the holder of the most unfortunate Test debut of all time when, in the first match against England at Bridgetown in 1960, he was run out off a no-ball which deflected from the bowler's hand. McMorris was backing up at the non-striker's end and had not faced a ball himself.

After this inauspicious start, things could only improve for the right-handed opener from Jamaica. They did when, in spite of an injury, McMorris hit a solid 73 in front of his home crowd in the third match at Kingston. He seemed to have done enough to secure his passage to Australia the following season, but was surprisingly omitted from the tour party.

McMorris was back in favour by the time the Indians visited the Caribbean in 1962 and justified his selection with an excellent century in the second game at Kingston, adding 255 in a record second wicket partnership with Rohan Kanhai. This helped the home side to victory by an innings. The Jamaican followed this up with two half centuries in the fourth game at Port-of-Spain, ending the series with a fine average of 58.16.

McMorris visited England in 1963 and 1966, and although he scored 878 runs on his second trip, he failed to leave his mark in the Tests, where he struggled against the moving ball.

The Jamaican was far more at home on hard, true pitches and played spin bowling with particular panache. A difficult player to dislodge when well set, he was a prolific run-maker in the Shell Shield. For a while McMorris was the leading scorer in the competiton and captained Jamaica successfully for several years.

Career details

Born: *4 April 1935*
Role: *Right-hand batsman*
Club: *Jamaica*
First-class record: *[1956-72] 5,906 runs (42.18) including 18 centuries*
Tests: *13*
Test debut: *v England 1960*
Test runs: *564 (26.85); HS: 125 v India, Kingston, 1962*
Tours: *England 1963; England 1966.*

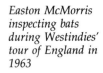

Easton McMorris inspecting bats during Westindies' tour of England in 1963

Clifford Aubrey McWatt

Clifford McWatt was one of several distinguished wicket-keepers tried by Westindies' Test selectors during the 1950s. He demonstrated his considerable skills from the early 1940s for Guyana and toured India in 1948-49 as deputy to Clyde Walcott. But McWatt didn't win his first Test cap until England visited the Caribbean in 1954, and then retained his place for the whole series. Even so, when Australia toured Westindies the following year, McWatt only played in the second match at Port-of-Spain.

Besides being a gifted wicket-keeper, McWatt was also a talented left-handed batsman, and the luck he enjoyed while batting earned him the nickname McCatt (nine lives). He made 56 and 123 not out against Trinidad at Port-of-Spain in 1946-47, and treated them with similar disdain when they visited Georgetown in 1953, this time helping himself to 128. After his elevation to Test status, he made 54 in the first innings of the first match against England at Kingston and an unbeaten 36 in the second, adding 90 runs with Everton Weekes.

McWatt scored another half century in the third game at Georgetown, sharing in a stand of 99 for the eighth wicket with John Holt, after the first seven wickets had fallen for just 139 runs. Then the Guyanese sparked off a disturbance in the crowd when he was run out trying to secure the century partnership. His home supporters showed their frustration at his dismissal by hurling bottles on to the ground.

When given the opportunity, McWatt performed well at the highest level but he was a casualty of the vagaries of selectorial policy that applied to wicket-keepers at that time, and faded from contention after Australia visited the Caribbean in 1955.

Career details

Born: *1 February 1922*
Role: *Wicket-keeper, left-hand batsman*
Club: *Guyana*
First-class record: *[1943-57] 45 catches and 6 stumpings, and 1,673 runs (28.84) including 2 centuries*
Tests: *6*
Test debut: *v England 1954*
Test catches: *9*; Test stumpings: *1*
Test runs: *202 (28.85); HS: 54 v England, Kingston, 1954 and 54 v England, Georgetown, 1954*

Malcolm Denzil Marshall

Malcolm Marshall first caught the selectors' eye after many of the leading Westindian bowlers had defected to World Series Cricket. After a patient apprenticeship, the young Barbadian went on to become the fastest bowler in the world.

Born in St. Michael, Marshall attended St. Giles' Boys' School, the same one as Wes Hall. Encouraged as a youngster by his grandfather, Oscar Welch, he captained the Barbados youth team in the Westindies school championships, playing as a batsman and a medium-pace bowler. Marshall remembers: "I started as a gentle-medium pacer, with an out-swinger from wide of the crease; then I realised that I could be quicker if I bowled nearer the stumps."

Besides his grandfather, Marshall was helped by William Bourne of Warwickshire, Charlie Griffith and Seymour Nurse; with Nurse being particularly impressed by the youngster's fluent batting. Marshall graduated through the junior ranks to play for Spartan Cricket Club, before appearing for the Banks Brewery team in Barbados' Division One.

The loose-limbed Barbadian made his first-class debut in the final match of the 1977-78 Shell Shield season, and made an immediate impact by taking six for 77 against Jamaica at Bridgetown. This performance was sufficient to secure his place in the tour party to India later that year, although he struggled on the sluggish Test wickets. Even so, he was the leading wicket-taker in all first-class matches with 42. Dicky Rutnagur remarked in *Wisden* that Marshall "showed exceptional promise in the subsidiary games, but his Test performances suffered from want of experience".

When he arrived back in the Caribbean, Marshall took 25 wickets in the Shield, which was a record for Barbados. This performance helped him to keep his place in the Westindies squad for the 1979 World Cup after the Packer players had returned. He did not play in any of the matches, but enjoyed considerable success that year in his first season with Hampshire,

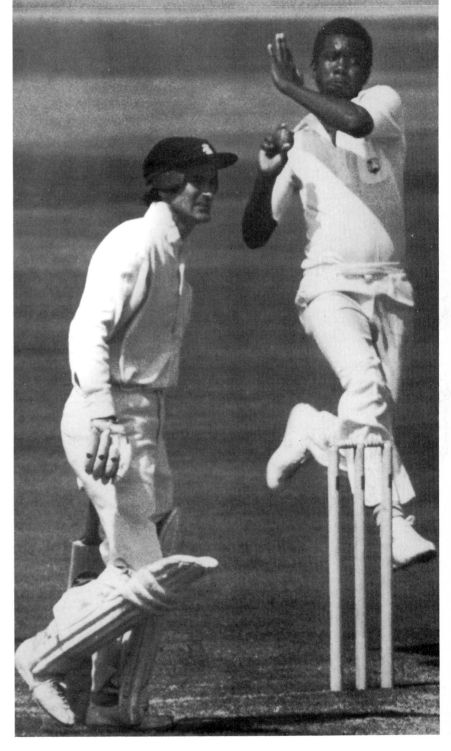

...colm Marshall ...t to release one of ...bullet-like ...veries. Alan ...tt is the non-...king batsman

taking nine wickets on his debut against Glamorgan.

Marshall has had a remarkably injury-free career and, despite his sparse frame, he can generate phenomenal pace with his powerful arm action which hurries even the best batsmen. He explains his success: "It's a lot to do with my approach to the wicket where I more or less sprint to the wicket, my whippy action, co-ordination and balance...so that I tend to come off a lot faster than the batsmen expect, to skid off, so to speak."

A fitness fanatic – he does between 50 and 60 sit-ups a day – the Barbadian is driven by a burning desire to be the best. He has tremendous staying power which allows him to bowl flat out for long periods, while, according to Wes Hall, who has managed recent Westindian teams, Marshall's attitude has been a crucial element in his success. He says: "There is more to being a great fast bowler than the ability to bowl fast. It takes fitness, stamina, common sense, commitment and aggression and Marshall has got them all."

As a batsman Marshall has a sound technique and, in a team less well endowed than Westindies, he could have developed into an all-rounder. The paceman muses on his missed opportunities: "I've not fulfilled my batting potential", he says, "because I come in too low down the order." Even so, his expertise with the willow has often paid rich dividends for Hampshire, as when he hit an unbeaten century off Lancashire at Southampton in 1982.

From 1979, Marshall toured regularly with Westindies. He says: "(I) found myself playing alongside some great bowlers and some great players...You had to learn in that company." He got an extended run on the tour to Pakistan, while Andy Roberts stayed in the Caribbean. He took four for 25 in Pakistan's total of 145 in the second match at Faisalabad, and finished the Test series with 13 wickets at 24 apiece. After five tours, Marshall still only had 12 Tests to his name; but, after clearing up a nagging back injury following the trip to Australia in 1981-82, his stunning success with Hampshire in 1982 catapulted him into pole position in the Test team.

That summer Marshall took 49 wickets more than anyone else in the English county championship, as

his 134 victims set a record for a 22-match season, and included a purple patch of four matches when he snapped up 39 wickets. Between 1981 and 1986, Marshall was one of the top three wicket-takers in the championship, while his ambition is to do the double of one hundred wickets and 1,000 runs in an English season.

In 1983 Marshall became a permanent member of Westindies' pace quartet, and was acknowledged as the fastest bowler in the world. He took 21 wickets at 23.57 each against India when they visited the Caribbean, including five for 37 bowling round the wicket on a rain-affected pitch in the second Test at Port-of-Spain.

Marshall is a great friend of Joel Garner and the pair used to egg each other on to success. Marshall says: "Before a series started, we usually set ourselves a target. If we were playing five Test matches, I'd aim for 25 wickets and anything over that was a bonus. So when I'm out there, I'm always bowling at something, to achieve something. Joel would do the same and when he got a wicket I always felt I must get one too and vice-versa."

By the time Westindies visited India at the end of 1983, Marshall was at his most deadly. The Barbadian enjoyed his most successful series ever as he equalled the record in India by collecting 33 wickets at 18.81 each. He took four wickets in each innings of the Test at Kanpur, and then slammed 92 with the bat taking the visitors to a comprehensive victory. In the fifth Test at Calcutta, Marshall was even more devastating than Roy Gilchrist a generation earlier, as he scythed through the Indian batting to finish with six wickets for 37. He finished a memorable series by taking five for 72 in India's only innings in the sixth Test at Madras, including the removal of the first two batsmen without a run on the board.

When Australia visited the Caribbean in 1984, despite being tired from continuous cricket, Marshall took five for 42 in the third match at Bridgetown, scuttling the tourists out for 97 in their second innings (the lowest Test score ever recorded at Kensington Oval). The Barbadian wrapped up the series with five for 51 in the fifth Test at Kingston, to take his tally of wickets to 21 at 22.85 each – ideal preparation for his assault on England's batsmen later that summer.

Once again Marshall was in lethal form. In the first Test at Edgbaston, England's opener, Andy Lloyd, was forced to retire hurt after misjudging the length and bounce of one of the Barbadian's thunderbolts.

Perhaps Marshall's greatest moment came in the third match at Headingley, after he had broken his left thumb in the field. Despite his injury he joined Larry Gomes at the wicket, enabling the Trinidadian to reach his century and, even more remarkably, managed to hit a boundary himself. Then, back in the field, he savaged England in their second innings, returning his best Test figures of seven for 53 off a shortened run. His performance took on the bizarre when he hung on to a return catch off his own bowling from Graeme Fowler, the top-scorer in the innings. Immediately on taking the catch, he tossed the ball into the air, as he felt his injury, before removing the next batsman with his next ball. Marshall ended a splendid series by taking five for 35 at The Oval, as Westindies completed their clean sweep.

Established as Westindies' premier strike bowler, Marshall humbled the Australians in 1984-85. His pace accounted for five wickets in an innings on four successive occasions, and he dismissed 10 batsmen in the third game at Adelaide. When he failed to take a wicket in the fifth match at Sydney, Westindies lost their first Test for three years. Marshall finished the campaign with 28 wickets (19.78) which was enough to secure him the Man of the Series award – an award which he won in the next two rubbers.

Against New Zealand in 1985, the Barbadian, who makes up in aggression what he lacks in stature, was again at his best. In the first Test at Port-of-Spain he accounted for three batsmen for 25 runs in 11 overs of blistering pace. Even so, Marshall saved his real magic for his home crowd in the third match at Bridgetown. There, he dismissed two batsmen for a duck as, at one stage, the visitors' first innings stood at a precarious one run for three wickets. Then, after continuing his fine form with the bat, this time scoring a half century, Marshall dominated New Zealand's second innings as he captured seven wickets for 80, coming round the wicket.

He was in dynamic form again in the last game at Kingston, prompting complaints from the tourists similar to those by the Indians after Holding's devastating assault on the same ground in 1976. Marshall swung the match in Westindies' favour after catching centurion, Jeremy Coney, and then dismissed four second innings batsmen to finish the series with 27 wickets from four Tests at an average of 18.16.

England incurred the full force of the slim Barbadian's pace when they toured the Caribbean in 1986: in the first one-day international in Jamaica he broke Mike Gatting's nose while, in the Test series, he took 27 wickets at 17.85 each and continued his splendid form with the bat, which has taken him to the verge of being an all-rounder.

Marshall took his 200th Test wicket in the second match at Port-of-Spain. He reached the landmark in a shorter time than any other Westindian bowler and celebrated by thrashing an unbeaten 62 off the English attack and followed this assault with a scintillating 76 in the fifth match at St. John's. Delighted at his success, he said: "It was great to get my 200 Test wickets and, seeing I've got there so soon, I could go on to pass 300 or 350, who knows?" He also has his sights set on a Test century; to date his highest score is 92, which he made against India at Kanpur in 1983.

Marshall was appointed vice-captain for Westindies' visit to Pakistan in 1986, and celebrated by finishing as the leading wicket-taker again. He took 16 at 16.62 each, including a splendid five for 33 in the first innings of the second Test at Lahore, dismissing the first three batsmen for a mere nine runs. He was a little less sprightly in New Zealand in 1987, when his nine wickets cost over 32 runs each.

Yet, with seemingly boundless energy and insatiable enthusiasm, Marshall still has an important role play in the Westindies side. When time allows, the likeable Barbadian enjoys playing tennis, darts, pool and golf; while his musical tastes include Teddy Prendergast, Luther Van Dross and Whitney Houston.

Career details

Born: *18 April 1958*
Role: *Right-arm fast bowler, right-hand batsman*
Clubs: *Barbados, Hampshire*
First-class record: *[1978-   ] 1,126 wickets (17.99) and
6,283 runs (22.35) including 4 centuries*
Tests: *51*
Test debut: *v India 1979*
Test wickets: *240 (21.64); BB: 7-53 v England,
Headingley, 1984*
Test runs: *1,068 (18.73); HS: 92 v India, Kanpur, 1983*
Tours: *India 1978-79; England (World Cup) 1979;
Australia and New Zealand 1979-80; England 1980;
Pakistan 1980-81; Australia 1981-82; England (World
Cup) 1983; India 1983; England 1984; Australia 1984-85;
Pakistan 1986; New Zealand 1987.*

Roy Edwin Marshall

Roy Marshall, who has the highest first-class aggregate of any Westindian player, with 35,725 runs

A tall bespectacled man, Roy Marshall was a brilliant opening batsman who always sought to entertain the public. He made his debut for Barbados at the tender age of 15 and, at 19, came within nine runs of a double century against Trinidad at Bridgetown in 1949.

Marshall was included in the tour party to England in 1950 and, as the youngest member of the team, enjoyed great success. The prolific Barbadian made over 1,000 first-class runs (39.89) including a magnificent 188 against Leicestershire, 143 against Surrey and 135 against Hampshire, but failed to penetrate the dependable opening partnership of Allan Rae and Jeff Stollmeyer in the Tests.

Nonetheless Marshall's potential had been noted and he became a professional with Lowerhouse in the Lancashire League in 1951. The following season he was included in Westindies' side to Australia and New Zealand, where he finally made his Test debut. But, in four international appearances his highest score was only 30, as he frequently came in lower down the order to buttress the middle batting which had been hit by injury. Even so, the Barbadian scored impressive hundreds against New South Wales at Sydney and against Otago at Dunedin.

Marshall, however, curtailed his career at Test level when he made his first-class debut for Hampshire in 1953 and didn't return to the Westindies. For almost two decades, Marshall's punishing style of play – which was occasionally unorthodox, demonstrated by his habit of cutting sixes over point – entertained the English public and, on his day, he could pulverise any bowling attack. One of the first Westindians to appear on the county circuit, Marshall's attractive style of play set the tone for the Caribbean stars who followed him into county cricket in the 1960s. During his years with Hampshire the fluent opener was sorely missed by the Westindies Test team.

It was Marshall's brilliant batsmanship, particularly in the last few crucial games, that helped his adopted county to their first county championship in 1961. In that summer the carefree Barbadian scored 2,455 runs

and, in one memorable game against Somerset at Bournemouth, brought off a famous victory for Hampshire with a magnificent double century.

During a distinguished career with Hampshire spanning 19 years – Marshall captained the county for five of them – he scored 30,303 runs, including 60 centuries, in 504 first-class matches, while his overall first-class aggregate is the highest by any Westindian player. Besides his renowned batting talents, the Barbadian was a useful off-spin bowler who could often be relied upon to break a frustrating partnership. He was also an agile fielder.

After he retired, Marshall moved to Somerset to coach at King's College, Taunton, and nowadays he can be found entertaining his customers in the Westgate Inn, also in Taunton, in the same relaxed manner which was such a prominent feature of his batting.

Career details

Born: *25 April 1930*
Role: *Right-hand batsman, off-spinner*
Clubs: *Barbados, Hampshire*
First-class record: *[1945-72] 35,725 runs (35.94) including 68 centuries, and 176 wickets (28.93)*
Tests: *4*
Test debut: *v Australia 1951*
Test runs: *143 (20.42); HS: 30 v Australia, Brisbane, 1952*
Tours: *Australia and New Zealand 1951-52.*

Frank Martin, who carried his bat to help set up Westindies' first victory over Australia in 1931

Frank Reginald Martin

Frank Martin, a determined and watchful left-handed batsman, was immensely strong off the back foot, and could be difficult to remove when well set. The sturdy Jamaican had an auspicious start to his first-class career when he hit 195 for his island against Barbados at Bridgetown in 1925-26, and then batted outstandingly against the Hon. F.S.G. Calthorpe's touring MCC side later the same year. He maintained his momentum into the following season, helping himself to an unbeaten double century off Lord Tennyson's England touring team at Kingston.

The relaxed Martin, who epitomized calmness and sobriety, was selected for the first four series of Test matches played by Westindies against England and Australia between 1928-33. In the inaugural rubber, against England in 1928, Martin topped the Test batting averages with 29.16, as he hit 44 in the first match at Lord's, adding 86 for the first wicket with George Challenor, and another 40 in the third game at The Oval.

Martin was the leading scorer on the tour, accumulating nearly 1,500 runs, while his slow bowling brought him 22 wickets, as he, along with Learie Constantine and Herman Griffith, lived up to their home reputations.

The resolute Jamaican was one of several leading players who had to miss some of the Tests in the first series against England in the Caribbean in 1930, because he couldn't get time off from his job. In fact, Martin only played in the fourth game at Kingston, but he made the trip to Australia later that year.

After being beaten comprehensively in the first four Tests, Martin lifted the beleaguered tourists to victory in the fifth game at Sydney. He carried his bat for 123, adding 70 for the first wicket with Clifford Roach, and 152 for the second with his compatriot, George Headley. Martin kept his concentration as the wicket deteriorated, helping the visitors to their highest score of the series, and their first ever victory over Australia.

The Westindians arrived in Australia believing that the pitches would suit their pace attack but, apart from Sydney, they were slow and lifeless. The tourists turned to Martin's slow off-spin, and the Jamaican was catapulted into an all-rounder's role as he bowled more overs than anyone else on the tour.

On his second visit to England in 1933, Martin recorded some good all-round performances in the first six county matches before he stood on a ball and wrenched his ankle in the game against Middlesex, which put him out of the Tests.

Martin was an enigmatic batsman in that he often played the most difficult bowling well and then fell to a bad ball. He failed to show the consistency that his ability warranted, yet, just as he seemed to have used up his opportunities, he would play a peerless innings like the one at Sydney.

His unflustered approach complemented some of the more exuberant members of the side and was important in steadying the batting on the early tours. Martin was sometimes promoted to open the innings with Roach, as had happened at Sydney, where his more circumspect style provided the perfect foil for the flamboyant Trinidadian.

Career details

Born: *12 October 1893*
Died: *23 November 1967*
Role: *Left-hand batsman, off-spinner*
Club: *Jamaica*
First-class record: *[1925-33] 3,589 runs (37.78) including 6 centuries, and 74 wickets (42.55)*
Tests: *9*
Test debut: *v England 1928*
Test runs: *486 (28.58); HS: 123* v Australia, Sydney, 1931*
Tours: *England 1928; Australia 1930-31; England 1933.*

Emmanuel Alfred Martindale

Manny Martindale was the first great Westindian fast bowler to develop after the granting of Test match status and, during those early years, he carried the burden of their pace attack.

Martindale hailed from a long line of pacemen produced by Barbados, and was influenced by Herman Griffith, his team-mate at Empire. Martindale was quite short for a fast bowler at 5ft 8½ins, but his solid physique enabled him to generate a lot of pace and his deceptively late out-swinger worried most batsmen.

He made his Test debut against England in 1933 and, along with Learie Constantine, provoked a lot of comment by bowling 'bodyline' at the Englishmen. The fiery Barbadian kept the batsmen on their toes and split Wally Hammond's chin with a ball that reared sharply off a good length in the second Test at Old Trafford.

These tactics brought Martindale five scalps for 73, to complement his four for 85 in the first match at Lord's, where he dismissed both openers; while his five for 93 in the final game at The Oval, gave him 14 wickets at 17.92 apiece in the series. With only three innings available to him, Martindale's performance compares with any fast bowling feat of modern times. The next most successful bowler was 'Puss' Achong, whose left-arm 'chinamen' brought him five wickets.

Martindale was one of the few successes on a generally disappointing tour for Westindies, snapping up 103 wickets altogether, including eight victims in an innings three times. Ironically, having shouldered the bowling almost single-handedly for most of the tour, he was also the not out batsman in both innings of the final Test. Perhaps, if Martindale could have shared the attack with Constantine, the result would have been different, or at least closer; but the great Trinidadian had commitments with the Lancashire League which restricted his Test appearances.

Martindale was at his peak for the four match series

Manny Martindale, the first great Westindian fast bowler to develop after the granting of Test match status.

against MCC in the Caribbean in 1935. On a virtually unplayable Bridgetown wicket, the local bowler dismissed five English batsmen for just 22 runs after their captain, Bob Wyatt, had juggled the batting order in an effort to keep his best batsmen until the pitch improved. Even though he finished with match figures of eight for 61, as so often, Martindale lacked the support to brush England aside decisively, and Hammond's fortuitous unbeaten 29, which included a winning six over extra-cover off Martindale, brought the tourists victory by four wickets.

Westindies went into the final Test at Kingston with the series level. In England's first innings Martindale produced a wicked delivery wide of the off-stump, which came back to fracture Wyatt's jaw; and caused similar havoc in England's second innings taking four for 28, to dismiss the tourists for 103. This performance brought Westindies victory by an innings and, with it, their first ever series' win as the home side enjoyed the rare luxury of Martindale and Constantine bowling in tandem.

After the 1935 tour by England, Westindies did not play another Test series until 1939 and, although Martindale followed Constantine and George Headley into league cricket, playing for Burnley during those years, when international competition finally returned, the Barbadian, then approaching 30, could not recapture the zest of his earlier days.

In his Test career, which spanned six years, Martindale played just 10 matches – no more than modern cricketers play in a year – preventing him from achieving the statistical feats associated with the contemporary game.

Like many Westindian pacemen, the Barbadian enjoyed batting and made 134 in an inter-territorial match against Trindidad, sharing in a partnership of 255 for the eighth wicket with 'Foffie' Williams in 1935-36, which is still a Westindian record.

After his retirement, Martindale coached for a while in Bermuda, before returning home to be appointed a national coach by the Barbados sports ministry.

He died in hospital in 1972, leaving behind the memory of one of the most gifted bowlers ever to wear Westindian colours.

Career details

Born: *25 November 1909*
Died: *17 March 1972*
Role: *Right-hand fast bowler*
Clubs: *Barbados, Lancashire League*
First-class record: *[1931-39] 205 wickets (25.64) and 972 runs (15.18) including 1 century.*
Tests: *10*
Test debut: *v England 1933*
Test wickets: *37 (21.72); BB: 5-22 v England, Bridgetown, 1935*
Tours: *England 1933; England 1939.*

Everton Hugh Mattis

Everton Mattis is a delightfully hard-hitting right-handed batsman, who graduated to Test honours against England in 1981, after scoring prolifically for Jamaica in the Shell Shield. He also enjoyed considerable success playing in Ireland after his Test debut.

Like many before him, the tall and elegant Mattis took a while to bridge the gap between island and Test cricket, and his highest Test score was 71 in the fourth match at St. John's.

An exhilarating 132 against Guyana rocketed him into the Test team in place of Alvin Kallicharran, but Mattis could not hold on to the position for the tour to Australia in 1981-82. Instead the Jamaican was selected to go with Westindies' under-26 side to Zimbabwe, where he was a notable success.

After making solid progress in Zimbabwe, and finishing as Jamaica's leading batsman in the Shell Shield in 1980-81 and 1981-82, Mattis seemed on the verge of a glowing international career. But, he suddenly compromised any prospect of a Test recall when he agreed to tour South Africa in 1982-83, claiming that he was in dire financial straits. He told the Jamaica *Daily News:* "I'm a Rastaman. That is my philosophy. I am not supporting apartheid, I am dealing with survival. At one stage I did not want to go but I had to think about my family."

It was an untimely end to a promising career. Besides being an accomplished batsman who was especially strong off the back foot, Mattis was a superb athlete who could field anywhere and who also bowled useful off-breaks.

If Mattis had been included on the trip to Australia in 1981-82, the young Jamaican could have developed into one of Westindies' finest batsmen. Instead he fell into the lucrative obscurity of playing in South Africa.

Career details

Born: *11 April 1957*
Role: *Right-hand batsman*
Club: *Jamaica*
First-class record: *[1977-84] 2,064 runs (33.29) including 3 centuries*
Tests: 4
Test debut: *v England 1981*
Test runs: 145 (29.00); HS: 71 v England, St. John's, 1981
Tour: *Zimbabwe (under-26 side) 1981.*

‑ton Mattis hits ‑r Willey straight over his head in ‑irst Test Match played in ‑gua, against ‑land in 1981

Bob Thomas

153

David Anthony Murray

David Murray was a gifted wicket-keeper kept out of the international limelight by his illustrious Trinidadian namesake, Deryck. David was Barbados' premier gloveman for many years and was included in the Westindies Young Cricketers side that toured England in 1970. He created a favourable impression on that trip and graduated smoothly to the senior team for the tour of England three years later, when he was chosen as reserve wicket-keeper. In 20 games Murray enhanced his all-round standing: he took 26 catches and made five stumpings, and averaged 35.62 with the bat, which was bolstered by an unbeaten century against Kent.

Murray was given an unexpected opportunity at the highest level against Australia in 1978, when Deryck Murray was dropped during the Packer crisis. The Barbadian performed admirably, collecting 11 victims in the last three games of the series, and underlined his ability on the subsequent tour of India by making 18 dismissals. He had been on the verge of selection as a specialist batsman, and averaged almost 30. In the first Test at Bombay he hit a splendid 84, sharing in a fifth wicket partnership of 167 with Alvin Kallicharran, after the early batting had floundered; and in the third game at Calcutta he top-scored with 66. Murray completed a successful trip by taking five catches in India's only innings in the fifth Test at New Delhi, and hit his career-best score of 206 not out against Central Zone at Jamshedpur.

Murray finally became Westindies' first choice wicket-keeper on the short tour to Pakistan in 1980-81, where he made a useful contribution to the visitors' success. He kept tidily and hit fifty in the first Test at Lahore, and despite a pair in the fourth game at Multan, he still collected 142 runs from six innings and returned to the Caribbean to continue his good work against England in 1981.

It was unfortunate for Murray that the first Test against England was in Trinidad, Deryck Murray's home island, and there were rowdy protests at the latter's omission. But the recently installed Test

'keeper, David, performed soundly and was taken on the subsequent trip to Australia. In the first Test at Melbourne the Barbadian set a new record for the number of dismissals in a match by a Westindian wicket-keeper when he caught nine batsmen.

It came as a surprise, therefore, having just established himself in the Test side after playing in the Trinidadian's shadow for so long, that Murray opted to join the rebel Westindians in South Africa. Still in his early thirties, he threw away his chance of playing official Test cricket again at the very moment he seemed to have secured the succession.

Married to an Australian, Murray now lives with his family in Adelaide.

Career details

Born: *29 May 1950*
Role: *Wicket-keeper, right-hand batsman*
Club: *Barbados*
First-class record: *[1970-84] 297 catches and 31 stumpings, and 4,503 runs (30.84) including 7 centuries*
Tests: *19*
Test debut: *v Australia 1978*
Test catches: *57*; Test stumpings: *5*
Test runs: *601 (21.46)*; HS: *84 v India, Bombay, 1978*
Tours: *England (WIYC) 1970; England 1973; India and Pakistan 1974-75; Australia 1975-76; India 1978-79; Australia and New Zealand 1979-80; England 1980; Pakistan 1980-81; Australia 1981-82.*

Deryck Lance Murray

Fresh out of Queen's Royal College in Trinidad, Deryck Murray was selected for Westindies' tour of England in 1963, as deputy wicket-keeper to David Allan. But, after keeping well in the first match of the tour, when Allan was ruled out of the first Test at Old Trafford through illness, the precocious teenager won his first Westindies cap and maintained his position throughout the series, making a record 24 dismissals.

Thereafter, Murray played intermittently for Westindies for more than 15 years. His university studies and involvement with World Series Cricket were the main reasons for his absence, although when he lost form the prodigious Jackie Hendriks was available to take over his mantle.

Born into an affluent business and cricketing family –his father, Lance, played for Trinidad – the reserved Murray spent two years at Cambridge University, for whom he played in 1965 and, as captain, in 1966, before moving to Nottingham University. There he got his degree and, after playing cricket for the university, he appeared for Nottinghamshire between 1966-69 and for Warwickshire between 1972-75 at county level. Murray scored 1,000 first-class runs in England three times, including 1,358 in 1966 when he remained unbeaten on 166 against Surrey at The Oval, and was later an important figure in Warwickshire's championship success in his first year with the club.

After his splendid tour of England in 1963, when he kept admirably to Wes Hall and Charlie Griffith, Murray stayed to continue his studies before rejoining the Test side for the series against England in the Caribbean in 1968, after Hendriks had dropped out through injury. But, the dapper Murray had been away from the Test scene for too long and his poor form saw him relinquish his place to Hendriks again for the subsequent tour to Australia. This prompted Murray to return to England to complete his studies at Nottingham University.

The Trinidadian returned to the Test fold for Australia's visit to the Caribbean in 1973. After the

incumbent, Mike Findlay, had a poor game in the first match, Murray secured the position with competent wicket-keeping and a sound 90 in the second game at Bridgetown. He shared in a record stand of 165 with Rohan Kanhai in the first innings to see his team into the lead, and made another solid 40 in front of his home crowd in the next Test at Port-of-Spain.

When England visited Westindies in 1974 the Trinidadian collected an unbeaten half century in the third match at Bridgetown and, on the following tour

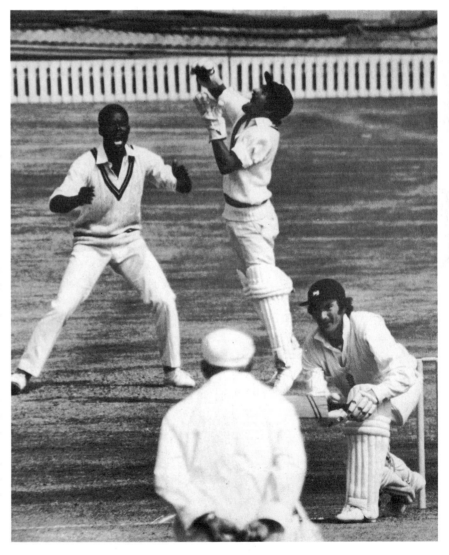

to India, Murray recorded his highest score of 91 in the last Test at Bombay, sharing in a record stand of 250 with Clive Lloyd.

Having established the wicket-keeper's position as his own, Murray's batting continued to buttress his side's fortunes. In a preliminary round match in the 1975 World Cup, he conjured a remarkable win for Westindies out of an impossible situation against Pakistan at Edgbaston. When Murray was joined by the last man, Andy Roberts, 64 more runs were still required. But an unbeaten 61 from the wicket-keeper, who coaxed Roberts to stay with him, brought Westindies a spectacular victory with two balls to spare.

On Westindies' disastrous tour to Australia in 1975-76, Murray again shone with the bat. In the first Test at Brisbane, he top-scored in the first innings with 66 and made 55 in the second. He followed this up with 63 in the next match at Perth, before completing another half century out of a total of 128 in the fourth Test at Sydney.

With the marked improvement in Westindies' batting in 1976, Murray was not involved in so many repair jobs with the willow. Even so, he scored a crucial 71 in the first innings of the fourth Test against India at Kingston that year, and hit 52 in a sixth wicket partnership of 151 with Lloyd in the first Test against Pakistan at Bridgetown in 1977. In the second Test against Australia in 1978, again at Bridgetown, Murray showed his all-round worth as he helped the home side to a lead by scoring 60 runs and taking five catches in the match. Murray's batting alone would not have won him a Test place, but he had an uncanny habit of saving his best innings for a crisis.

Besides his skill on the cricket field, Murray was a key figure in the Westindies Test Players' Association. The Trinidadian was a driving force in the campaign for improved wages for cricketers and was one of the main negotiators on behalf of the Westindians who signed for Kerry Packer – a role which incurred the wrath of the Westindies Board of Control. When he and two other WSC players were dropped from the third Test against Australia at Georgetown in 1978, the remaining Packer players boycotted the game. He was replaced by his namesake, David Murray, but once the rift with the

establishment was resolved, Deryck returned to the official fold where he stayed until the end of the 1980 tour to England. He was dropped for the series against England in the Caribbean in 1981 in favour in David Murray, which prompted his supporters to organise a protest during the opening game which, unfortunately for his successor, was played on Deryck Murray's home ground at Port-of-Spain.

As his country's longest serving wicket-keeper, Murray was the first Westindian to claim over one hundred Test victims and also holds the record for the highest number of dismissals for Westindies with 189. The quiet Trinidadian kept to two generations of pace bowlers at their peak: Hall and Griffith, and Roberts and Michael Holding.

He played a crucial role in maintaining morale during the lean years in the early 1970s and, with the emergence of a new team, he was appointed as vice-captain to Lloyd for the tour to India in 1974-75. Murray led Westindies when Lloyd was injured in the first Test against Australia at Brisbane in 1979, and was only injured himself once in a Test, when he was hit on the head by a ball deflected by Dennis Amiss at Port-of-Spain in 1974.

After his first-class career was over, Murray became more heavily involved in the administration of the game, and served as Trinidad & Tobago's representative on the Westindies Board with his father. He has also represented his country at a diplomatic level at the United Nations.

Career details

Born: *20 May 1943*
Role: *Wicket-keeper, right-hand batsman*
Clubs: *Trinidad, Cambridge University, Nottinghamshire, Warwickshire*
First-class record: *[1960-81] 741 catches and 108 stumpings, and 13,289 runs (28.33) including 10 centuries*
Tests: *62*
Test debut: *v England 1963*
Test catches: *181*; Test stumpings: *8*
Test runs: *1,993 (22.90); HS: 91 v India, Bombay, 1975*
Tours: *England 1963; England 1973; India and Pakistan 1974-75; England (World Cup) 1975; Australia 1975-76; England 1976; England (World Cup) 1979; Australia and New Zealand 1979-80; England 1980.*

Robert Karl Nunes

Karl Nunes was a polished left-handed batsman, who captained Westindies in their first official Test series against England in 1928. A product of Wolmer's Boys' School, Nunes completed his education at Dulwich College and had all the social prerequisites for guiding the visitors through their first international series.

Nunes was an accomplished opening batsman with a wealth of strokes and an impeccable defence. But, as Westindies had not included a specialist wicket-keeper in the party, Nunes filled that position and dropped himself down the batting order. This was a costly mistake for Nunes and his team, as he scored just 87 runs from six Test innings.

Behind the stumps the Jamaican put down a number of chances, while Herbert Sutcliffe had the dubious honour of being Nunes' only victim in the three match series. *The Cricketer* sympathised with Nunes' plight commenting: "He has a horrid job. He does not consider himself or his hands. As captain, he could give himself a rest from acting all day long as target for fast bowling."

One of six players in the Test side to have toured England in 1923, Nunes had been a more prolific scorer on his earlier visit when he was free from the constraints of keeping wicket and the captaincy. Even so, as vice-captain he often stood in for the elderly skipper, Harold Austin, who, in fact, had originally been appointed as captain for the 1928 series, until his age of 52 prompted the selectors to reconsider. Perhaps, if the calm left-hander, Nunes, had been able to open with the more boisterous right-hander, Clifford Roach, with Austin's experience at the helm, the series might have been closer.

Nunes demonstrated his best form against the Hon. F. S. G. Calthorpe's touring MCC side when he hit 83 and 140 not out opening for Jamaica in 1925-26 and, the following season, confirmed his outstanding ability with an unbeaten double century and 108 for Jamaica against Lord Tennyson's team.

Nunes captained Westindies again in the fourth Test against England at Kingston in 1930, and,

batting where he was most comfortable, as opener, he top-scored in Westindies' first innings with 66, as the home side struggled in the face of the visitors' massive score of 849. Calthorpe declined to enforce the follow-on and in the end Westindies were set 836 to win. Nunes hit 92, adding 228 for the second wicket with his compatriot, George Headley, to the delight of the home fans, before the rains swept down from the Blue Mountains to bring about a premature end to the celebrated "timeless Test".

Nunes was a member of the Jamaican Board of Control from its inception in 1926 until his death more than 30 years later and President of Westindies Board of Control from 1945-52. He played an important role in consolidating Westindies' Test status in the years immediately following the Second World War, and the R.K. Nunes Trophy, which is awarded to the Westindian who makes the most impact in each Test series, means that his memory lives on. He was also awarded a CBE for public services as chairman of the Agricultural Societies Loan Board.

Career details

Born: *7 June 1894*
Died: *22 July 1958*
Role: *Left-hand batsman, wicket-keeper*
Club: *Jamaica*
First-class record: *[1920-30] 2,695 runs (31.34) including 6 centuries*
Tests: *4*
Test debut: *v England 1928*
Test runs: *245 (30.62); HS: 92 v England, Kingston, 1930*
Tour: *England 1928.*

Seymour McDonald Nurse

A brilliant and exuberant batsman, Seymour Nurse delighted in scoring at a tremendous rate. A hard-hitting right-hander, blessed with a wealth of natural talent, Nurse scored prolifically in First Division cricket in Barbados and soon built up an enthusiastic following in Bridgetown. He was also an outstanding footballer, but it was in cricket that Nurse made his impact.

In his second first-class match, the Barbadian hit a splendid 128 not out against Jamaica in 1957-58, demonstrating his strength on both sides of the wicket. Nurse had an insatiable appetite for runs, but the unorthodox manner in which he accumulated them meant that, for many years, the Test selectors considered him too much of a risk to be included in the Westindies side. The consensus was that Nurse made eye-catching forties and fifties, but did not transform them into big hundreds, as his gregarious approach often cost him his wicket prematurely.

The flamboyant Nurse eventually made his international debut against England in the third Test at Kingston in 1960, after hitting a double century off the visitors for Barbados. In his first Test innings Nurse made a commendable 70, but was dropped to make room for Clyde Walcott.

A tall man, who drove powerfully off the back foot, Nurse regained the selectors' confidence for Westindies' tour to Australia in 1960-61. In the second Test at Melbourne, Nurse hammered another 70 as he and Rohan Kanhai put on 123 out of a total of 181. But, perhaps, 70 was an unlucky number for Nurse as he was dropped again and only got one other opportunity in a series where he was handicapped by a niggling injury, which left him reliant on crutches for a while.

Nurse played in one game against the touring Indians in the following series and was included in the tour party to England in 1963 but, once again, a pulled muscle precluded him from taking an active role in the Tests. Altogether he had played in eight

Seymour Nurse, one of Westindies' most exciting stroke-makers

Tests over four series and had yet to make a century. But, with the retirement of Frank Worrell and a return to full fitness, Nurse was given an extended run in the side.

When Australia visited the Caribbean in 1965 Nurse was promoted to open the innings in the first Test at Kingston; but the experiment failed, and he returned to the middle order in time to play at his majestic best in front of his home crowd in the fourth Test at Bridgetown. He stroked his way to a double hundred, as his fluent play lit up Kensington Oval, and almost lifted his side to a surprise win. Fittingly, before the match was over, Nurse's wife produced her own double when she gave birth to twin girls.

By the time of the 1966 tour to England, Nurse was a senior member of the team even though he had only played in 10 Tests. He scored over 500 runs in the Tests and finished second in the averages to Gary Sobers, with 62.62. The Barbadian top-scored with a sparkling 64 in the first innings of the Lord's Test, and followed this up with 93 and 53 in the third match at Trent Bridge. By the time of the fourth game at Headingley, Nurse was well into his stride and treated the crowd to 137, as he added 265 for the fifth wicket with Sobers, paving the way for an innings victory by the visitors. In the final match at The Oval Nurse collected a duck in the first innings but was Westindies' main defender in the second innings with 70 as, this time, the tourists collapsed to an innings defeat.

The Barbadian didn't shine so brightly on the following tour to India, and with Conrad Hunte's early retirement, he was tried in the opener's position again when England visited Westindies in 1968. Nurse was not at home in this role, but helped Sobers to save the second Test at Kingston with a resolute 73. Then, batting at first wicket down, he made a brilliant 136, sharing in a scintillating partnership of 273 with Kanhai, in the fourth Test at Port-of-Spain.

Nurse continued to score prolifically in Australia later that year, hitting 74 in the second Test at Melbourne, as he shared in a century stand with Sobers, before stroking his way to a magnificent hundred in the last match at Sydney. This proved to be the prelude to his most successful Test series, which came on the New Zealand leg of the tour.

Seymour Nurse (right) and Jackie Hendriks run for cover during a storm at one of the early matches on Westindies' tour of England in 1966

In the first match at Auckland Nurse signalled his intentions by crashing 95, as he added 172 for the second wicket with Joey Carew. After the visitors had conceded an unlikely lead, Nurse made sure that Westindies finished as victors by hitting 168 in a brilliant display of stroke-making lasting just over three-and-a-half hours. In the final Test at Christchurch he powered his way to a career-best 258 – the highest score recorded on the ground – out of a Westindies total of 417. His innings contained a six and 35 fours, as he and Carew shared in a stand of 231. At the end of a remarkable tour in which the Barbadian had scored 1,520 runs (52.41) including four centuries, he announced his retirement, thus depriving Westindies of a masterful batsman who could have led them into the 1970s.

In five innings Nurse made 558 runs and left the Test scene at his peak. His splendid footwork and strong wrists, together with his quick eyesight and magnificent timing, contrived to make him one of the most gifted batsmen of his generation. Besides his batting prowess, Nurse was also a magnificent close to the wicket fielder, who often brought off athletic catches.

On his retirement, Nurse became a government coach and has been instrumental in the development of many of the players in the current Test side. Nurse still plays over-40s cricket in Barbados and has toured Britain several times as a club cricketer.

Career details

Born: *11 November 1933*
Role: *Right-hand batsman*
Clubs: *Barbados, Lancashire League*
First-class record: *[1958-72] 9,489 runs (43.93) including 26 centuries, and 12 wickets (32.41)*
Tests: *29*
Test debut: *v England 1960*
Test runs: *2,523 (47.60); HS: 258 v New Zealand, Christchurch, 1969*
Tours: *Australia 1960-61; England 1963; England 1966; India 1966-67; Australia and New Zealand 1968-69.*

Bruce Hamilton Pairaudeau

Bruce Pairaudeau began his cricket career with a stunning string of scores at a tender age, which suggested that he would enjoy a long and distinguished career at the highest level. The Guyanese scored his maiden first-class century, 130, against Jamaica in 1947, aged 16 years and five months, having made his debut just before his 16th birthday.

Several seasons of consolidation paid the youngster rich dividends in the 1952-53 season, when he hit three successive hundreds, including a magnificent 115 on his Test debut, against India in the first match at Port-of-Spain, adding 219 for the fourth wicket with Everton Weekes. After this performance, Pairaudeau was promoted to open the innings as Westindies attempted to find a successor to the illustrious pairing of Allan Rae and Jeff Stollmeyer.

Bruce Pairaudeau

The bespectacled Pairaudeau's auspicious Test debut seemed to confirm the promise he had shown for Guyana and a half century in the final game at Kingston suggested that he would make the opener's position his own. But it wasn't to be, as he failed to sustain his initial form at international level. Pairaudeau was weaned on the Indian spinners in his early Tests, but, later, seemed vulnerable against high-class fast bowling. The reason was often blamed on the fact that he wore glasses and that he was more naturally suited to batting in the middle-order.

The right-hander shone briefly against England in the second Test at Bridgetown in 1954, as he stroked his way to 71, adding 165 with Clyde Walcott, whose double century turned the game in favour of Westindies.

Pairaudeau was replaced by John Holt for the Tests against the visiting Australians in 1955, but continued to score prolifically for Guyana and returned to the Test side for the tour to New Zealand in 1956. He met with considerable success, making 68 in the first innings of the third Test at Wellington, and was the only Westindian player other than Everton Weekes to hit a hundred on the tour.

Pairaudeau was included as a specialist opener on the 1957 tour of England, but, once again, failed to establish himself in the role. In the first Test at Edgbaston, the Guyanese was dismissed for a single, but spent most of the first innings in the middle as runner for Clyde Walcott and Frank Worrell, and was at the wicket as 387 runs were added.

The Guyanese enjoyed several seasons of cricket in the Lancashire League and played with great success for Northern Districts in New Zealand between 1958-67. Pairaudeau settled in New Zealand, like his Test colleague, Simpson Guillen, and was one of the first overseas players to captain a provincial side.

Career details

Born: *14 April 1931*
Role: *Right-hand batsman*
Clubs: *Guyana, Northern Districts*
First-class record: *[1946-67] 4,930 runs (32.01) including 11 centuries*
Tests: *13*
Test debut: *v India 1953*
Test runs: *454 (21.61); HS: 115 v India, Port-of-Spain, 1953*
Tours: *New Zealand 1956; England 1957.*

Derek Ricaldo Parry

Derek Parry was born on the tiny island of Nevis and became the second player from this Leeward Island to play Test cricket for Westindies. The most gifted spin bowler to emerge since Lance Gibbs, Parry was also a capable batsman which elevated him into the all-rounder's class.

He enjoyed an outstanding season for the Combined Leeward and Windward Islands in the Shell Shield in 1978, a year after his debut. He began with nine wickets and 94 runs against Barbados in the opening fixture, and a succession of excellent all-round performances catapulted him into Test match contention.

Parry was selected for the third Test against Australia at Georgetown in 1978, where he had a disastrous debut. He was out to the first ball he faced and then bowled a wide with his first delivery in Test cricket. He had steadied his nerves by the second innings, making 51 as nightwatchman, but this was not enough to hold the visitors at bay and Australia won by three wickets.

By the time of the fourth match at Port-of-Spain, Parry was reproducing his territorial form and, in the absence of the World Series players, he hit 65 in the second innings, helping to set the visitors a target of 293 to square the series. Australia were quickly reduced to 72 for five, before Parry chaperoned his side to victory in the series by collecting five wickets for six runs in 28 balls. Four of his five victims were bowled, as Australia were ushered out for 94.

The right-arm off-spinner was selected for the tour to India in 1978-79, but, apart from a sound 55 in the opening game at Bombay, he made little impression with the bat or the ball, making just 193 runs in six Tests and taking nine expensive wickets.

Parry was taken on the following tours to Australia and New Zealand, and England and Pakistan between 1979-81 but, like many outstanding slow bowlers before him, he found himself sidelined by the fast men who monopolised the bowling positions. Larry Gomes and Viv Richards were relied upon as the compulsory fifth bowler in the limited-overs games and sometimes turned their arms over in

the Tests, making the prospects for the inclusion of a specialist slow bowler even bleaker.

On the tour to England in 1980, Parry bowled well against the counties, with his 40 wickets costing a mere 20 runs each, but, after several years heading the reserve list, Parry's patience ran out and he joined the two rebel tours to South Africa in 1983 and 1984.

Career details

Born: *22 December 1954*
Role: *Right-arm off-spinner, right-hand batsman*
Club: *Leeward Islands, Cambridgeshire*
First-class record: *[1975-84] 251 wickets (28.96) and 2,522 runs (26.58)*
Tests: *12*
Test debut: *v Australia 1978*
Test wickets: *23 (40.69); BB: 5-15 v Australia, Port-of-Spain, 1978*
Test runs: *381 (22.41); HS: 65 v Australia, Port-of-Spain, 1978*
Tours: *India 1978-79; Australia and New Zealand 1979-80; England 1980; Pakistan 1980-81.*

ek Parry

Balfour Patrick Patterson

Alan Cozzi

A splendid athlete, Patrick Patterson appeared from nowhere to blast himself to the forefront of the Westindies pace attack in time for England's visit to the Caribbean in 1986, having tamed the cream of Westindies' own batting with a superb performance in the Shell Shield.

Included in the Westindies side for the first one-day international against the tourists on his home ground at Kingston, the 6ft 2in Jamaican collected two wickets for 17 runs in seven overs of blistering pace. This was merely a prelude to his magnificent Test debut on the same ground a few days later when, this time, he collected match figures of seven for 73. On his first day of Test cricket, encouraged by an excited crowd, which included most of his family, Patterson returned figures of four for 29. At the end of the game, Westindies' latest bowling discovery was presented with the Man of the Match award.

The Times reported that some of Patterson's short balls were "just about as fast as a man can bowl", while Malcolm Marshall, hitherto regarded as the fastest bowler in the world, agreed that by the end of the season Patterson was "the quickest around".

Yet the strapping youngster's rise was far from meteoric: Patterson made his first-class debut in 1983 and, prior to 1986, had been struggling to become a regular member of the Jamaican team. But, even if he lacked consistency, he had a burning desire to bowl fast and, after sprinting up to release his bullet-like delivery, his follow-through invariably carried him through to the unfortunate batsman on the receiving end. Besides sheer speed, the Jamaican has a savage yorker in his repertoire.

Born in Portland, Patterson comes from a cricketing family. His grandfather and father both played club cricket at a high standard and, like most youngsters, Patterson played cricket in the street and on the beach, and consolidated his remarkable talent at his two schools, Happy Grove and Wolmer's in Kingston. Patterson remembers: "I used to pay the

Patrick Patterson, whose fearsome pace brought him four wickets for 29 on his first day in Test cricket, against England at Kingston in 1986

other boys at school to bowl at me and let me bowl at them." This enthusiasm, together with his considerable natural ability, prompted his selection for Jamaica in the annual youth championships in 1980 and 1981; and he had two games for the full squad in 1983, including one against the touring Indians.

When Australia visited the Westindies the following year, Clive Lloyd asked Patterson to bowl at him in the nets. The Jamaican says: "He seemed impressed because he got me to come to Lancashire that season and also arranged a contract for me the following season in Tasmania. It was the break I needed." But Patterson didn't make a startling impression with either team, taking 32 wickets for his Australian club at 38 each – even though he hit the headlines when he was dropped from the side for bouncing the captain in the nets – and 41 at 27.27 apiece when he joined Lancashire in 1985. In England he was hampered by the slower wickets and lacked support from any other genuinely quick bowler, while the *Daily Telegraph Cricket Year Book* said of his performances for Lancashire: "Patterson could be as fast and as hostile as any bowler in England but was erratic, unpredictable and prone to injury."

Patterson returned to the Westindies after his summer at Lancashire to work on his game for the imminent Shield season and, later, for the English visitors. He recalls: "I started bowling a bit faster for longer periods and with better line, bowling straighter than I'd done before."

On the first day of the Shield competition, Patterson took seven for 24 from 7.1 overs against Guyana in front of his home crowd and took seven wickets in the next match against the Leeward Islands, also at Kingston. He accounted for Richie Richardson in both innings and also dismissed the Westindies' captain, Viv Richards. In addition, the Jamaican sent the Leewards' opener, Luther Kelly, to hospital with a badly cut mouth. Although Patterson was not as rampant in Jamaica's three away games, his 22 wickets were sufficient to catapult him into the Test side.

His performance against England in 1986, when he took 19 wickets at 22.36 apiece, secured his passage to Pakistan at the end of that year, but he only managed three fairly expensive wickets in the three match series, and was not selected for the subsequent tour to New Zealand.

Patterson's critics believe his success has been too centred on the fast wicket at Sabina Park, with its unpredictable bounce; but his compatriot, Jeff Dujon, who has kept wicket to all the great fast bowlers of recent years, says: "I think he has it in him to go all the way."

Time will tell, but if Patterson, who works as an accounts clerk when not playing cricket, can carry his success out of Jamaica he seems likely to have a prominent role to play in the Test team in the coming years.

Career details

Born: *15 September 1961*
Role: *Right-arm fast bowler*
Clubs: *Jamaica, Lancashire, Tasmania*
First-class record: *[1982-] 232 wickets (27.83) and 238 runs (4.76)*
Tests: 6
Test debut: *v England 1986*
Test wickets: *22 (23.90); BB: 4-29 v England, Kingston, 1986*
Tours: *Pakistan 1986; New Zealand 1987; India and Pakistan (World Cup) 1987.*

Norbert Phillip

A superbly fit cricketer, Norbert Phillip was an enthusiastic right-handed batsman and sharp medium-fast bowler who always gave his best to the Windward Islands and Essex. Renowned for his passion of being on the winning side, Phillip took over Keith Boyce's mantle at Essex, maintaining the Caribbean bravado in the county.

Phillip came from a cricketing family: his father played club cricket at a high standard, while, as a youngster, the Dominican often indulged in impromptu nets with his four brothers. Phillip played at school and was included in the Dominican school team for the annual Windwards tournament at the age of 16. He progressed to the Combined Islands team, where he took part in the only schools championship to be held in the Westindies, in 1966.

He appeared for the Combined Islands five years later, and pushed himself into contention for a Test place in 1978 when he averaged 76.66 with the bat in the Shell Shield and took 21 wickets (17.71). He had

Norbert Phillip

an outstanding match against Guyana, collecting 10 wickets and making 70 and 90 not out.

The tall, broad-shouldered Phillip won his first Test cap against Australia in the third game at Georgetown in 1978, where he opened the attack with Sylvester Clarke and took six wickets in the match. Phillip's batting helped Westindies to win the fourth match at Port-of-Spain, as his 46, before he was last man out, gave the home side the initiative and eventually swung the match in their favour.

The man from Dominica maintained his momentum with a splendid first summer at Essex in 1978. He took 71 wickets for his county and scored 645 runs, including a magnificent 134 against Gloucestershire. His continued success ensured his selection for the tour to India in 1978-79, where he helped himself to 19 wickets (34.21) in six Tests. His tally would have been higher if several chances off his bowling had been accepted. Phillip's best performance came in the third match at Calcutta where he took four for 64 in India's first innings and then hit a sparkling 47 to help Westindies to a lead. He took seven for 85 in the fourth game at Madras and supplemented his bowling with a batting average in excess of 35.

In 1979 Phillip was one of the leading players in Essex's double success in the county championship and the Benson & Hedges Cup, and was instrumental in their success in the John Player League two years later, when he hit a match-winning 83 against Surrey in the deciding game at The Oval.

Phillip maintained this all-round form for the Windwards, when they competed in the Shield for the first time on their own in 1982, snapping up 21 wickets at 16.3 apiece and averaging 31 with the bat. His bowling figures included seven for 33 in the second innings of the match against the Leeward Islands (at one stage he took six wickets for nine runs, including three in four balls) and a splendid 62 runs at Bridgetown, as he ushered his side to their historic victory over Barbados. In the end, the Windwards were runners-up to Barbados in the Shield, while Phillip was second only to Joel Garner in the overall bowling averages. The likeable all-rounder succeeded to the captaincy of the Windwards in 1983, and celebrated his appointment by taking five wickets

Norbert Phillip

Tony Edenden

against the touring Indians.

Phillip eventually lost his Test place to Malcolm Marshall after the Packer crisis was resolved, as Westindies put their faith in an all-out pace attack.

Career details

Born: *22 June 1949*
Role: *Right-hand batsman, right-arm medium-fast bowler*
Clubs: *Windward Islands, Essex*
First-class record: *[1971-85] 7,013 runs (23.61) including 1 century, and 688 wickets (24.75)*
Tests: *9*
Test debut: *v Australia 1978*
Test runs: *297 (29.70); HS: 47 v India, Calcutta, 1979*
Test wickets: *28 (37.18); BB: 4-48 v India, Madras, 1980*
Tour: *India 1978-79*

Allan Fitzroy Rae

Known for his virtually inpenetrable defence, Allan Rae was Westindies' anchorman for several years and, with Jeff Stollmeyer, formed their first reliable opening partnership at Test level.

A product of Wolmer's Boys' School, Rae's solid defence was underpinned by huge powers of concentration. Certainly not a flamboyant player, the kindly Jamaican was a reliable accumulator of runs and drove the ball ferociously.

Rae was selected for the tour to India in 1948-49, 20 years after his father, Ernest, made the first trip to England. The younger Rae had only a few first-class matches behind him, although in one of them, against Trinidad at Kingston in 1946-47, he had scored a hundred in each innings.

The quiet left-hander was a resounding success in India, collecting his maiden Test century in the second match at Bombay, as he added 134 with Stollmeyer. Rae played well for another skilful hundred in the fourth game at Madras, in the face of some feeble leg-theory bowling from the Indians. This time he shared in a record double century partnership with Stollmeyer which stood until 1983. In the final match at Bombay, the Indian bowlers were more in command, but a resolute innings of 97 from the tall Jamaican ended the home side's hopes of giving the visitors a fright, as Rae finished the series with an average of 53.42.

This performance secured his passage to England in 1950 – familiar territory for Rae who had studied law there and who occasionally turned out at club level for Winchmore Hill and the BBC. Once again the broad-shouldered Jamaican was among the leading run scorers, as he hit two Test centuries and shared in a record first wicket stand of 355 with Stollmeyer against Sussex at Hove, hitting a career-best 179.

Rae's partnership with Stollmeyer was a vital component in Westindies' winning combination in England in 1950, as the pair always gave the visitors a sound start. Rae's best moment came on the first day of the second Test at Lord's. He scored 106, after seeing off some testing early deliveries, and then consolidated the visitors' position in two substantial partnerships with Frank Worrell and Everton Weekes.

In the third match at Trent Bridge Rae played well to score 68 in the first innings, before he and Stollmeyer erased the 102 runs required for victory in the second without being separated. Rae finished the series with a determined century at The Oval, adding 172 for the second wicket with Worrell. This completed another satisfying tour for the Jamaican, in which he scored over 1,000 first-class runs and returned a Test average of 62.83.

The watchful Rae struggled on the subsequent tour to Australia against the aggression of Ray Lindwall and Keith Miller. He never really recovered from losing his wicket to Lindwall for a duck to the third ball of the Test series, as his extravagant backlift failed to come down in time on a scything yorker, and he finished with a paltry average of 14.50 from three Tests. But Rae returned to his more consistent ways in New Zealand, when he made 99 in the second match at Auckland, adding 197 for the first wicket with Stollmeyer.

Back in the Caribbean, Rae played his first Test at home, against India at Port-of-Spain in 1953. He made an unbeaten 63, sharing in an unbroken stand of 142 with Stollmeyer, in the second innings. Then the selectors decided to promote Bruce Pairaudeau to the opener's role in place of Rae, and end the best first wicket pairing Westindies had known. This seemed harsh on the Jamaican, whose batting had returned from its depths in Australia to its more familiar dependability.

Rae continued to play first-class cricket until 1960, the year in which he secured a Jamaican record by sharing in a partnership of 258 with Easton McMorris against Trinidad. By this time Rae was captain of Jamaica and already involved in cricket administration.

On his retirement, Rae concentrated on his legal career, although he remained heavily involved in the administrative side of the game and is currently President of the Westindies Board of Control. Often the situations Rae has had to deal with have been as pressing as those he met on the field of play, and include involvement in the negotiations with Kerry Packer and coping with the aftermath of the rebel tours to South Africa.

Career details

Born: *30 September 1922*
Role: *Left-hand batsman*
Club: *Jamaica*
First-class record: *[1946-60] 4,798 runs (39.65) including 17 centuries*
Tests: *15*
Test debut: *v India 1948*
Test runs: *1,016 (46.18); HS: 109 v India, Madras, 1949*
Tours: *India 1948-49; England 1950; Australia and New Zealand 1951-52.*

Sonny Ramadhin

Sonny Ramadhin whose mystique entranced England in 1950

Sonny Ramadhin really was an overnight sensation. Included in the tour party to England on a hunch after he had taken 12 wickets in two trial matches, the little spinner, along with his partner Alf Valentine, soon became the talk of the Caribbean. The first pair of world-class Westindian slow bowlers to operate together at Test level, Ramadhin and Valentine were instrumental in securing Westindies' first victory on English soil.

Born in south Trinidad, Ramadhin was the first East Indian to appear for Westindies in a Test match. An orphan who was brought up by friends and relatives, Ramadhin was spotted as a youngster by a Barbadian cricketer, who noticed others struggling to read his bowling. He persuaded the Trinidadian to join the Trinidad Leaseholds Oil Company, where he got his first opportunity to play senior cricket regularly.

The slightly-built spinner made an unusual sight, with his cap seemingly glued to his head and his shirt-sleeves buttoned to the wrist, while his bowling mystified cricketers all over the world. With his unorthodox grip he baffled the best of batsmen, who could not distinguish his leg-break from his off-break. This, along with his immaculate control and subtle variations in flight meant that, for many years, he was a match-winner for Westindies.

The 1950 tour to England was the first time that Ramadhin had left Trinidad, but he adapted quickly from the matting surfaces that he was used to at home and, with his friend Valentine, proved to be Westindies' trump card.

The right-armer, who was the youngest member of the side, took 135 wickets, including 26 wickets at 23.23 each in four Tests. After losing the first match at Old Trafford, Ramadhin rallied his side with five for 66 in the first innings of the second game at Lord's, and mesmerized the batsmen with six for 86 off 72 overs in the second innings to complete Westindies' first win in England, which fittingly came at headquarters. *Wisden* commented: "No blame could be attached to the pitch...Ramadhin bowled with the

guile of a veteran. He pitched a tantalising length, bowled straight at the wicket and spun enough to beat the bat. No English batsman showed evidence of having mastered the problems of deciding which way Ramadhin would spin."

His magic continued in the next game at Trent Bridge, where he took five for 135 to usher the tourists to a 10 wicket victory. When the team returned victorious to the Caribbean, they were given an enthusiastic reception and public holidays were granted in the islands. Calypsos sung the praises of the two spinners: "We want Ramadhin on the ball" said one line. A law unto himself, Ramadhin had more than fulfilled his potential as his mystique entranced the opposition as much as his spin.

After the tour to England Ramadhin was a stalwart in Westindies' side for over a decade. He tended to have most impact on his first meeting with the opposition, although the Pakistanis and New Zealanders never mastered him.

Like several of his contemporaries, Ramadhin played in the Lancashire League in the early 1950s. He was taken to Australia in 1951-52 but, after taking five for 90 in the opening match at Brisbane, he suffered at the hands of the Australian batsmen whose deft footwork upset his rhythm. He was more effective on the friendlier pitches in New Zealand, and took nine wickets in the first Test at Christchurch.

When India visited the Caribbean in 1953, record crowds turned out to see Ramadhin and Valentine in action on their home territory. Yet Ramadhin was never as potent in the Westindies and seemed to have lost some of his mystique after his trip to Australia. Even so, he won the second Test at Bridgetown for his side, when he dismissed India's five leading batsmen for 26 in the second innings, to hand Westindies the initiative in the series.

The right-armer was still a handful for the English when they visited the Caribbean in 1954, even though he lacked support. He collected four wickets in the first innings of the first two Tests, and then took six for 113 in the third game at Georgetown. The most successful bowler on either side, he finished with 23 wickets at 24.30 each.

During these years, Ramadhin was often forced to

carry Westindies' bowling attack and showed admirable consistency in the face of strong English and Australian batting line-ups. His performances put paid to the view that he cracked under pressure, first mooted when a thigh injury forced him to leave the field in the last few minutes of the fourth Test against Australia at Melbourne in 1952. Indeed, the gifted spinner maintained his place in the side even with the resurgence of the pace attack at the end of the 1950s.

Nonetheless, Ramadhin struggled against the powerful Australian tourists in 1955, but returned to his best form against the New Zealanders in 1956. In the first Test at Dunedin, he rekindled his old magic by taking six for 23 off 21.2 overs, including four batsmen before they had scored. He maintained his momentum for the second game at Christchurch, as he collected nine wickets in the match, including five for 46 in the first innings. His 15 Test wickets cost 15.80 apiece, while his batting was a revelation as he hit 44 at Dunedin and 33 at Christchurch. The same year, Ramadhin ushered a Westindies X1 to victory by eight wickets over a touring team of English county cricketers, which boosted his confidence further for the tour to England the following year.

A little more portly than on his previous trip, the jovial Ramadhin seemed, nonetheless, to have found some new tricks to confound the opposition in the early games of the tour. By the time of the first Test, he had already captured a phenomenal 38 wickets. Then, bowling on an unhelpful Edgbaston wicket, he dismissed England cheaply in their first innings by taking seven for 49 in 31 overs. After removing two batsmen early in the home side's second innings, it seemed that Ramadhin might repeat his earlier efforts. Then Colin Cowdrey and Peter May devised a method to nullify Ramadhin's effectiveness, making judicious use of their front pad. Their ploy served England well as the pair added a record 411 runs for the fourth wicket. England saved the match and destroyed Ramadhin's reputation, but the tactics employed prompted a public outcry and eventually led to a change in the LBW law.

The Trinidadian bowled the longest stint ever recorded in a Test innings, as he sent down 98 overs – and a record 129 overs in the match – in the absence of the injured Frank Worrell and Roy Gilchrist. It was a mammoth spell from which Ramadhin never recovered for the rest of the series, although he shared in a match-saving last wicket stand of 55 with Worrell in the third game at Trent Bridge, and took four wickets in the final game at The Oval when the rubber had been decided. Even so, he still headed the bowling in all first-class matches with 119 wickets at 13.98 apiece.

In the subsequent series against India and Pakistan, Ramadhin kept a low profile, although he helped Westindies to victory in the third game against Pakistan at Lahore with four wickets for 25. He also took four in the final match against the English tourists at Port-of-Spain in 1960, before retiring from Test cricket after the tour to Australia the following year.

Although some of Ramadhin's mystery evaporated towards the end of his career, between them he and Valentine provided the most entrancing spin partnership in the history of cricket for one immortal season in 1950.

After many years playing in the Lancashire League, Ramadhin appeared for the county in 1964 and 1965. He also turned out for Lincolnshire and Commonwealth X1s and, even in his fifties, still played in the Bolton Association. Ramadhin has made his home in England and now runs a pub in Lancashire.

Career details

Born: *1 May 1930*
Role: *Right-arm spinner*
Clubs: *Trinidad, Lancashire, Minor Counties, Lancashire League*
First-class record: *[1949-65] 758 wickets (20.24) and 1,106 runs (8.77)*
Tests: *43*
Test debut: *v England 1950*
Test wickets: *158 (28.98); BB: 7-49 v England, Edgbaston, 1957*
Test runs: *361 (8.20); HS: 44 v New Zealand, Dunedin, 1956*
Tours: *England 1950; Australia and New Zealand 1951-52; New Zealand 1956; England 1957; India and Pakistan 1958-59; Australia 1960-61.*

Isaac Vivian Alexander Richards

Batting in an era of unrivalled Westindian supremacy in world cricket, it is indicative of his genius that Viv Richards is generally regarded as the best batsman of his generation. Like George Headley before him, Richards has reached a level of excellence that no other can emulate.

The distinctive feature of his batting is his unqualified confidence. He has never worn a helmet, once remarking: "My personal view is that a helmet with a visor takes a little of the batsman's vision – and just a little of the challenge out of the game" – an attitude which typifies his whole approach to cricket.

Born into a cricketing family – for many years his father, Malcolm, was Antigua's leading fast bowler, while his two brothers have also played for the island – Richards made rapid progress and appeared for Antigua at cricket and soccer while still at school.

From an early age Richards won the adoration of his country: he has come to embody the island of Antigua that stands alone of the Leewards to compare with the other great cricketing regions of the Caribbean. He, more than any other individual, put Antigua on the sporting map and, largely as a result of his phenomenal exploits, the Recreation Ground in the capital, St. John's, was granted Test match status in 1981; while his marriage, a few days earlier, to Miriam, his long-time girl-friend, in St. John's, attracted intense media coverage.

On one famous occasion the support of his partisan followers proved to be his downfall: in a Leeward Islands' tournament in 1969, his adoring fans forced an official to overrule the umpire and reinstate Richards after he had been caught behind. The incident resulted in a two year suspension for the young Antiguan which delayed his entry into first-class cricket until 1972. Then, he was chosen for the Combined Islands against the touring New Zealanders and hit a stylish half century.

Richards' talent was so obvious that, in 1973, he was sent with another promising youngster, Andy

Viv Richards during his peerless double century against England at Trent Bridge in 1976

170

Roberts, to the Alf Gover School in England, courtesy of Antigua's Volunteers' Cricket Committee. Richards made a favourable impact and, later on, impressed Colin Cowdrey with a splendid fifty against the Englishman's side in Antigua. Then, he came to the attention of Somerset committee member, Len Creed, who interrupted Richards as he practised for his Antiguan club, the Rising Sun, to invite him to England.

The right-hander joined Somerset in 1974 and soon benefitted from the fatherly advice proffered by Brian Close, the county's captain, who took the young Richards under his wing and instilled professional values into his game. In his first year with Somerset the gifted youngster made over 1,000 first-class runs and was consistently high in the English county averages, scoring over 1,000 runs every season until he was controversially released by the club in 1986. He enjoyed a vintage summer in 1977 when he scored 2,161 first-class runs for an average of 65.48 and set a record for hitting the most sixes in the Sunday League, with 26.

With Joel Garner, Richards catapulted Somerset from the periphery to the centre of English cricket. In 1985, the Antiguan helped himself to a triple century off Warwickshire at Taunton. It was Richards' highest first-class score and the highest innings ever played for Somerset, coming off 258 balls with eight sixes and 42 fours. He hit eight other championship centuries that summer, and finished with an average of 76.50.

Standing 5ft 11in tall, Richards' build and looks have often been compared to those of the great American boxer, Joe Frazier – hence his nickname "Smokin'". The Antiguan has an upright stance, and makes full use of his powerful arms and shoulders. Equally at home against pace or spin, Richards is a superb cover-driver, a brilliant hooker and master of on-side play. He is also one of the best fielders in the world, while his accurate bowling has often broken dangerous partnerships in Test matches.

Richards was the surprise choice for the tour to India and Pakistan in 1974-75, but demonstrated his calibre immediately by scoring a match-winning 192 not out in the second Test at New Delhi, as he dominated partnerships with Clive Lloyd and Keith Boyce. He hit fifty in a losing cause in the fourth game at Madras, but his youthful impetuosity cost him his wicket in the other matches.

In 11 glorious Tests, beginning in Australia in 1976 against the fearsome pace of Dennis Lillee and Jeff Thomson, the remarkable Antiguan scored 1,710 runs. In his last three Test innings on the tour to Australia he scored 101, 50 and 98; while his return to the Caribbean to face the Indians only accelerated his run-scoring. He hit 142, 130, 20 run out, 177, 23 and 64. England were the next team to suffer at Richards' hands: he pillaged them for 232, 63, 4, 135, 66, 38, and a brilliant 291 at The Oval to take his total to 1,710 in eight unforgettable months. *Wisden* wrote of his feats that year: "If he fails to make another run in Test cricket his performance in this single year will always be a source of conversation for the enthusiasts and inspiration to young batsmen".

Alec Bedser wrote of the Antiguan Goliath: "There are academic discussions centred on the fine point of whether Richards is a bludgeoning murderer or a clinical assassin when he is in his pillaging mood. It matters little. Either descriptions could fit for he has the confidence – perhaps arrogance is the right word – and other coordinated gifts of the eye, balance and timing to meet any occasion."

Like his colleagues, Richards struggled on the tour to Australia in 1975-76. Early on he treated Western Australia to a splendid 175 but opened his Test account with a duck at Brisbane, and failed to get into his stride until he was promoted to open the innings for the fifth Test at Adelaide. This happened after he had opened the batting against Tasmania and scored centuries in each innings. He made 30 and 101 at Adelaide, as he began his sequence of scores that would take him to his record-breaking aggregate in England later in 1976.

Richards returned to the middle order for the following home series against the Indians and, after a shaky start, hammered a superb 142 in the first Test at Bridgetown. The Antiguan secured a draw for his side with an equally magnificent 130 in the next game at Port-of-Spain and helped himself to his third and best hundred, a chanceless 177, in the following match, also at Port-of-Spain.

In his last five Tests, Richards had scored four

hundreds and 98, but became more sedate in the final match at Kingston, where he hit a mere 64 in his only innings, for an average of 92.66 in the series. In both the Trinidad Tests his individual scores were more that the combined total of the rest of the team and, apart from Lloyd, no other Westindian made a century in the rubber.

Against England Richards was irrepressible. In the first Test at Trent Bridge he hit 232, dominating a triple century third wicket partnership with Alvin Kallicharran. The Antiguan's innings lasted 465 minutes and contained four sixes and 31 fours. He missed the Lord's Test with 'flu – which made his eventual batting aggregate even more incredible – and, after failing in the first innings of the Old Trafford Test, he made amends in the second with a brilliant 135, before thrashing 66 runs off the beleaguered English attack at Headingley.

Richards was at his brilliant best in the final game at The Oval. Glowing with confidence, he helped himself to 291 runs in just under eight hours. His innings contained 38 majestic fours, as he shared in successive century partnerships with Roy Fredericks, Lawrence Rowe and Lloyd. The Antiguan's performance overhauled Frank Worrell's record for the highest individual score by a Westindian in England and, for a while, it seemed as though he might surpass Gary Sobers' all-time record. But, finally, having reached 291 with a six, he succumbed to tiredness trying to repeat the stroke, having been at the wicket for 472 minutes and after facing 386 balls.

From seven innings, Richards plundered 829 runs for an average of 118.42. It was the highest aggregate ever by a Westindian: only three other batsmen have hit more runs in a series, but they all needed five matches. On the whole tour the Antiguan scored 1,724 runs, with four other hundreds, to finish with an average of 71.83.

Of his performances in that glorious summer, *Wisden* wrote: "Richards was exceptionally brilliant and must be ranked among the finest West Indian batsmen of all time, worthy to be coupled with the great George Headley of pre-War fame, even if perhaps he did not have to deal with the same class of bowling...Mere figures cannot convey his perfect style and stroke-play. His cover driving was superb and with his feet always in the right position the way he flicked the ball on his leg-stump to square-leg had to be seen to be believed."

After all this frenzied activity, it seemed that Richards must be due for a quieter patch and it came the following year – after a season of Sheffield Shield cricket for Queensland – against Pakistan. In that series the Antiguan limited himself to two half centuries, including 92 in the opening game at Bridgetown, adding 130 with Fredericks for the second wicket.

As he got older, Richards revealed another tell-tale sign of his enviable talent: namely his ability to save his best performances for the big occasion. He relishes Lord's, and coolly shattered the English bowling attack to retain the World Cup for Westindies in 1979 with 138, sharing in a match-winning fifth wicket partnership with Collis King. At the end of that season, the Antiguan hit another match-winning century at Lord's, this time for Somerset in the Gillette Cup final. He repeated the feat for his county in the Benson & Hedges Cup final of 1981, and collected half centuries in the B&H final the following year and in the NatWest final in 1983, the day after the birth of his son.

In the three match rubber against Australia in 1979-80, Richards averaged nearly one hundred runs each time he went to the wicket. He began with 140 at Brisbane, got 96 at Melbourne and finished with 76 and 74 at Adelaide, being instrumental in Westindies winning their first series in Australia.

The right-hander excelled against England in 1980 and was again at his best at Lord's. He stroked the ball around the ground for 145 glittering runs, with a six and 25 fours, and in the third Test at Old Trafford, hit 65, sharing in a three figure partnership with Gordon Greenidge. Predictably, Richards finished the tour as Westindies' leading batsman in the Tests and the first-class matches.

He played well in Pakistan in 1980-81, reaching 120 in the last Test at Multan and, after a quiet start against England later that year – including a duck in the first innings of the third match at Bridgetown – he crashed a superb 182 not out in the second, in a magnificent prelude to the first ever Test to be played in Antigua.

Pelham Cricket Year aptly summed up the inevitability of Richards' success there, remarking: "That the man would hit a Test century on his own ground to mark its use as an international arena for the first time was one of cricket's more predictable happenings. He began in dominant mood, rested for a while, then flourished again before easing off to his hundred. It was his first week of married life, his home ground and his fourteenth Test hundred."

Richards was more restrained in Australia in 1981-82, although he still hit two forties and a half century in the three match series. Even so the Antiguan was clearly in need of a rest and, after captaining the Leeward Islands for the first time and a successful benefit with Somerset in 1982, he took one before returning refreshed to face the visiting Indians in 1983.

He began with a whirlwind 60, which included four sixes, to bring Westindies victory in the opening Test at Kingston, and followed this with a scintillating century in the third at match Georgetown. It was a long-winded affair: he ended the first day on 97 not out and had to hold his fire through Good Friday, the washed out Saturday and Sunday morning before reaching three figures.

With the passing years and his continued prominence, some critics have questioned Richards' approach, claiming that his attitude oscillates between arrogance and casualness. It is perhaps most easily explained by the surfeit of cricket played these days, which makes even the keenest contemporary batsman stale, and recently, the master, perhaps a little jaded by the intense competition, has restricted himself to one century per series.

When Australia visited the Caribbean in 1984, Richards hit 76, sharing in a three-figure partnership with Gus Logie in the second Test at Port-of-Spain, but was at his most savage in the fourth game at St. John's. He made 178 and, appropriately, added 308 runs with his compatriot, Richie Richardson, prompting headlines that read: "Richards and Son, specialists in batting."

Later that year he hit 117, with a six and 17 fours, sharing in a double century stand for the third wicket with Larry Gomes in the first Test against England at Edgbaston. Generally, by his own lofty standards, Richards had a modest tour, but left spectators with an innings to cherish when he slammed 189 chanceless runs off 170 balls in the first one-day game at Old Trafford. It was the highest innings in the history of limited-overs cricket and included five huge sixes and 21 fours. Richards made his runs out of a total of 272, after Westindies' ninth wicket had fallen at 161.

He had another lean spell in Australia and fell for a duck in the third Test at Adelaide, which seemed to inspire him for the next encounter at Melbourne where he stroked his way to 208, with three sixes and 22 fours – the highest score by a Westindian in Australia – and, surprisingly, only the third double century of his Test career. He revealed his technical prowess with a polished 58 on a difficult wicket in the final Test at Sydney.

The first player from the Leeward Islands to captain Westindies, Richards was appointed for the home series against New Zealand in 1985. He opened his account with two fifties in the first match at Port-of-Spain and crashed a splendid hundred, with three sixes and 13 fours, in the third Test at Bridgetown to bring victory in the match and the rubber. Thus, by beating New Zealand, Richards began his reign by achieving one of the few feats to elude Lloyd, and went on to emulate the Guyanese by defeating England 5-0 in the subsequent series in the Caribbean.

Once again the right-hander was high in the averages, as he finished the series with 331 runs at 66.20, including 51 in the third match at Bridgetown, 87 in the fourth at Port-of-Spain and a scintillating 110 not out in the fifth at St. John's, with seven sixes and seven fours. In terms of balls, his century in Antigua was the fastest in the history of Test cricket coming off only 56 deliveries – 11 less than the previous record – after he had used up 15 balls without scoring!

Richards had a quieter time in Pakistan later in 1986. His best performance came in the third and final Test at Karachi, where he hit 70 in the visitors' first innings, as Westindies shared the rubber.

The Antiguan struggled for an average of under 20 in another drawn series against New Zealand the

Happiness is a century: Viv Richards is congratulated on his 117 against England at Edgbaston in 1984

Viv Richards in a typically majestic mood against England at Lord's in 1984

following year, which prompted talk of the end of Richards' and, indeed, Westindies' world dominance. Not only were they struggling in Tests, but they were being knocked out of limited-overs tournaments, notably the Benson & Hedges Challenge Trophy and World Series Cup, both held in Australia before the New Zealand tour.

But, after a summer playing Lancashire League cricket with Rishton, Richards returned to the international fold for the World Cup later in 1987. In a preliminary round match against Sri Lanka, the Westindies captain powered his way to the highest score ever recorded in the competition: 181 off a mere 125 balls, including six sixes and 16 fours, in a brilliant display of batting from a man hungry for success. He later became the first player to score 1,000 runs in the World Cup – a landmark doubtless overshadowed, in Richards' eyes, by Westindies' failure to reach the semi-finals for the first time.

Politically astute, Richards is fiercely patriotic and proud of his origins. As a national figure of international standing, his snubbing of South Africa and the pride with which he wears his Rastafarian wristband both reveal his strong personal beliefs and, on a wider level, provide inspiration for the peoples of the Caribbean.

Richards was awarded an honorary doctorate of letters by Exeter University in 1986. He is involved with Amnesty International and, at home, helps to sponsor young cricketers, footballers and basketball players. He is also a patron of the Antiguan Blind Society as, since his early thirties, he has suffered from an eye complaint.

Yet, the majesty of Richards' batting continues to dominate the cricketing landscape and, however much longer he goes on, the Antiguan has assured his place in cricket's history as one of the finest players the game has known.

Career details

Born: *7 March 1952*
Role: *Right-hand batsman, off-spinner*
Clubs: *Leeward Islands, Somerset, Queensland, Lancashire League*
First-class record: *[1972-] 29,061 runs (49.67) including 93 centuries, and 176 wickets (44.03)*
Tests: *88*
Test debut: *v India 1974*
Test runs: *6,472 (52.61); HS: 291 v England, The Oval, 1976*
Test wickets: *22 (54.90); BB: 2-19 v Pakistan, Lahore, 1980*
Tours: *India 1974-75; England (World Cup) 1975; Australia 1975-76; England 1976; England (World Cup) 1979; Australia 1979-80 (missed New Zealand leg through injury); England 1980; Pakistan 1980-81; Australia 1981-82; England (World Cup) 1983; India 1983; England 1984; Australia 1984-85; Pakistan 1986; New Zealand 1987; India and Pakistan (World Cup) 1987.*

Richie Benjamin Richardson

Richie Richardson won a place in Westindies' tour party to India in 1983 after collecting centuries off Barbados and Jamaica, whose respective bowling line-ups included Malcolm Marshall and Michael Holding, in the Shell Shield earlier that year. His first tour innings against the President's X1 at Nagpur, like his maiden first-class innings against Barbados in 1982, was inauspicious as, on both occasions, he failed to score. He made it a hat-trick of ducks when he collected one on his Test debut in the fourth match at Bombay – his only game of the series.

However, he revealed his class in the finals of the subsequent one-day series in Australia, and eventually recovered his five-day form when Australia visited the Caribbean in 1984. But Richardson's path was far from smooth. He greeted the tourists with his customary duck when they played the Leeward Islands and lost his Test place after two indifferent matches, batting in an unfamiliar position at number three.

But, as so often happens, a quirk of fate gave him another chance. Immediately before the third match at Bridgetown, Gus Logie withdrew through illness, and his replacement, Richardson, made full use of his unexpected opportunity. He hit 131 stylish runs, sharing in a partnership of 155 with Desmond Haynes, and followed this up with 154 in the next game at St. John's, demonstrating great maturity and concentration. He and his mentor, Viv Richards, added a record 308 for the third wicket in front of their adoring home crowd, prompting the predictable headline: "Richards and Son, specialists in run-making", as the pair brought their side victory by an innings. Just to prove that his impetuosity hadn't left him completely, Richardson was dismissed for nought in his next innings at Kingston. Even so, he finished second in the averages with a splendid 81.75.

Richardson enjoyed a prolific sporting career as a youngster, excelling at both cricket and football, and

ie Richardson out against cestershire on tindies' tour of land in 1984

was sponsored by a businessman, Victor Michael, to come to England to improve his cricket.

Born in Five Islands, a village about four miles from the capital, Richardson was brought up in a sporting environment: his father had been a capable cricketer and his whole family encouraged Richie, the third of four children, to practise his cricket and football skills. Richardson joined his eldest brother, Adolphus, in Antigua's youth soccer team which won the Cable & Wireless trophy in Dominica in 1977.

But two years later cricket had the bigger draw for Richardson and he visited England with an Antiguan schools team, and in 1980 was selected for the Westindies Youth team in their one "Test" against the touring England Youth team. He moved smoothly into Antigua's senior side and made his first-class debut for the Leewards in 1982. He made a duck in the first innings, but collected 76 runs in the second.

Besides his family, Richardson was encouraged from many other quarters. He spent two seasons playing county cricket, one at Glamorgan, then one at Somerset, thanks to further support from Michael and Richards, while the coaching he had received from Danny Livingstone and Guy Yearwood, a former Leewards' Shield player, was also paying handsome dividends.

The gifted right-hander lost his Test place to Larry Gomes on the tour of England in 1984, but renewed his splendid form against the unfortunate Australians in the subsequent series. In the second Test at Brisbane he made 138, with 24 fours, sharing in a century partnership for the fifth wicket with Clive Lloyd, after being dismissed for a duck in the first match at Perth.

In the home series against New Zealand in 1985, he was the most successful batsman: in the first Test at Port-of-Spain, he made a resolute 78 in trying conditions, adding 185 for the third wicket with Gordon Greenidge. He followed this up with a scintillating innings in the second match at Georgetown, cutting and driving his way to 185 glorious runs – after being dropped near the start of his innings – as he shared in a partnership of 181 with Desmond Haynes for the second wicket.

The Antiguan continued to bat fluently against England when they visited Westindies in 1986 and finished the series with an average of 55.28, including two dazzling centuries in the second Test at Port-of-Spain and in the third at Bridgetown. In the Leewards' game against the tourists, Richardson collected the only first-class wickets of his career, five for 40, with his medium pace, when he was pressed into service as the island's opening bowler after an injury to George Ferris.

Richardson was taken on the short tour of Pakistan in 1986 and finished third in the batting averages, having hit a commendable half century in the first Test at Faisalabad; and was third again after Westindies' tour to New Zealand the following year.

A superbly gifted batsman, Richardson has the qualities to become a permanent and successful member of Westindies' batting line-up over the next few years. If he can become more consistent by taming the more exuberant aspects of his batting, he seems assured of a glittering future.

Career details

Born: *12 January 1962*
Role: *Right-hand batsman*
Club: *Leeward Islands*
First-class record: *[1982-] 3,934 (37.11) including 11 centuries, and 5 wickets (22.80)*
Tests: 26
Test debut: *v India 1983*
Test runs: *1,636 runs (44.21); HS: 185 v New Zealand, Georgetown, 1985*
Tours: *India 1983; England 1984; Australia 1984-85; Pakistan 1986; New Zealand 1987; India and Pakistan (World Cup) 1987.*

Clifford Archibald Roach

Clifford Roach, who achieved some notable "firsts" in Test cricket

Clifford Roach was one of the few Westindian batsmen to succeed in the early Tests, although his inconsistency typified the best and the worst aspects of the pre-War Caribbean style. He was widely regarded as the natural successor to George Challenor but, more accurately, he provided an important link before the emergence of George Headley.

On the first tour of England in 1928, despite his inconsistency, demonstrating itself in a mixture of dazzling stroke-play and reckless impetuosity, Roach still scored 1,000 runs. He put on 56 with Joe Small in the second innings of the first Test at Lord's, and made a superb half century in the second match at Old Trafford, before adding 91 runs in 80 minutes of stupendous hitting with Challenor, against the bowling of Harold Larwood, in the final game at The Oval, but found himself on the losing side on each occasion.

When MCC toured the Caribbean the next year, Roach cut and drove his way to the first Test century by a Westindian in the opening game at Bridgetown. His 122 runs were made out of 179 while he was at the wicket, and included 20 boundaries, four of them in the first two overs off Bill Voce; and he followed it up with a similarly entertaining 77 in the second innings, sharing in a partnership of 156 with Headley.

Then he revealed his inconsistency as his next six first-class innings for Trinidad and Westindies yielded just 24 runs, including a pair at the hands of Voce on his home ground in the second Test at Port-of-Spain. Indeed, Roach's run famine was so severe that he cabled the selectors suggesting that they leave him out of the third match at Georgetown. The selectors declined his invitation and he arrived at the Bourda ground, where he surpassed his earlier feat at Bridgetown, by becoming the first Westindian to score a Test double century. Roach hit a career-best 209, including three sixes and 23 fours, scoring 122 of his runs in 98 minutes after tea on the opening day, and was instrumental in securing Westindies' first ever Test victory, sharing in partnerships of 144 with Errol Hunte and 196 with Headley for the first two wickets.

The lithe Trinidadian returned to his less prolific ways on the tour to Australia in 1930-31, scoring just one fifty in the first Test at Adelaide and, when Westindies visited England in 1933, he bagged another pair, this time in the first Test at Lord's. He rallied with a bright 64 in the next match at Old Trafford and, in the third game at The Oval, amongst the debris of some poor Westindian batting which left them facing a deficit of 212 runs, Roach thrashed 56 off the slow bowlers in just over half an hour, as the visitors slid to an innings defeat. Roach seemed to enjoy batting at The Oval, as he hit 180 at more than a run-a-minute in the tourists' match against Surrey, reaching his century before lunch on the first day.

The pugnacious Roach was a magnificent batsman, equally strong on the back or the front foot, with all the strokes at his command. He was an outstanding close fielder, as well as being nimble in the covers. His career was a mixture of spectacular firsts: the first Westindian to receive a ball in Test cricket, he went on to become their first Test centurion and double centurion while, on the other hand, he was also run out without scoring in his first Test innings.

Indeed, it was his peerless inconsistency which marred his claims to be looked on as Challenor's successor. Yet, Roach's overriding priority was to entertain, and he was often a casualty of his own impatience. He was also hampered, like many of his successors, by not having a regular opening partner with the same flair and ability and, in 12 consecutive Tests between 1928-35, Roach went out with nine different partners, four of them in 1930.

It was a particularly cruel and ironic blow that, for someone who liked to score his runs quickly and who was very fast between the wickets, diabetes caused Roach to have both his legs amputated in later life.

Career details

Born: *13 March 1904*
Role: *Right-hand batsman*
Club: *Trinidad*
First-class record: *[1925-35] 4,851 runs (28.04) including 5 centuries*
Tests: *16*
Test debut: *v England 1928*
Test runs: *952 (30.70); HS: 209 v England, Bridgetown, 1930*
Tours: *England 1928; Australia 1930-31; England 1933.*

Anderson Montgomery Everton Roberts

Andy Roberts was the first of the fearsome quartet of fast bowlers, who catapulted Westindies to the top of world cricket in the 1970s, to gain international recognition. A relatively late starter, the Antiguan did not play cricket seriously until he left school at 16; while his parents wanted their son to become an architect.

But, it was cricket that captured the young man's attention and he began playing regularly at the Rising Sun club of St. John's, with Viv Richards. Roberts made rapid progress and played his first representative game for the Leeward Islands in 1970, taking four for fifty. Two years later Roberts received his first formal coaching when he and Richards were sent by the Volunteers' Cricket Committee in Antigua to Alf Gover's cricket school in London for six weeks.

By the time England visited the Caribbean in 1974, Roberts had matured into a lively opponent. He took four for 75 for the Leewards against the tourists and, after collecting five for 62 in a Shell Shield game against Trinidad & Tobago, Roberts became the first Antiguan to play for Westindies. He made his Test debut in the third match at Bridgetown, but failed to maintain his place after struggling on a placid wicket.

Even so, Roberts was on his way to becoming one of the best fast bowlers in the world. He enjoyed his first full season with Hampshire in 1974, giving cricketers on the English county circuit a taste of genuinely quick bowling as he collected 119 wickets at 13.62 apiece from 21 games. His performance wasn't impaired by his aversion to the English climate or his belief that one of the main criterion for playing in England was "being able to plough your way through a ton of lettuce". Roberts headed the first-class averages, and excelled in the limited-overs competitions, prompting *Wisden* to say that his bowling "stirs the blood".

Roberts had a straight, easy run-up, which sometimes appeared to have a touch of laziness, before he exploded into action releasing the ball fast and straight. A calm, resilient character, Roberts generated an exceptional amount of pace without any noticeable effort; while the resigned, expressionless look on his face when a catch was dropped off his bowling became his hallmark.

For many, Roberts was, apart from Dennis Lillee, the most complete fast bowler of the early Seventies and for the second half of the decade he was one of the most feared in the world. The phlegmatic Antiguan took one hundred Test wickets in a record time of two years and 142 days – a record later overhauled by Ian Botham.

The Antiguan came of age as a fast bowler on the tour to the Indian subcontinent in 1974-75. He shouldered the bulk of the work and finished with 32 wickets from five Tests in India – the highest number of wickets taken by a Westindian in a series in India – and another 12 from two matches in Pakistan.

Ironically, Roberts' best returns came in the two games Westindies lost, when he took five for fifty in the first innings of the third match at Calcutta and was even more deadly in the fourth game at Madras, as he finished with match figures of 12 for 121. He completed a splendid double tour by taking another nine wickets on a lifeless pitch in the first Test in Pakistan at Lahore.

John Arlott said of the Antiguan paceman: "His mind works coolly and clearly behind his rather brooding, veiled look. He observes batsmen with the care of a slow bowler; employs varied methods; has studied the mechanics of his cricket...In 1975 Andy Roberts is the rare combination of fire, settled physique and mature mind in a young fast bowler – and he is not yet at his peak."

By the time of the World Cup in 1975, Roberts had established a formidable reputation as a world-class bowler, but it was as a batsman that Roberts made his mark in that competition. In Westindies' preliminary round game against Pakistan at Edgbaston, Roberts, the number 11 batsman, joined Deryck Murray with 64 more runs still required to win. Roberts' calm and patient temperament was stretched to the limit as Murray coaxed him to stay at the wicket, while the wicket-keeper masterminded a famous victory. Roberts finished unbeaten on 24, as Westindies scampered home with two balls to spare.

Bob Woolmer faces up to one of Andy Roberts' lethal deliveries, during the Antiguan's vintage summer against England in 1976

When Westindies visited Australia later that year, Roberts had the luxury of a partner to share the pace attack: Michael Holding. Even so, the experienced Roberts continued to dominate the bowling, finishing as the leading wicket-taker with 22 victims at 26.36 each. The Antiguan enjoyed his greatest success in the second Test at Perth where, after the home side trailed by 256 runs on the first innings, Roberts ripped through their second innings. He dismissed both openers for a second time, as the pair failed to score, and another two batsmen before the end of the third day. Roberts accounted for the first seven batsmen for 54 runs, to catapult Westindies to victory.

Hampered by injury, Roberts was less effective against the visiting Indians in 1976, but he was back to his best for the tour to England later that year. In the second match he became the first Westindian bowler to take 10 wickets in a Test at Lord's. He was in top form in the next game at Old Trafford when, after taking three first innings wickets, he found himself on a hat-trick twice in the second innings. Drinks were taken before Roberts returned to see his second hat-trick ball dropped in the slips. Characteristically Roberts looked up to the heavens and returned to the start of his run-up. The Antiguan finished with six wickets for 37 and played an important role in securing Westindies' decisive victory.

Well supported for a change, Roberts finished the series with 28 wickets at 19.17 apiece. His captain, Clive Lloyd in *Living for Cricket*, said: "(Roberts') stint in county cricket has taught him a lot about bowling and about the game in general, and he has developed into a shrewd reader of the game who puts his knowledge into his bowling. His striking rate of wickets per Test is one of the highest among all fast bowlers and his value to me as a skipper has been enormous."

In 1977, Roberts was partnered by Joel Garner and Colin Croft against the visiting Pakistanis. The Antiguan paceman bowled modestly, failing to repeat his overseas conquests, as he finished the series with 19 expensive wickets.

Before the World Series schism midway through the 1978 home series against Australia, Roberts was instrumental in Westindies' victory in the first Test at Port-of-Spain as he returned another five wicket haul in the second innings. Somewhat jaded by continuous cricket, Roberts left Hampshire halfway through the English summer that year to concentrate on his World Series commitments. However, he returned to the official Test fray later, refreshed and enthusiastic, to become the third Westindian bowler to take 200 Test wickets.

He visited Australia and New Zealand in 1979-80 but, after a modest tour to England in 1980 – his most notable performance being five for 72 in Westindies' victory in the first Test at Trent Bridge – Westindies' selectors gave the Antiguan paceman a sabbatical and he was left out of the subsequent trip to Pakistan. The break from Test cricket recharged his batteries and Roberts returned with renewed vigour to snap up 24 Shield wickets from four games before the English tourists arrived in 1981.

When he lost his place for the final Test and was dropped in the second match of the subsequent tour to Australia, Roberts' international prospects were again written off. As usual the reserved bowler, whose shyness was often misinterpreted as gloominess, allowed his figures to speak for him. He returned to the team for the final match at Adelaide to set up his side's victory with four wickets for 43 in the first innings; and returned to the Caribbean to take another 24 wickets in four Shield games.

Roberts was lethal against the visiting Indians in 1983, finishing as the leading wicket-taker with 24 scalps at 22.70 each. He enjoyed another vintage Shield season in which he captained the Leeward Islands by example, collecting 28 wickets at 18.35 each, to make him the highest wicket-taker in the history of the competition.

In his opening game he took a hat-trick against Barbados and in his last game, against the Windward Islands, he collected 11 wickets for 114, including eight for 62 in the second innings – his best figures in a first-class match. A week before that Roberts had set up Westindies' victory in the first Test at Kingston, with an inspired performance. He took nine wickets in the match, including five for 39 in the second innings as the last four Indian batsmen succumbed in the space of 20 balls.

Roberts appeared in the last two Tests in India in 1983 and, in the fifth one at Calcutta, he took his 200th Test wicket. The Antiguan celebrated the feat by scoring 68, his highest first-class innings, sharing in a record ninth wicket stand of 161 with Lloyd, as Westindies romped to victory by an innings.

Towards the end of his Test career, Roberts was used in short bursts to open up the batting order for his younger colleagues, but he invariably returned later in the innings to end an awkward partnership and hand the initiative to Westindies.

Roberts was the first of the new wave of fast bowlers which is still flowing, and his success prompted other cricketing nations to turn to speed for their salvation. He was also the first Antiguan quick bowler to receive worldwide recognition.

In the absence of Richards, Roberts proved a capable captain of the Leewards and in spite of his overseas commitments – after leaving Hampshire, he played part-time for Leicestershire and Haslingden in the Lancashire League – Roberts returned to Antigua to nurture cricket on the island that he took to the forefront of the game.

Career details

Born: *29 January 1951*
Role: *Right-arm fast bowler*
Clubs: *Leeward Islands, Hampshire, New South Wales, Leicestershire, Lancashire League*
First-class record: *[1970-1984] 889 wickets (21.01) and 3,516 runs (15.69)*
Tests: *47*
Test debut: *v England 1974*
Test wickets: *202 (25.61); BB: 7-54 v Australia, Perth, 1975*
Test runs: *762 (14.94); HS: 68 v India, Calcutta, 1983*
Tours: *India and Pakistan 1974-75; England (World Cup) 1975; Australia 1975-76; England 1976; England (World Cup) 1979; Australia and New Zealand 1979-80; England 1980; Australia 1981-82; England (World Cup) 1983; India 1983.*

William Vincente Rodriguez

Willie Rodriguez, who also represented Westindies at football

Willie Rodriguez was a capable all-rounder who played several resolute innings for Westindies. He underpinned his batting contribution with some useful leg-breaks, but never seemed able to make a sufficient impression to secure a permanent place in the Test side.

A Trinidadian, Rodriguez made his Test debut against India in 1962, hitting a worthy half century in the fourth Test at Port-of-Spain in front of his home crowd.

He made a favourable impact with his steady approach and was included on the trip to England in 1963. But, before the first Test at Old Trafford, he went down with cartilage trouble which hampered him for several weeks. Rodriguez had recovered by the fifth game at The Oval, where he was promoted to open the innings with Conrad Hunte. The pair shared in a substantial opening stand of 78 in the second innings, laying a solid foundation for Rohan Kanhai to blast the tourists to victory by eight wickets.

Thereafter, the all-rounder made isolated Test appearances at home against Australia in 1965 and England in 1968, before managing the Westindies team in Australia and New Zealand in 1979-80.

Rodriguez was even better known as a footballer, and achieved the unique double of representing Westindies at both cricket and football at international level.

Career details

Born: *25 June 1934*
Role: *Right-hand batsman, medium-pace bowler*
Club: *Trinidad*
First-class record: *[1953-70] 2,061 runs (24.83) including 1 century, and 119 wickets (28.08)*
Tests: *5*
Test debut: *v India 1962*
Test runs: *96 (13.710); HS: 50 v India, Port-of-Spain, 1962*
Test wickets: *7 (53.42)*
Tour: *England 1963*

Lawrence George Rowe

Lawrence Rowe is one of modern cricket's most famous enigmas. Blessed with prodigious natural talent, the graceful Jamaican saved his best performances for the highest level, but was hampered by an unfortunate number of injuries and bouts of ill health.

Nonetheless, he provided the history books with a unique record on his Test debut, as he carved his way to a double century in the first innings of the first Test against New Zealand at Kingston in 1972, sharing in a second wicket stand of 269 with Roy Fredericks, and went on to a single century in the second innings, to take his match aggregate to 314 for once out. Rowe finished the series against the New Zealanders with an average of 69.83, scoring his runs with such style and fluency that he was compared, in many quarters, with George Headley, Don Bradman and the three "W"s.

A classical batsman, beautifully balanced and equally strong on the front or the back foot, Rowe had a confidence that bordered on arrogance, as he wore down the opposing bowlers with his impeccable timing and placement of the ball – not to mention his incessant whistling!

Rowe scored 76 in the first Test against Australia at Sabina Park – his favourite home ground – in 1973, but wrenched his ankle on the opening day of the third match in Trinidad. The injury put him out of the game and the series, and a damaged knee ruled him out of the tour to England in 1973, as he embarked upon an almost endless battle to return to full fitness.

Indeed, after his remarkable international debut, Rowe made only one other fifty that season and his 76 against Australia was his highest score over the next three years. If other players had been available, it is unlikely that Rowe would have been given the opportunity to enjoy his most prolific series, against England when they visited the Caribbbean in 1974, as he regained his earlier spectacular form to help the home side to a sound start in nearly every match. Having gone 19 Tests without an opening stand of three figures, Rowe filled the void for a while as, in the five match series, he and Fredericks enjoyed four century partnerships.

Predictably, Rowe scored a century for his home fans, sharing in a double hundred stand with Fredericks in the second Test at Kingston, and emphasised his deep reservoir of talent with a masterful 302, which included a six and 34 fours, in the third Test at Bridgetown. It was only the second Test triple century by a Westindian, and he shared a record second wicket partnership of 249 with Alvin Kallicharran.

Tony Cozier described in the *Nation* newspaper how, on the Sunday of the Test, with Rowe unbeaten overnight on a double century, the crowds poured in to see history made as he recorded the first Test triple century at Kensington Oval and his own maiden first-class hundred outside Jamaica. Cozier wrote: "The whole of Barbados, it seemed, was there to see him bat…Gates were broken, walls were scaled and even high-tension electric cables were used as a means to enter. Rowe himself and the other players had to be escorted through the mass to enter the ground through a fence."

Patrick Eagar

Lawrence Rowe, who made 314 runs on his Test debut against New Zealand in 1972

rence Rowe

Just to confirm his genius, Rowe hit a brilliant defensive 123 in seven-and-a-quarter hours, on a turning wicket in the the first innings of the fifth Test at Port-of-Spain. He added 110 for the first wicket with Fredericks and 102 for the third with Clive Lloyd, before the quality of his innings was underlined as the remaining batsmen succumbed quickly in difficult conditions.

Thereafter, this superbly gifted player was frustrated by injury again as, at different stages in his career, he was exiled from the cricket field by problems with his knees and ankles, and even his eyesight, before finally developing an allergy to grass! On top of all these difficulties Gordon Greenidge had emerged as an opening batsman with world class potential, to add another dimension to Rowe's unfavourable situation.

But, Rowe recovered, once again, to tour Australia in 1975-76, this time going in at number three, and recorded his first Test century overseas, as his matchless timing took him to 107 in the opening game at Brisbane. He shared in an exhilarating stand of 198 for the fourth wicket with Kallicharran, which could have turned the match, had Lloyd not been dismissed for a duck immediately upon Rowe's departure and then Viv Richards ran himself out to seal the tourists' fate.

On the subsequent trip to India, after Greenidge's nightmare tour of Australia and with Richards monopolising the number three position, Rowe was promoted to open the innings again. Although he put on 105 with Fredericks in the fourth Test at Kingston, the Jamaican failed to reach fifty that season, and surrendered his place to Greenidge for the tour to England in 1976. Even so, Rowe was included in the tour party and summoned into the side when Kallicharran was injured. In the two games in which he played, the Jamaican hit fifty in the fourth Test at Headingley and 70 in the fifth match at The Oval, sharing in a stand of 191 with Richards.

After this Rowe's career was blighted by injury again, thwarting his chance to become one of the great post-War batsmen. Nevertheless in his erratic Test career, he still managed seven centuries and over 2,000 runs, and one can only muse on what he might have achieved had his health matched his

cricketing ability.

Rowe had an adoring following in Jamaica and stood second only to George Headley in public esteem; indeed, many remained loyal to him even after his defection to South Africa, when he captained the rebel tour there in 1983.

Many astute judges regarded Rowe as a more natural stroke-maker than either Greenidge or Richards, but, apart from rare and magical occasions, other factors colluded to prevent the full flowering of his talent.

Career details

Born: *8 January 1949*
Role: *Right-hand batsman*
Clubs: *Jamaica, Derbyshire*
First-class record *[1968-84] 8,755 runs (37.58) including 18 centuries, and 2 wickets (112.00)*
Tests: *30*
Test debut: *v New Zealand 1972*
Test runs: *2,047 (43,55); HS: 302 v England, Bridgetown, 1974*
Tours: *Australia 1975-76; England 1976; Australia and New Zealand 1979-80.*

Reginald Osmond Scarlett

A towering figure, with a personality to match, Reg Scarlett is a testing off-spin bowler and capable batsman. A product of Wolmer's Boys' School, he played Senior Cup cricket for Kingston before the age of 16 and, at 17, became the youngest player to appear for Jamaica. Later on, his younger brother, Bobby, also played for the island.

Meanwhile, Reg was soon making his mark in the side and was regarded as a player of international calibre. He was on the verge of Test selection for several years and, after performing well in a quadrangular tournament, he was selected for the first Test against England in 1960. He was then dropped, but, an outstanding all-round performance for Jamaica against the tourists, when he scored 72 not out and 59, and dismissed three leading batsmen, earnt him another two appearances in the Test series.

Later in 1960 the big Jamaican, who stands 6ft 4in tall and weighs 17 stone, came to live in England. Two years later he qualified as a cricket coach, then as an Advanced coach, before becoming a Staff coach with the National Cricket Association. He is also a founder member of the Association of Cricket Coaches.

The off-spinner spent 15 years playing league cricket in Scotland and the North of England, where he set many records and won even more friends with his engaging charm. He is a leading figure in charity cricket in England, notably with the Vic Lewis team which has raised over £3m since its beginnings in 1960. Scarlett also appears regularly for the Forty Club and Cricket Society, two other organisations

The Westindies team for the first Test against England at Bridgetown in 1960: Back row (l-r) Basil Butcher, Conrad Hunte, Chester Watson, Reg Scarlett, Wes Hall, Easton McMorris, Rohan Kanhai. Front row (l-r) Sonny Ramadhin, Frank Worrell, Gerry Alexander, Gary Sobers

Scarlett

dedicated to the safe-guarding of the game.

The Jamaican returned home to the Westindies for four years in 1975 where he was co-opted, and later elected, onto the Jamaican Board of Control, and was given special responsibility for youth development. He also gained a following for the technical expertise and humour he brought to radio during those years, when he commentated on Shell Shield and Test matches played on the island.

Scarlett re-settled in England in 1979 where his experiences of cultivating youth cricket in Jamaica stood him in good stead, and he became a driving force in many sporting activities promoted by the Greater London Council.

Perhaps his greatest contribution to the game is his untiring commitment to the revival of grass roots cricket in England. He is cricket consultant with the London Community Cricket Association and chief coach at Haringey Cricket College, two organisations set up to promote cricket, especially among young people and deprived groups. At Haringey he organises their annual tour to the Westindies which, although funded largely by the trainees themselves, is made easier by Scarlett's own wealth of personal contacts.

As long ago as 1969 Scarlett was instrumental in taking teams of professional cricketers, many of whom played on the English county circuit, on overseas tours. He has been an inspiration and example to players at all levels of the game, as well as a great ambassador for his country.

Career details

Born: *15 August 1934*
Role: *Off-spinner, right-hand batsman*
Clubs: *Jamaica, Scottish and North of England Leagues*
First-class record: *[1951-60] 48 wickets (34.12) and 477 runs (23.85)*
Tests: *3*
Test debut: *v England 1960*
Test wickets: *2 (104.50); BB: 1-46 v England, Bridgetown, 1960*
Test runs: *54 runs (18.00); HS: 29* v England, Georgetown, 1960*

James Edward Derek Sealy

While still at Combermere School, Derek Sealy became the youngest player in the history of Test cricket when he made his debut at the age of 17 years and 122 days against England in the first Test in the Caribbean, at Bridgetown in 1930. Although younger players have since appeared, Sealy remains the youngest man to play for the Westindies, when he hit 58 and 15, in a commendable start to his international career. Sealy later recounted how Joe Hardstaff Senior, the former England player, who was umpiring in the game, had kept encouraging him to play straight!

Along with the rest of the team, Sealy fared poorly in the subsequent series against Australia, but returned to his best form against England in 1935, when he hit a cultured 92 in the second Test at Port-of-Spain.

Sealy was disappointingly dismissed in the nineties again in the fourth Test at Kingston, as he added a record 202 runs for the third wicket with George Headley. Sealy played an unexpected role as a bowler in winning that match, when he was introduced into the attack to allow Learie Constantine and Manny Martindale to change ends. During his over the Barbadian collected the wicket of Errol Holmes, before Constantine returned to complete the damage and usher Westindies to victory and their first Test rubber. The series was a personal triumph for Sealy, who averaged 45.

Surprisingly left out of the tour party to England in 1933, the right-hander was included for the next visit six years later. He achieved little of note in the Tests, apart from being the second highest scorer in the opening match at Lord's with 29 in the visitors' second innings. Even so, the Barbadian scored nearly 1,000 runs in the other matches, including a magnificent career-best innings of 181 in three-and-a-half hours against Middlesex, also at Lord's. His most valuable contribution in the Tests came when he kept wicket in the final two matches when Ivan Barrow's

Derek Sealy (right), the youngest player ever to appear for Westindies, walking out with Herman Griffith in the first Test played in the Caribbean, against England at Bridgetown in 1930

188

recall, after the untimely death of Cyril Christiani, was not as successful as anticipated.

Besides being an accomplished batsman and a useful wicket-keeper, the strongly built Sealy was a capable medium-pace bowler, who could produce a surprising amount of lift. In 1942 he returned the best first-class figures ever recorded in Westindies when he took eight for eight for Barbados against Trinidad on a wet Bridgetown wicket, as the latter were bowled out for 16.

After the War was over, Sealy moved to Trinidad and appeared regularly in inter-territorial competition, keeping wicket for his new island between 1945-46. He made his last first-class century, for Trinidad against Barbados in 1949, at Kensington Oval – scene of his great bowling triumph seven years earlier.

Sealy worked in Trinidad's oilfields and, after retiring from cricket, became a selector and administrator on the island and was the official scorer at Queen's Park Oval for a while.

A superb and versatile athlete, Sealy represented Barbados at football as well as cricket.

But, perhaps, Sealy's greatest contribution to Westindian cricket was the influence he had on the young Frank Worrell, who was one of his pupils at his old school, Combermere, in Barbados, where he was a sports teacher. Sealy also advised the emerging Clyde Walcott, thus nurturing two of the finest players of the next generation of Westindies cricketers.

Career details

Born: *11 September 1912*
Died: *3 January 1982*
Role: *Right-hand batsman, wicket-keeper, medium-pace bowler*
Clubs: *Barbados, Trinidad*
First-class record: *[1929-49] 3,831 runs (30.40) including 8 centuries, 67 catches and 13 stumpings, and 63 wickets (28.60)*
Test: *11*
Test debut: *v England 1930*
Test runs: *478 (28.11); HS: 92 v England, Port-of-Spain, 1935*
Test catches: *6, Test stumpings: 1*
Tours: *Australia 1930-31; England 1939.*

John Neil Shepherd

An enthusiastic and gifted all-rounder, John Shepherd became an integral part of the English county scene after he joined Kent in 1965. His reliable medium-pace swing bowling and cavalier approach to his batting brought him a harvest of wickets and runs in a first-class career stretching over nearly two decades. He came close to the double of 1,000 runs and one hundred wickets on several occasions, nearly making it in 1968 when he fell just four wickets short.

The muscular Barbadian made his first-class debut for Barbados in 1964-65 and in 1967 played his first full season with Kent, the year they won the Gillette Cup. Two years later he was elevated to Test honours, when he played against England. His bowling was full of aggression and he finished the three-match series with 12 wickets at 22.16 apiece, including five for 104 off 58.5 overs in the second Test at Old Trafford. Generally, he was overworked on the tour so that by the third Test, hampered by back problems, he was operating at less than full throttle.

Shepherd returned to fitness by the time the Indians visited the Caribbean two years later. He played in two Tests, but failed to distinguish himself on wickets less conducive to his style of bowling than the green English ones.

The Barbadian became the first black cricketer, along with Younis Ahmed, to tour South Africa when he went there with the Derrick Robins team in 1973. This caused controversy in the Westindies but, undeterred, Shepherd went on to play Currie Cup cricket for Rhodesia in 1975-76, and enjoyed two prolific seasons playing grade cricket for the Melbourne Club, Footscray. Speaking to *The Cricketer* in 1986, Shepherd said: "When I went to South Africa in 1973, the Westindies Board did not disapprove, but when Younis Ahmed, who was also out there, was banned by Pakistan the Westindies Board then banned me. I was never offered coaching jobs in Jamaica and Guyana or even Barbados, where I offered my services free, but I could secure a coaching job tomorrow in South Africa. I wouldn't go

John Shepherd

190

back, however, even to coach black kids because it doesn't matter whether they are black, white, pink or whatever, the common denominator is South Africa."

The all-rounder is probably best remembered for his performances at Kent. He hit 170 against Northamptonshire at Folkestone in 1968 and returned figures of eight for 83 against Lancashire at Tunbridge Wells in 1977. In a match against Sussex in 1975 he bowled unchanged in both innings, and finished with the remarkable figures of eight for 93 in the first innings off 32.5 overs and seven for 54 off 39 overs in the second.

Shepherd moved to Gloucestershire in 1982 and was capped the following year. His most valuable contributions have been as coach and he is currently doing a splendid job with Gloucestershire's Second X1, although he appears occasionally for the First team.

Career details

Born: *9 November 1943*
Role: *Right-hand batsman, right-arm medium pace bowler*
Clubs: *Barbados, Rhodesia, Kent, Gloucestershire*
First-class record: *[1964-] 3,353 runs (26.44) including 10 centuries, and 1,155 wickets (27.28)*
Tests: 5
Test debut: *v England 1969*
Test runs: *77 (9.62)*
Test wickets: *19 (25.21); BB: 5-104 v England, Old Trafford, 1969*
Tour: *England 1969*

Cameron Wilberforce Smith

Renowned for taking the attack to the bowlers, Cammie Smith could always be relied on to entertain the crowd with his exciting stroke-making. A fine player of fast bowling, the right-handed opener was selected for the tour to Australia in 1960-61 and had no qualms about taking on the home side's pacemen. His innings were usually peppered with sixes but, apart from a rapid 55 in the third Test at Sydney, the Barbadian failed to live up to his early promise, struggling in the face of the spinners.

As well as being an extravagant batsman, Smith was a useful wicket-keeper and stood in for Jackie Hendriks after the Jamaican had broken his finger on the opening day of the first Test against India at Port-of-Spain in 1962.

Yet, when the ebullient Barbadian's style of play came off, he provided the spectators with marvellous entertainment, as he showed when Barbados played the MCC tourists in 1959. Barbados made 533 for five declared, before the visitors struggled against the then unknown Charlie Griffith. Just as MCC seemed to have saved the game, Smith hit a whirlwind innings in bad light and rain to bring his side an unlikely win by 10 wickets, as the last 58 runs came up in 25 minutes.

A jovial character, this tall and handsome opener played league cricket in England in the 1960s. Now a businessman in Barbados, he has been on the management of several Westindian teams overseas. Smith is an active member of the Barbados Cricket Association, enthusiastically helping to develop and promote the game on the island, as well as being a regular personality at festival matches.

Career details

Born: *29 July 1933*
Role: *Right-hand batsman, wicket-keeper*
Club: *Barbados, North of England leagues*
First-class record: *[1951-65] 2,277 runs (37.32) including 5 centuries*
Test matches: *5*
Test debut: *v Australia 1960*
Test runs: *222 (24.66); HS: 55 v Australia, Sydney, 1961*
Test catches: *4; Test stumpings: 1*
Tour: *Australia 1960-61*

O'Neil "Collie" Gordon Smith

Perhaps what made the irrepressible "Collie" Smith so popular was that he brought the spirit of club cricket into the Test arena. Growing up in one of Kingston's poorest districts, he first came to the attention of the selectors playing senior cup cricket for Boys' Town, a club for youngsters from the capital's deprived areas.

The stocky and immensely fit Jamaican was a gregarious batsman and top class off-spinner, as well as a magnificent fielder. Indeed he seemed to have all the ingredients to become one of the game's great players.

Having played just two matches for Jamaica, Smith was included in the island team for their game against the strong touring Australian side of 1955, and hammered 169, putting on 277 for the sixth wicket with wicket-keeper, Alfie Binns. This performance won him selection to the Westindies team, and he enjoyed an auspicious debut in front of his home crowd, hitting 44 in the first innings of the first Test at Kingston, as he shared in a century partnership with Clyde Walcott. The Jamaican followed this with his maiden hundred in the second innings, against the speed of Keith Miller, Ray Lindwall and Ron Archer, as four other frontline batsmen failed to reach double figures.

Yet, his first Test was as delightful as his second one was dismal. At Port-of-Spain, Smith bagged a pair, on both occasions trying to keep the score ticking over after a large stand between Everton Weekes and Walcott, and was promptly dropped. The youngster must have been comforted by the overwhelming sympathy he received from the mass of the people but, on his return, later in the series, he struggled to find his form and made little impression.

Nonetheless, Smith was selected for the tour to New Zealand in 1956, along with Gary Sobers, as the two prodigious youngsters, who later became close friends, were fully blooded. The series was dominated by Weekes, but the ebullient Smith held

his own with 64 in the first Test at Dunedin, adding 162 with Weekes; while his four for 75, including the important wicket of one of New Zealand's most accomplished batsmen, John Reid, in the home side's second innings, was a major factor in Westindies' handsome victory in the second match at Christchurch.

Smith was one of the few players to improve his standing on the disastrous tour of England in 1957, as he thrashed his way to 161 in the first Test at Edgbaston, earning him the nickname of "mighty mouse". Smith began carefully, knowing that Frank Worrell and Walcott were both injured, before opening out once Westindies had secured a lead, eventually adding 190 with Worrell, to stretch the tourists' first innings advantage to 288.

In the third game at Trent Bridge, the young Jamaican scored 168 in seven hours to salvage another difficult draw for his beleaguered team. Curbing his attacking instincts, Smith added over a hundred with Denis Atkinson and shared in a match-saving seventh-wicket partnership of 154 with John Goddard, against the pace battery of Fred Trueman and Brian Statham.

Smith performed consistently with the bat and the ball when Pakistan visited the Caribbean in 1958. His bowling in the second Test at Port-of-Spain was instrumental in seeing Westindies to victory, as his

Smith during scintillating ...ry against ...nd at ...aston in 1957

Collie Smith on the attack during his vintage summer against England in 1957

scalps included Hanif Mohammad, Intimaz Ahmed and Saeed Ahmed, while his 86 in Westindies' defeat in the fifth Test, also at Port-of-Spain, represented almost solitary resistance against the medium paced leg-cutters of Fazal Mahmood.

Smith was included on the tours of India and Pakistan in 1958-59 but, as other rising batsmen consolidated their positions and a new generation of pace bowlers made their presence felt, the likeable all-rounder had a less prominent role to play. Despite their eventual runaway sucess, the tourists had an uneasy start in the first Test at Bombay and it was left to Smith and Rohan Kanhai to rally the first innings against the accurate bowling of the leg-spinner, Subhash Gupte, with Smith scoring 63 and a valuable 58 in the second innings.

He displayed his all-round strengths in the final Test in New Delhi, after injuries to the fast bowlers. He ended Chandrakant Borde's innings of 109, which was India's only century of the series, and then Smith hit a hundred himself, before returning in India's second innings to collect five wickets for 90, although the Jamaican couldn't quite lift his side to victory, as Borde batted gallantly for 96, before hitting his wicket in the last over of the match.

In the summer of 1959, Smith played cricket for Burnley in the Lancashire League and, in the last week of the season, travelling to a charity match in London, he was involved in a car accident in which he sustained fatal injuries. His death was a stunning blow to the whole cricket community and when his body was flown back for the funeral in Jamaica, an estimated 100,000 people thronged the streets to pay their respects to a man who had remained one of them at heart.

This punishing stroke-maker, who was quick between the wickets, was missed for the joy he brought into an increasingly competitive game. Smith was missed, too, for the way he attacked international bowlers regardless of their reputation: once, as England were developing a stranglehold on Westindies, he hit a straight six off the precise Statham.

Smith was one of the few who attended church on the Sunday of a Test, while his approachable manner, as he signed autographs for delighted school-boys,

further endeared him to the cricketing public. Smith's untimely death was a sad loss to the cricket world as a whole, and for Westindies in particular, to whom he still had much to offer. As J.F. Dare, President of the Westindies Board of Control, commented: "He was one of a diminishing band who play a game for the game's sake and he had a great future before him."

Career details

Born: 5 May 1933
Died: *9 September 1959*
Role: *Right-hand batsman, right-arm off-spinner*
Clubs: *Jamaica, Lancashire League*
First-class record: *[1954-59] 4,031 runs (40.31) including 10 centuries, and 121 wickets (31.02)*
Tests: *26*
Test debut: *v Australia 1955*
Test runs: *1,331 (31.69); HS: 168 v England, Trent Bridge, 1957*
Test wickets: *48 (33.85); BB: 5-90 v India, New Delhi, 1959*
Tours: *New Zealand 1955-56; England 1957; India and Pakistan 1958-59.*

Sir Garfield St. Aubrun Sobers

Gary Sobers enjoys the distinction of being universally acknowledged as the most complete cricketer the game has known.

His unique place in cricket history is secured by his all-round versatility: a master batsman, who bowled incisive fast-medium, orthodox left-arm spinners and, for good measure, slow chinamen and googlies. He was also a brilliant fielder, who contributed greatly to the success of Lance Gibbs with his close to the wicket catching.

Sobers came from a family of seven and grew up in the district of Bayland, just outside Bridgetown. Born with five fingers on each hand – the extra two were removed during childhood – the Barbadian was brought up by his mother after his father had been killed in the Second World War.

Sobers' cricketing genius was recognised from his early days when he excelled at soft-ball cricket, while his all-round sporting gifts were such that he played football and basketball for Barbados. He is also a low handicapped golfer and currently represents Barbados.

He rose rapidly in Barbadian cricket and made his international debut at the age of 16, playing for Barbados against the touring Indians in 1953. He took seven wickets in the match, which proved to be the start of a peerlessly successful international career.

Sobers made his first Test appearance in the final game against England at Kingston the following year - becoming Westindies second youngest debutant at 17 years and 245 days – and took four for 75. In the following series against Australia, he scored 47 in the second Test at Port-of-Spain and, in the fourth game at Bridgetown, roared on by his home crowd, crashed four fours off Keith Miller's first over, and scored 40 of his 43 runs in boundaries. He completed a promising series with 64 in the final match at Kingston.

The prodigious colt had another taste of Test cricket on the "blooding" tour to New Zealand in

y Sobers, whose ous styles of ling helped to e him cricket's test all-rounder

1956 and, on his first trip to England the following year, he scored over 1,600 first-class runs, passing 40 in four of the five Tests, and took 37 wickets.

Even so, Sobers had played in four Test series without scoring a century. But, when it came, in the third match against Pakistan at Kingston in 1958, he made it a big one: a world record 365 not out. It took him just over 10 hours, three hours less than Len Hutton had needed for one run less, and included 34 fours. When the young left-hander reached the landmark, crowds poured onto the field and play was abandoned for the day. Earlier on, he and Conrad Hunte had added a record 446 runs for the second wicket.

It was a golden season for Sobers which established him as the best batsman of his generation. He began with an unbeaten 183 for Barbados in the opening match of Pakistan's tour and went from strength to strength: he hit fifties in his first three Test innings and, after his triple hundred at Kingston, contented himself with two singles centuries in the fourth game at Georgetown.

For more than a decade afterwards, the rest of the world worshipped at Sobers' court, as he dominated every aspect of the game and set the standards by which others were judged. Despite the phenomenal amount of cricket he packed into those years, and the publicity that accompanied his every feat, Sobers' appetite for the game never waned until late in his career. A supremely fit athlete, Sobers is remembered not so much for the remarkable trail of statistical records that he left in his wake but, rather, for the quality of his cricket and the way he enjoyed the game.

The 6ft tall all-rounder had no formal coaching, but was an admirer of the batting techniques of Everton Weekes, Frank Worrell and Roy Marshall. Blessed with a natural grace, he was beautifully balanced, with quick footwork and keen eyesight. Never afraid to experiment, the Barbadian worked assiduously to perfect every facet of his cricket.

Sobers scored over 500 runs in a Test series on six occasions: beginning with his triumph against Pakistan in the Caribbean in 1958 when he scored 824 runs for an average of 137.33 – including, at one stage, 599 runs for once out. Against India in 1958-59

he hit 557 runs at 92.83; against England in 1960 he hit 709 runs at 101.28, in 1966 722 runs at 103.14 and in 1968 545 runs at 90.83 and, finally, against India in 1971 he scored 597 runs at 74.62.

On the trip to India in 1958-59, Sobers hit centuries in the first three games: 142 not out at Bombay, 198, with 28 fours, before he was run out, in the second match at Kanpur, and an unbeaten hundred in the third game at Calcutta. The Barbadian also bowled splendidly throughout the tour to finish third in the averages behind Roy Gilchrist and Wes Hall.

When Westindies visited Pakistan in early 1959, Sobers maintained his momentum with 45 in the second Test at Dacca and a stylish 72 in the third and final game at Lahore, after being dropped off his first ball.

The Barbadian's run glut continued into the series against England in the Caribbean the following year. He made three scores of over 140, including a masterful double century in front of his home crowd in the first Test at Bridgetown – adding a record 399 for the fourth wicket with Worrell – and fell for 92 in the final match at Port-of-Spain. Despite these performances, which outshone those of any other player on either side, Westindies narrowly lost the rubber. His efforts were even more remarkable when one considers that, before the start of the series, there was speculation that he might not take part, having recently been in the car accident that killed his great friend Collie Smith.

On Westindies' tour to Australia in 1960-61, Sobers

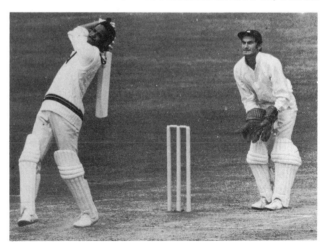

Gary Sobers and his extraordinary follow-through, like a golf swing, as he hits to leg with perfect balance. Alan Knott is the wicket-keeper

established himself as the best all-rounder in the world. Up until then his mantle had been confined to the best batsman in the world. By now his mastery with the willow seemed inevitable but, on that trip, as well as supporting Alf Valentine as the slow left-armer, Sobers shared the new ball with Hall and, to underline his phenomenal gifts, treated the Australian crowds to some spectacular catching.

The all-rounder scored 132 to set the scene for the thrilling tie in the opening game at Brisbane. His breath-taking innings lasted 174 minutes and included 21 fours, prompting Don Bradman to visit the dressing-room to congratulate Sobers, while Johnny Moyes concluded that "it ranks with the most outstanding seen in Australia since the halcyon days of Bradman and (Stan) McCabe."

In the third match at Sydney, Sobers hit a brilliant 168 in four-and-a-half hours, with a six and 25 fours – which many consider to be his best Test innings – crashing Alan Davidson and Richie Benaud to all parts of the ground at will, as he brought Westindies level in the rubber. In the fifth and deciding game at Melbourne, the Barbadian top-scored with 64 in the tourists' first innings, and then took five wickets for 120 in Australia's reply. In the end, it took a dubious umpiring decision and a fortuitous extra to clinch the game – and the series – for the home side. Yet nothing could detract from Sobers' dominance and he was invited to play for South Australia in the Sheffield Shield.

The Sobers juggernaut gained even more momentum against the inadequate Indian tourists in 1962. In the opening Test at Port-of-Spain he began the visitors' slide by taking four wickets for 22, and hit 153, his highest score of the series, in the second match at Kingston. His innings contained four sixes and 11 fours, as he shared in a double century stand for the second wicket with Rohan Kanhai. The Barbadian completed a rousing series by scoring a delightful 104 in the first innings of the final game, also at Kingston – always his favourite ground – and fifty in the second, before collecting five second innings Indian wickets for 63 runs, after bowling well throughout the rubber.

By the time of Westindies tour to England in 1963, Sobers must have been tired from the intense level of competition and in that series he restricted himself to two fifties and just one century, in the fourth Test at Headingley, when he batted against medical advice with a septic finger; while his best bowling performance came in the third game at Edgbaston, when he took five for 60 in England's first innings.

The all-rounder was made captain for the series against the visiting Australians two years later, a post he held for 39 of his 93 Tests. Again, he had a lean time with the bat, but confirmed his tactical know-how by leading Westindies to their first victory over Australia. His best performance came when he scored 69 in the second match at Port-of-Spain and, in a splendid all-round contribution in the third game at Georgetown, he hit two forties, took four wickets in each of his bowling styles and claimed four catches.

If Sobers had been below par in the last two series,

Gary Sobers, pictured during Westindies' tour of England in 1957. Just a year later, he made the world record individual score of 365*

it was the English who bore the brunt of his rejuvenation when Westindies toured in 1966. Leading from the front, the Barbadian scored 722 runs from five Tests, took 20 wickets at 27.25 each – often opening the attack despite the presence of Hall and Charlie Griffith – held 10 catches and, for good measure, won the toss on each occasion.

He top-scored with 161 in the first Test at Old Trafford; he reached his century by lifting John Snow over the long-off boundary, prompting Colin Milburn at forward short-leg to remark: "You know something, Gary? You're ruining this bloody game!"

In the second match at Lord's the all-rounder headed the batting with a splendid 163 not out, as he shared in an unbeaten sixth wicket partnership of 274 with his cousin, David Holford, after the tourists had conceded a first innings lead. Sobers' bold declaration was quickly rewarded with four cheap English wickets, but the home side held out having seemed to be in a winning position earlier in the match.

A quick-fire 94 in the next game at Trent Bridge allowed the Barbadian time to declare and win the match before he set up an unassailable lead in the series in the Headingley Test. In his only innings Sobers hammered 174 – scoring one hundred of those runs between lunch and tea on the first day – as he added 265 for the fifth wicket with Seymour Nurse. He also took eight wickets for 80 in the match, bowling pace and spin, including five for 41 in England's second innings.

Although the series was won, Sobers' competitive edge never wavered and, in the fifth Test at The Oval, he hit 81 when Westindies batted first and bowled 10 overs more than anyone else in England's only innings, as the home side secured victory. His second innings duck, however, probably came as a relief to everyone: he was human after all.

In the following series in India, Sobers hit fifties in each of the three Tests, but had little opportunity to go on to a really big score as, since becoming captain, he had batted at number six and invariably ran out of partners. He scored two half centuries in the first match at Bombay to usher his side to success and, in the second game at Calcutta, brought off another conclusive win with 70 runs and four wickets for 56 in India's second innings; while his 95 and 74 not out –

after he was dropped twice in the second innings before he was 10 – in the drawn Test at Madras nearly secured a clean sweep of victories for the tourists.

Westindies lost their first rubber for five series when England visited the Caribbean in 1968. Sobers saved his side with an unbeaten 33 after Westindies had been forced to follow-on in the opening Test at Port-of-Spain. In the next game at Kingston, he hit a superb 113 on a difficult pitch – having been dropped on seven and after a first innings golden duck – which allowed him to declare after the home side had followed on for a second successive time. It seemed that Sobers might orchestrate an incredible win for Westindies when he dismissed two batsmen before the tourists had scored but, in the end, England hung on for a draw.

The home captain hit 68 in the drawn Test at Bridgetown, before his "infamous" declaration at Port-of-Spain where England scored 215 runs in 164 minutes to win the match and, as it turned out, the rubber. He was without one of his frontline bowlers, Griffith, and the visitors reached their target with seven wickets and eight balls to spare. Sobers slumped to an all-time low in the popularity stakes and his effigy hung in Independence Square in the city that night, as a gesture of the crowds' disapproval.

This was not the last time that the Barbadian was to incur the wrath of his followers as it happened again, two years later, when he played cricket in white-dominated Rhodesia. He later conveyed his "sincere regrets" for this action to the Westindies Board, a diplomatic statement which prevented a potential crisis in Westindian cricket after Guyana had said that he would not be welcome to lead the Test side against India in 1971 in their country.

Meanwhile, in the series against England, after the débâcle at Port-of-Spain, Sobers answered his critics in the best possible manner in the fourth Test at Georgetown. He stroked his way to 152, adding 250 for the fourth wicket with Kanhai in the first innings, and was left high and dry on 95 not out in the second. He took six wickets in the match, but even this performance failed to salvage the rubber.

Away from the Test arena, Sobers was leaving his mark in the domestic competitions in Australia and

y Sobers

England. He became the only man to score 1,000 runs and take 50 wickets in an Australian season – a feat he achieved twice; and also played what is regarded as one of the great innings of all time in that country, when he hit 254 for the Rest of the World against Australia in Melbourne in 1971-72.

The Barbadian proved to be an enterprising captain for South Australia and provided similar inspiration in England at Nottinghamshire. In his first season with the club, in 1968, he led them from 15th to fourth in the county championship, as he topped the batting averages, finished second in the bowling and held more catches than anyone else apart from the wicket-keeper. In the same year he provided cricket's archives with one of its favourite television clips: his savaging of Glamorgan's Malcolm Nash, whom he crashed for six sixes off a six ball over at Swansea. Altogether he scored over 7,000 championship runs for an average of nearly fifty and took more than 250 wickets. Prior to playing in the championship, he had a distinguished career in the leagues in the north of England.

When Westindies toured Australia in 1968-69, Sobers was one of the leading bowlers. In the first Test at Brisbane, he returned his best Test figures of six for 73 in Australia's second innings, leading the visitors to a decisive victory. But, thereafter, little went right for Westindies and Sobers was criticised for his lack of leadership, as he was accused of having too many diversions off the field.

Yet the criticism failed to affect his personal performances: he scored 67 and took four for 97 in the defeat at Melbourne, hit 110 – with two sixes and 14 fours – and 52 in the drawn game at Adelaide and another scintillating century in another losing cause in the final match at Sydney. According to Sobers many of his side's problems stemmed from their poor fielding and the captain estimated that 34 catches were dropped, often at decisive moments, during the rubber.

Sobers' failure to maintain his usual high standards in the short series against England in 1969 probably had a decisive effect on its outcome. An injury hampered his bowling in the drawn second Test at Lord's, but, with the help of a runner, the Barbadian rallied his side with an unbeaten fifty the second

innings. Sobers took five wickets for 42 in England's second innings in the third and final match at Headingley, which put his side in a position to level the series, but the visitors lost their momentum in the subsequent run-chase when their captain was dismissed for a duck.

It is said that Sobers' new restrained approach as captain against India and New Zealand in the Caribbean in 1971 and 1972 contributed to nine of the 10 matches being drawn. But, if his captaincy lacked inspiration, his own remarkable individual performances continued unabated. In the five-match series against India, he failed to reach 90 only in the second game at Port-of-Spain. He hit a match-saving 93 in the opening Test at Kingston and ended the series with three successive centuries.

Against New Zealand he played another match-saving innings, this time 142, in the third Test at Bridgetown, sharing in a record double century partnership with Charlie Davis on the last day. Even so his captaincy continued to be cautious and, when Westindies held the early advantage in the last game in Trinidad, he failed to capitalise on it.

By the time of Australia's visit to the Caribbean in 1973, there seemed to be a question mark over Sobers' position. The all-rounder was struggling for fitness after the removal of a cartilage in England the previous summer, and Westindies hadn't won a Test in their last 15 matches. At his own request he missed the first Test, but when the selectors asked him to prove his fitness before returning to the side, the Barbadian chose to miss the series, saying that he had always informed the Board when he was unfit in the past. Australia won the series, but their captain, Ian Chappell, was quick to point out that it would have been more meaningful if Sobers had taken part.

The Barbadian was back in the side for the tour to England later that year – without the worry of the captaincy – and ended his Test career abroad on the high note that the cricket world had come to expect. In his final appearance at Lord's, in the third Test, he hit an unbeaten 150 – even though he was forced to retire at one stage with a stomach complaint – and took a record six catches close to the wicket, having scored fifties in the previous two matches.

Sobers bowed out of the international scene after

the return rubber against England in 1974, tired but jubilant, in the knowledge that he could be counted among the greats of the game. Indeed, for many, Sobers is *the* greatest cricketer the game has known.

In recognition of his unprecedented contribution to cricket, he was knighted by the Queen in 1975 on the Garrison Savannah in Barbados, less than a mile from where he grew up. Alec Bedser summed up his impact when he said: "Sobers has to be the supreme all-rounder, and, as with Bradman, cricket might never see his like again." On a more philosophical plane, C. L. R. James remarked: "A man of genius is what he is, he cannot be something else and remain a man of genius…Garfield Sobers I see not as an afortuitous combination of atoms which by chance have coalesced into a superb public performer…for me his command of the rising ball in the drive, his close fielding and his hurling himself into his fast bowling are a living embodiment of centuries of a tortured history."

Gary Sobers waits expectantly as Ray Illingworth tosses [a] the start of Englan[d] match with the Res[t] of the World at Lord's in 1970

Career details

Born: *28 July 1936*
Role: *Left-hand batsman, left-arm fast medium bowler, orthodox left-arm spinner, left-arm chinaman and googly bowler*
Clubs: *Barbados, South Australia, Nottinghamshire, North of England Leagues*
First-class record: *[1953-74] 28,315 runs (54.87) including 86 centuries, and 1,043 wickets (27.74)*
Tests: *93*
Test debut: *v England 1954*
Test runs: *8,032 (57.78); HS: 365* v Pakistan, Kingston, 1958*
Test wickets: *235 (34.03); BB: 6-73 v Australia, Brisbane, 1968*
Tours: *New Zealand 1956; England 1957; India and Pakistan 1958-59; Australia 1960-61; England 1963; England 1966; India 1966-67; Australia and New Zealand 1968-69; England 1969; England 1973.*

Joe Stanislaus Solomon

Joe Solomon is remembered, above all else, for his historic fielding in the first Test against Australia in Brisbane in 1960, when he gathered and threw the ball to run out Ian Meckiff by inches to secure the first tied match in Test cricket. This fleeting act ingrained Solomon's name in cricketing folk-lore and his other achievements paled by comparison.

Solomon was one of a group of excellent young batsmen to emerge from Guyana in the mid-1950s, after Clyde Walcott went there as coach. The right-hander, who was also a worthy change bowler, was selected for the 1958-59 tour to India and Pakistan and soon established himself as a batsman who could hold the middle-order together, when the more extravagant stroke-makers had failed.

On his debut in the second Test at Kanpur, he made 45 and 86 and, in the third game at Calcutta, he hit 69 not out in a run-a-minute century partnership with Gary Sobers. Solomon's unbeaten hundred in the fifth match at New Delhi, together with several other not out innings, helped him to head the batting averages. Against Pakistan he made 66 in the defeat in the first Test at Karachi, while his 56 contributed to Westindies' decisive win in the third match at Lahore.

When England toured the Caribbean in 1960, the selectors failed in their attempt to convert Solomon into an opening batsman, and he returned to his old position for the trip to Australia in 1960-61. In the Brisbane Test, even before he transformed the course of the match with his dynamic fielding, Solomon had already attracted attention in Westindies' first innings by standing on his wicket after he had made a sound 65. He scored 47 in the second innings, helping to set the home side their elusive target of 232.

The partnership between Alan Davidson and Richie Benaud of 134 had made victory almost certain for Australia, before Davidson, attempting a sharp single, was run out by a direct hit from Solomon, who had only one stump to aim at. Within two overs the scores were level: the last ball of the match was firmly struck by Lindsay Kline, who scampered off for the winning single, but Solomon swooped on the ball and, once again, with just one stump to aim at, threw down the wicket to dismiss the non-striker, Meckiff. Crucially, Solomon's pick-up and throw came in one movement as he beat Meckiff, while the Australian later admitted to momentary hesitation in setting off for the run, which proved fatal.

Solomon was a dependable batsman who, nonetheless, had a habit of getting out in unusual ways, such as the time when his cap fell on his wicket as he tried to pull a ball from Benaud. He never received the adulation of the likes of Rohan Kanhai, Sobers and Wes Hall, as, in his Test innings, he curbed his free-scoring style, for which he was renowned when playing for the strong Berbice team. He made his highest first-class score of 201 not out for Berbice against MCC in 1959-60, yet seemed prepared to play a more defensive role at the highest level. Solomon's supportive batting stabilised the team and his accurate bowling allowed the frontline attack to rest for a few overs, while his precision fielding became legendary.

The Guyanese made two good fifties at Lord's and Headingley on Westindies' tour of England in 1963, and his 76 against Australia in the first Test at Kingston in 1965, provided Westindies with a lead which proved beyond the tourists. When he left the international scene at the end of that season, although Solomon rarely found himself in the headlines, his all-round utilitarian performances were conspicuous by their absence.

After his playing days were over, Solomon became involved in the administration of the game in Guyana and, later, a Test selector.

Career details

Born: *26 August 1930*
Role: *Right-hand batsman, right-arm leg-spin bowler*
Club: *Guyana*
First-class record: *[1956-69] 5,318 runs (41.54) including 12 centuries, and 51 wickets (38.23)*
Tests: *27*
Test debut: *v India 1958*
Test runs: *1,326 (34.00); HS: 100* v India, New Delhi, 1959*
Tours: *India and Pakistan 1958-59; Australia 1960-61; England 1963.*

Joe Solomon

Jeffrey Baxter Stollmeyer

Jeff Stollmeyer has been a central figure in Westindies cricket since the 1930s. The tall, slim opener made his international debut at the age of 18 against England in the first Test at Lord's in 1939 and, with Allan Rae, went on to provide Westindies with their first dependable opening partnership in Test cricket.

A graduate of Queen's Royal College, Stollmeyer made a name for himself as a youngster scoring prolifically for Trinidad, after being coached by the Australian, Arthur Richardson, at school.

The discovery of the 1939 Westindies tour, Stollmeyer was originally selected as deputy to his brother, Victor. But when the latter fell ill, Jeff took his place at Lord's and confirmed his enormous potential. He scored 59 runs in his first Test innings, and hit the same score in the final match at The Oval,

sharing century partnerships with George Headley on both occasions.

Sadly, many of the best years of the young man's international career were lost during the Second World War, but Stollmeyer continued to flourish in inter-territorial matches. An orthodox, wristy player, with a penchant for the on-side, he hit 210 and 107 against Barbados and shared several double century partnerships with Gerry Gomez, and one with his brother, during these years. In 1947 the elegant Stollmeyer added a record 434 runs for the third wicket with Gomez against Guyana, as he reached his career-best score of 324 and the highest score in inter-colonial matches.

Stollmeyer was picked for the first post-War Test against England at Bridgetown in 1948, as a member of arguably the strongest side Westindies had fielded since the granting of Test status. He played fluently, scoring 78 and 31, before a back injury ruled him out of the next two Tests, including the second game at Port-of-Spain, where he had been nominated captain. Over the years, injury and poor health deprived

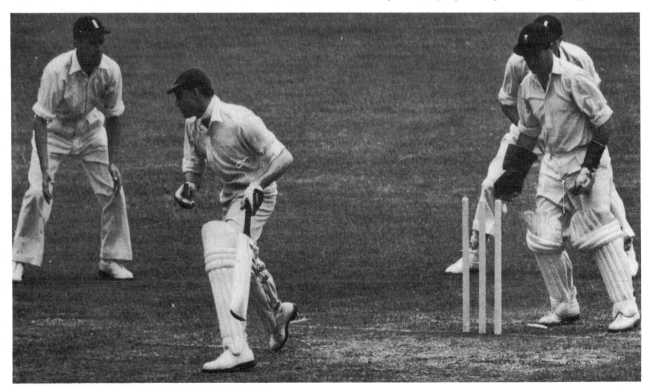

Jeff Stollmeyer is bowled for 30 by Roley Jenkins in the second Test at Lord's in 1950

Stollmeyer of the captaincy on several occasions, although in the series against England he returned to fitness for the last match at Kingston.

Stollmeyer was appointed as vice-captain to John Goddard on the tour to India in 1948-49. In the second Test at Bombay the Trinidadian's famous pairing with Rae was born, as the two batsmen put on 134 for the first wicket. After compiling a masterful unbeaten double century against South Zone, Stollmeyer scored his maiden Test hundred in the fourth match at Madras. It was a marvellous innings of 160 and cemented his fledgling partnership with Rae, as the openers hoisted a record 239 runs for the first wicket. During the Test series Stollmeyer scored 342 runs at an average of 68.40.

The right-hander continued to bat well on the tour to England in 1950 and was instrumental, along with Goddard, in securing the selection of the virtually unknown spinners, Alf Valentine and Sonny Ramadhin, who were to have such a decisive effect on the series. Stollmeyer played well himself, scoring over 1,000 first-class runs, including 198 against Sussex at Hove, as he and Rae put on a record 355 runs in just over four-and-a-half hours.

The pair gave Westindies regular sound starts in the Tests, which provided a launching pad for the powerful middle-order batting. In the third Test at Trent Bridge they added 77 in the first innings and then hit the 102 runs required to win in the second without loss. In this series Stollmeyer collected his runs quietly and unspectacularly, but still finished with a Test average of over fifty, including a top score of 78 out of a total of 183 on a trying pitch in the first Test at Old Trafford.

The unassuming opener went on Westindies' subsequent tour of Australia, and continued his good form in difficult circumstances. Stollmeyer showed particular resourcefulness and courage when he was showered with bumpers from Keith Miller and Ray Lindwall in the fifth Test at Sydney. Captaining the side in the absence of Goddard, Stollmeyer made the highest score of the match, when he hit a brave 104 out of a second innings total of 213, in a losing cause. He demonstrated a marvellous technique and superb temperament, as he became the first Westindian captain to score a century in a Test match.

In New Zealand, Stollmeyer batted well for a fine 152 in the second Test at Auckland, adding 197 with Rae, before being elevated to the captaincy for the series against India in 1953. His mature approach was important in lifting his side out of the doldrums after their defeat in Australia, as Westindies beat the touring Indians.

During that series Stollmeyer's illustrious partnership with Rae was broken when the selectors replaced the Jamaican with Bruce Pairaudeau, after the established openers had shared in an unbeaten stand of 142 in the second innings of the first Test at Port-of-Spain. In 21 Test partnerships, Stollmeyer and Rae averaged a startling 71 runs per innings, but the selectors felt that it was time for change.

Stollmeyer carried on with his usual consistency against the Indians, scoring 76 not out, 54 and 104 not out in the first three games, as he went on to play in his first complete home rubber since his Test debut 14 years earlier.

In the next series against England, Stollmeyer was not at his best as a batsman and his captaincy came under criticism when the visitors levelled the rubber, after trailing by two matches at one stage. Stollmeyer's decision not to enforce the follow-on in

John Goddard introduces Jeff Stollmeyer to George during the second Test at Lord's in 1950. Sir Pelham Warner is on the left of the picture, and Gerry Gomez on the right

the first game at Kingston caused considerable controversy but, in the end, after rapid scoring from Everton Weekes allowed Stollmeyer to declare, Westindies won by 140 runs.

When Australia visited the Caribbean in 1955, Stollmeyer was plagued by injury again, which restricted him to two Test appearances, and eventually forced him to retire the following year.

After his playing days were over Stollmeyer moved into the administrative side of the game. He became a selector and managed the Test team, and represented Westindies on the International Cricket Conference committee, before being elevated to the Presidency of the Board of Control in 1974 where, appropriately, he was succeeded by Rae. A key figure in the negotiations with Kerry Packer, Stollmeyer's natural diplomacy stood him in good stead as he strove to reconcile the antagonistic demands of conventional and commercial cricket.

Stollmeyer became involved in politics and is now a senator in the Trinidad legislature. He also looks after his own estates on the island.

Career details

Born: *11 April 1921*
Role: *Right-hand batsman*
Club: *Trinidad*
First-class record: *[1938-1956] 7,942 runs (44.61) including 14 centuries*
Tests: *32*
Test debut: *England 1939*
Test runs: *2,159 (42.33); HS: 160 v India, Madras, 1949*
Tours: *England 1939; India 1948-49; England 1950; Australia and New Zealand 1951-52.*

Alfred Lewis Valentine

Alf Valentine was one of the few Westindians to receive any coaching as a youngster, when he was taken under the wing of the former Jamaican left-arm spinner, George Mudie.

Jack Mercer, the English county cricketer, also helped him on his visits to Jamaica. Mercer said of the young Valentine: "I knew from the first time I saw him bowl that he was a winner: and from that time until he came to England he punctually turned up each afternoon with a small case and two old cricket balls. I told him that he must spin it more and I should not be satisfied until I saw his fingers bleeding. A few days later he turned up with two very bright red fingers carrying the little bag. I don't know where he got the red ink from! I saw him in a trial match bowling an eight ball over to an established Test batsman who played at the lot and connected once to mid-off, and that on a billiard table wicket. It was the best piece of bowling I ever saw in a very long association with the game."

In the two matches leading up to the trip to England in 1950, Valentine bowled expertly without taking as many wickets as Sonny Ramadhin. Even so, the gangling youth clearly had a wealth of talent and was included in the tour party. Like Ramadhin, Valentine, with just two first-class matches behind him, was virtually unknown on his own island and unheard of in the entire Caribbean.

After some indifferent performances early on the tour, the bespectacled Jamaican secured his place in the team for the first Test at Old Trafford after taking eight for 26 and five for 41 against Lancashire on that ground.

The youngster repaid the faith shown in him by returning the best figures by any bowler on his Test debut as he took the first eight wickets to fall for 104 runs on the first day, including five before lunch. In the third game at Trent Bridge he set a Test record by bowling 92 overs in an innings and in the last Test at The Oval he took 10 for 160, including six for 39 in the second innings, to complete a hat-trick of wins for Westindies.

Valentine who ︙ured 8 wickets ︙104 on his first ︙in Test cricket ︙nst England in ︙0

Valentine took a record number of wickets for his first Test series: 33 at 20.42 each from 422.3 overs, including Len Hutton's three times. Altogether on the tour he took 123 wickets at 17.94 apiece, including the remarkable figures of five wickets for six runs against Kent. His performances rocketed him to world fame, and he was featured in many calypsos: "Those little pals of mine, Ramadhin and Valentine".

Valentine, a tall, unassuming man, was easily recognisable on the field. His poor eyesight was often a source of amusement for his colleagues, especially when the ball came to him from one direction and he went off in another; while he was renowned for dropping return catches off his own bowling! However, his discovery, in England, that he needed glasses put an end to the entertainment for his colleagues.

Quick for a left-arm spinner, the Jamaican spun the ball prodigiously which meant that he extracted life from any wicket. This, combined with his excellent control and a well disguised quicker ball, made even the best batsmen struggle. Indeed the amount of spin he imparted left his fingers scarred, and it was a familiar sight to see him treating them with surgical

Alf Valentine bowls Graeme Hole in the second Test against Australia at Sydney in 1951

206

spirit after a match.

Valentine underlined his ability by bowling splendidly in Australia in 1951-52 and could have been as successful as in England if more catches had been held. He took 24 Test wickets at 28.79 each – more than anyone else on either side – including five for 99 in the first innings of the first Test at Brisbane.

He maintained his momentum throughout the series taking four for 111 at Sydney, six for 102 in the victory at Adelaide and five for 88 at Melbourne, including the scalp of Lindsay Hassett whose century saw Australia to victory by one wicket. Valentine's success was one of the few bright spots on a difficult tour, with the Australians hailing him as the best left-arm spinner since the War.

Valentine's performances with Ramadhin attracted record crowds for the home series against India, who were anxious to the see the spin twins in action in the Caribbean for the first time. The Jamaican did not disappoint them, as he collected 28 wickets in the series, including four for 58 in the second Test at Bridgetown, and another five wickets at Georgetown and Kingston. He reached the landmark of one hundred Test wickets in the unusually quick time for a spinner of three years and 263 days.

Valentine bowled well in New Zealand in 1956, spinning his side to victory in partnership with Ramadhin in the first Test at Dunedin. The Jamaican took two for 28 off 24 overs and, in the second match at Christchurch, collected five for 32.

However, on the trip to England the following year, Valentine was very ill and bowled only 26 overs in the entire Test series. He missed an important catch in the game at Lord's after the sun had reflected from his glasses, and was then cruelly injured on the eve of the fifth Test at The Oval, where the wicket would have suited his style.

After missing three series, Valentine was a surprise choice for a Westindies tour party for the second time in his career and, for the second time, he lived up to the selectors' expectations. He finished second in the bowling averages to Wes Hall on the tour to Australia in 1960-61, collecting eight wickets in Westindies' solitary win in the third match at Sydney and found himself at the centre of the excitement in the deciding game at Melbourne. With Australia surging for

victory, the Jamaican bowled Peter Burge and Richie Benaud, and then seemed to remove Wally Grout's bail. However, the unsighted umpire ruled the batsman not out and, although Grout got himself out immediately afterwards, the ensuing runs were allowed to stand and Australia scraped home by two wickets.

The Jamaican made the tour to England in 1963, but couldn't hold a regular place in the Test team.

The left-armer played in the Birmingham league for a while and was a familiar face at festival cricket. Unlike his partner, Ramadhin, when he retired, Valentine opted to stay on the other side of the Atlantic.

Career details

Born: *29 April 1930*
Role: *Left-arm off-spinner*
Clubs: *Jamaica, Birmingham League*
First-class record: *[1949-65] 475 wickets (26.20) and 470 runs (5.00)*
Tests: *36*
Test debut: *v England 1950*
Test wickets: *139 (30.32); BB: 8-104 v England, Old Trafford, 1950*
Test runs: *141 (4.70)*
Tours: *England 1950; Australia and New Zealand 1951-52; New Zealand 1956; England 1957; Australia 1960-61; England 1963.*

Clyde Leopold Walcott

A prodigiously gifted cricketer, Clyde Walcott, like his friend Frank Worrell, was playing for Combermere School team by the age of 12. He had little coaching, but was helped by Derek Sealy, the sports master at Combermere, and Stan Gittins, Barbados' opening batsman, who introduced him to the rudiments of batting. A splendid all-round sportsman, Walcott was a good footballer and also represented Combermere and Harrison College at athletics.

During the War years Walcott played against the cream of Barbados' cricketers and by the cessation of hostilites was one of the island's leading players. Indeed, while still at school, Walcott was selected to play for Barbados in an inter-territorial match against Trinidad at Port-of-Spain. At the tender age of 19, he hit his career-best score of 314 not out in a record unbroken stand of 574 with Worrell – which remains the record Westindian partnership for any wicket.

Standing at over 6ft, Walcott was the tallest and also the youngest of the three "W"s (the other members of the famous trio being Worrell and Everton Weekes). He quickly won a reputation as one of the hardest hitters of the ball in the game, and delighted in driving off the back foot. His square-cut was second to none and he excelled at the hook shot, a stroke he often played standing on tiptoes, as he took full advantage of his height.

His stand with Worrell brought the young Walcott to the notice of many influential figures and he made his Test debut against MCC in 1948 – the first series in which all three "W"s played together. Walcott had an inauspicious start to his Test career, after being invited to open the batting. Nonetheless, his competence as a wicket-keeper kept his place in the side. Despite his size Walcott was a nimble 'keeper and unchallenged in the position until a back injury forced him to give up.

After a less than impressive first series by his own standards, Walcott was selected for the subsequent trip to India. He returned to his more prolific ways immediately, top-scoring with 152 in the first Test at

Clyde Walcott in his less well-known position as Westindies' wicket-keeper during their tour of England in 1950

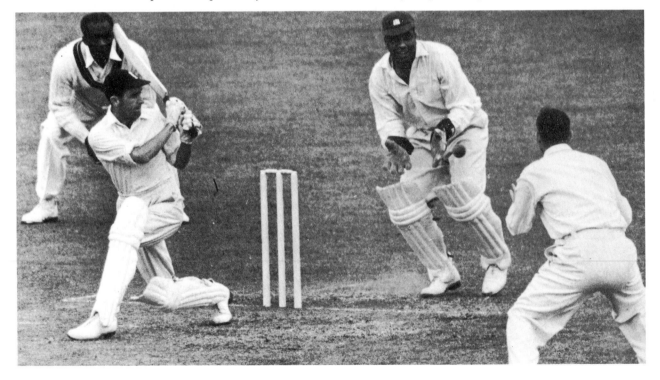

New Delhi, as he shared in a double century stand with Gerry Gomez. He maintained his momentum in the next two matches, hitting another century in the third game at Calcutta. Altogether he scored over 1,000 first-class runs, including five hundreds, at an average of 75.88. When it seemed that India might square the rubber in the final match of the series at Bombay, the Barbadian gave a further demonstration of his enthusiasm by chasing a ball to the boundary from behind the stumps. It proved a worthy effort, as the Indians failed to reach their target by just six runs.

Walcott continued his splendid form on Westindies' historic tour of England in 1950. He thrashed his way to a superb 168 not out in the second Test at Lord's, sharing in a record match-winning double century stand for the sixth wicket with Gerry Gomez; while his splendid wicket-keeping helped the young spinners, Sonny Ramadhin and Alf Valentine, to establish their supremacy. In England's first innings, Walcott stumped both openers and caught Bill Edrich to open up the inexperienced middle-order batting. Indeed, his later batting exploits often make people forget how capable a wicket-keeper he was.

The muscular Barbadian scored 1,674 runs on the tour, including seven hundreds, at 55.80, which booked him a permanent berth in the Westindies side. Despite some cultural differences – Walcott was surprised at the difficulty of obtaining such a basic ingredient as rice – he returned to England the following year to play for Enfield in the Lancashire League, before making the trip to Australia in 1951-52.

That tour was perhaps the only poor season of Walcott's Test career as he mustered just 87 runs from six innings, including one score of 60, against the pace of Ray Lindwall and Keith Miller. It also marked a watershed in his career as, after slipping a disc in his back, he gave up wicket-keeping on the advice of an Australian doctor. On that tour the unfortunate Walcott also had his nose broken.

But he perked up on the New Zealand leg of the trip, hitting 65 in the first Test at Christchurch and 115 in the second at Auckland.

When India visited the Caribbean in 1953, the right-hander hit 98 to give his side the initiative in the second match at Bridgetown, before being given out LBW by his uncle, who was umpiring. Walcott scored his first century in the Caribbean when he hit 125 in the fourth game at Georgetown, sharing in a century partnership with Weekes, and rounded off the series with 118 at Kingston.

By the time of England's visit to the Westindies the following year, Walcott was in rampant mood and firing on all cylinders. He began the series quietly with 65 in the first Test at Kingston as a prelude to his scintillating double century in the second game at Bridgetown, which underlined his world-class ability. His 220 – which he regards as his finest innings in Test cricket – came out of a total of 383 and transformed the course of the match. In the fourth game at Port-of-Spain, the Barbadian raced to 124 – the second time all three "W"s made centuries together – and finished a memorable series with fifty and 116 in a losing cause at Kingston. Altogether, he scored 698 runs for an average of 87.25.

Walcott saved his most memorable assault for the visit by the Australians in 1955, by which time he was widely acknowledged as the best batsman in the world. He scored five centuries in three Tests to wipe out memories of his traumas in Australia four years earlier. Against one of the best bowling attacks of all time, Walcott hit the then record Westindian aggregate for a series of 827 runs at 82.70.

After dismissing two Australian centurions with his slow off-cutters, Walcott hit 108 in the first Test at Kingston, sharing in a century partnership with Collie Smith. He and Weekes manufactured a draw for the home side in the second game at Port-of-Spain, as they built two substantial partnerships, including a record 242 runs in the first innings. Walcott scored 126 and 110 in that game.

In the third match at Georgetown, the right-hander hit 73, sharing a century partnership with Worrell, and 83 in the next game at Bridgetown. The Barbadian was at his majestic best in the fifth Test at Kingston. While five Australians hit hundreds, Walcott stood alone for Westindies as he thrashed his way to 155, and followed it up with 110 in the second innings, adding 179 for the fourth wicket with Gary Sobers. It was in a vain cause as Westindies slumped to an innings defeat, but it must have been of some consolation to Walcott that, in this match, he became the only player ever to score a century in each innings of a Test twice in the same series. In five successive matches at Kingston he had hit five hundreds and two fifties.

Walcott seemed to be in peak form for the trip to England in 1957 and he set about the county sides with relish in the early matches of the tour. He made 90 in the first Test at Edgbaston, albeit with the help of a runner after a thigh injury restricted his movement. However, after that innings he was disappointing in the other Tests and failed to pass fifty even though he scored nearly 1,500 runs on the entire tour.

On his return to the Caribbean, Walcott found his touch again and had a vintage season against Pakistan. In the third Test at Kingston he hit an unbeaten 88 and followed that with 145 at Georgetown, sharing in a partnership of 269 for the second wicket with Sobers, and wrapped up the series with 62 at Port-of-Spain. Altogether he scored 385 runs for an average of 96.25: a suitably high note on which to announce his retirement. Even so, he was persuaded to make a brief return for the series against England in 1960, and showed that he had lost none of his sparkle when he made a bright and breezy 53 in the fifth Test at Port-of-Spain.

The Barbadian, who played in various Commonwealth X1s, was a versatile all-round cricketer: as well as his swashbuckling batsmanship, which endeared him to millions, Walcott was an agile wicket-keeper. After his back injury ended his career behind the stumps, Walcott moved into the slips where his sharp reflexes and dexterity proved invaluable assets. A further demonstration of his all-round ability came in the second innings of the second Test against England at Old Trafford in 1950, when he opened the bowling.

After his retirement, Walcott went to live in Guyana where, as cricket organiser and coach on the estates of the Sugar Producers' Association, he uncovered a galaxy of hidden talent. His brightest stars included Rohan Kanhai, whom he nurtured on the 1957 tour to England, Basil Butcher, Joe Solomon, Lance Gibbs and Clive Lloyd. Walcott was instrumental in transforming the cricket landscape in Guyana, as he inspired a renaissance which has lasted until today.

The Barbadian has managed several Westindian teams abroad, including the triumphant side to England in 1976. This must have been a particularly satisfying trip for Walcott, who spoke of his faith in a rejuvenation of Westindian cricket, when he gracefully conceded defeat in a speech in the absence of John Goddard 19 years earlier.

Career details

Born: *17 January 1926*
Role: *Right-hand batsman, wicket-keeper, medium-pace bowler*
Clubs: *Barbados, Guyana, Lancashire League*
First-class record: *[1941-63] 11,820 runs (56.55) including 40 centuries, 175 catches and 33 stumpings, and 35 wickets (36.25).*
Tests: *44*
Test debut: *v England 1948*
Test runs: *3,798 (56.68); HS: 220 v England, Bridgetown, 1954*
Test catches: *53; Test stumpings: 11*
Tours: *India 1948-49; England 1950; Australia and New Zealand 1951-52; England 1957.*

A famous Westindian foursome, pictured at a cocktail party in England in 1957. (1-r) Frank Worrell, Everton Weekes, Sonny Ramadhin and Clyde Walcott

Courtney Andrew Walsh

A wealth of natural talent and a sound temperament helped Courtney Walsh rise rapidly through the fast bowling ranks to gain full membership of Westindies' Test elite.

Born in Kingston and educated at Excelsior High School, Walsh took 10 for 43 in an innings in school cricket in 1979. A year later, at the age of 17, he was included in the Jamaica youth team against the England youth team on its tour of the Caribbean, and played in the Westindies youth championships. The 6ft 5½in Jamaican joined the illustrious Melbourne Club on leaving school and made his first-class debut in 1982. He enjoyed a splendid debut and finished the season leading Jamaica's bowling averages with 15 wickets, including figures of six for 95 against the champions, Barbados.

That same year the promising youngster was included on Young Westindies tour to England. After creating a favourable impression in England, the slim paceman was selected for Westindies "B" tour to Zimbabwe in 1983. Walsh bowled superbly, and in the second first-class game returned match figures of eight for 122 off 42 overs. He maintained his momentum on his return to the Caribbean, and set a record for Jamaica by taking 30 wickets in the Shell Shield in 1984.

These performances made his graduation to the full Westindies team inevitable and he was selected for the tour to England later that year where, this time, struggling with his run-up, he managed only 14 expensive wickets and failed to get into the Test side. But, it was only a temporary difficulty, and he was selected for the subsequent trip to Australia. Early in the tour he bowled Western Australia to defeat, taking five for 60, a performance which helped him win his first Test cap. He took 13 wickets in the series at 33.23 each and finished as the leading wicket-taker overall, with 37.

A charming man, with a delightfully detached disposition, Walsh was instrumental in catapulting

urtney Walsh

David Munden

Gloucestershire 14 places up the county championship table in his first full season with them in 1985, as he finished with 82 wickets at 19.95.

He allowed England's batsmen no respite when they visited the Caribbean in 1986. Encouraged by his home crowd, Walsh bowled ferociously in the tourists' game against Jamaica to unsettle them early on and, in his only Test appearance of the series, in the second match at Port-of-Spain, he took a match-winning four for 74 in the second innings on a placid pitch. Among fast bowlers, Walsh was the leading wicket-taker in the Shield that season with 29 at 15.89 each.

The affable Jamaican maintained his momentum on his return to England, and was the first bowler to one hundred championship wickets in 1986. He reached the landmark on 9 August, earlier than anyone since Lance Gibbs in 1971. He headed the first-class bowling averages with 118 wickets at 18.17 apiece, including nine for 72 against Somerset at Cheltenham and returned five or more wickets in an innings in 11 other matches.

Against Pakistan later that year, Walsh took 11 wickets in the three match series at 17.72, including seven for 77 in the second Test at Lahore. In Sharjah Walsh produced one of the most remarkable bowling analyses in the history of one-day cricket, when he took five wickets for one run off 4.3 overs against Sri Lanka.

In the disappointing one-day competitions held in Australia at the beginning of 1987 Walsh was the only fast bowler to play in every match while, against New Zealand later that year, he was again the best bowler taking 13 wickets at 23.53 each, including his best Test figures of five for 73 in the second innings of the second match at Auckland.

In his short career, Walsh has been involved in some remarkable last over situations to rival those of Wes Hall. In the Geddes Grant-Harrison Line Trophy last year he won the match for Jamaica against the Leeward Islands, even though only two runs were required off his last over. However, against England and Pakistan in the World Cup, also in 1987, when entrusted with the final over in both games, he conceded 18 and 14 runs respectively, which meant that Westindies finished on the losing side. In the last

tense moments of the game against Pakistan, Walsh warned a batsman for backing up too far rather than removing the bails which would have won the game for Westindies. The next day a Karachi firm awarded Walsh a hand-woven carpet in acknowledgement of the Jamaican's sportsmanship, in what might be described as a gesture of poetic justice.

Lacking the boisterous nature of some of his colleagues, Walsh's normally calm disposition and splendid action have earned him early recognition. With continued application and fitness, the languid Jamaican can look forward to an illustrious career on the merry-go-round of international competition.

Besides cricket, Walsh also plays football, and is a keen follower of basketball and athletics. Like many Westindian cricketers, Walsh enjoys soul music, and likes to relax in front of the television.

Career details

Born: *30 October 1962*
Role: *Right-arm fast bowler*
Clubs: *Jamaica, Gloucestershire*
First-class record: *[1982-] 494 wickets (22.57) and 1,058 runs (10.07)*
Tests: *13*
Test debut: *v Australia 1984*
Test wickets: *45 (24.66); BB: 5-73 v New Zealand, Auckland, 1987*
Tours: *England (WIYC) 1982; Zimbabwe ("B"team) 1983; England 1984; Australia 1984-85; Pakistan 1986; New Zealand 1987; India and Pakistan (World Cup) 1987.*

Chester Watson

Chester Watson was originally selected for Test honours as a replacement for his fiery compatriot, Roy Gilchrist. A right-arm bowler, Watson's wristy action disguised the speed of his deliveries, and helped him to 16 wickets (37.06) in his only full series against England in the Westindies in 1960. In front of his home crowd, the Jamaican took four for 62 in an inspired spell of pace bowling in the second innings of the third Test at Kingston.

He went on the subsequent tour to Australia, but was eventually overshadowed by the development of Gary Sobers as a fast bowler.

Watson spent many profitable seasons playing cricket in the Lancashire League and has served the Jamaican Board of Control loyally for many years, where he is currently the treasurer.

Career details

Born: *1 July 1939*
Role: *Right-arm fast bowler*
Clubs: *Jamaica, New Delhi, Lancashire League*
First-class record: *[1958-64] 85 wickets (32.07) and 197 runs (7.57)*
Tests: *7*
Test debut: *v England 1960*
Test wickets: *19 (38.10); BB: 4-62 v England, Kingston, 1960*
Tour: *Australia 1960-61*

Everton De Courcey Weekes

After some notable batting exploits in the Caribbean during the War years, a wealth of natural ability and no small measure of confidence rocketed Everton Weekes to the top of world cricket.

Weekes had no early coaching, but developed his potential playing at St. Leonard's school, where, by the age of 12, he was a regular member of the team. For a while, the Barbadian experimented as a wicket-keeper, but soon gave it up in favour of a more profitable career as a batsman.

A powerful man with tremendous strength in his arms and shoulders, Weekes was spotted by the former Westindies captain, Teddy Hoad, while serving with the Barbados Battalion of the Caribbean Regiment. His ability was such that, by the age of 18, he was opening the batting for Barbados.

By the time of the first Test series against England after the War, in 1948, Weekes had staked his claim for Test recognition and, having played with Frank Worrell for Empire, the pair joined forces with Clyde Walcott to complete the unique batting triumvirate, which quickly became known as the three "W"s.

However, Weekes' international baptism was not an auspicious one and, after some indifferent performances, where his top-score was 36, he was dropped for the final Test at Kingston to make room

Everton Weekes snaps up Australia's Ken Archer at slip off Gerry Gomez in the second Test at Sydney in 1951

for George Headley. But an injury caused Headley to withdraw and the young Barbadian was given a second chance, much to the chagrin of the Jamaican crowd who wanted John Holt to play and they booed Weekes every time he fielded the ball, after he had arrived late from Barbados.

The amiable Weekes answered his critics in the best way possible with a magnificent innings of 141, which included 15 fours. After being dropped early on, the Barbadian demoralised the English bowlers with a superb display of stroke-making and deft footwork, which helped him to the highest score of the rubber.

This splendid performance secured his place for the following tour to India – the setting for Weekes' most prolific series. He thrashed his way to a glorious 128 runs in the opening match at New Delhi, which proved to be the prelude for a superb 194 in the next game at Bombay. He was so dominant that the bowlers were reduced to impotency, while the helpless fielders dived for cover.

The Barbadian was in irrepressible form again for the third Test at Calcutta. He galloped to 162 in the first innings and followed this with 101 in the second, as his remarkable run of scoring established a world record of five successive Test hundreds. In the next game at Madras, the explosive right-hander was controversially run out for 90. Many still claim that the decision was wrong, and it almost certainly prevented him from making his sixth consecutive Test century. However, it must have been of some consolation to him that he set the then Westindian record aggregate for a series by scoring 779 runs at an average of 111.28.

A pugnacious player, Weekes' insatiable appetite for runs entrenched him firmly in the Test team and he was soon scoring as freely in the Lancashire League. He signed for Bacup and, in 1949, hit the highest score ever in the League with an unbeaten 195 against Enfield. Indeed, in six seasons with the club, the Barbadian scored 8,036 runs for an average of 91.32. During this time, he became the first player to score over 1,000 runs in six seasons in the League and in 1951, exceeded 1,500.

Fleet of foot, Weekes had the complete array of attacking strokes at his disposal, and showed no mercy if a bowler lost his line or length as he closed in on his unfortunate victim. By the time of Westindies' tour to England in 1950, Weekes was developing a reputation as one of the most murderous of post-War batsmen.

The Barbadian scored 2,310 first-class runs that summer for an average of 79.65 although, by his own lofty standards, he was a little disappointing in the Tests. Weekes restricted himself to 338 runs (56.33) including the top-score of 52 in difficult conditions in the first innings of the opening match at Old Trafford; and 129 in the third game at Trent Bridge, as he added 283 for the fourth wicket with Worrell.

But, if England didn't suffer directly, Weekes treated Cambridge University to an unbeaten triple century and the counties to four double hundreds and two single centuries. As well as his batting, Weekes was also a superb close fielder and snapped up many catches off Sonny Ramadhin and Alf Valentine, including five in England's defeat in the last game at The Oval.

Selected for the tour to Australia in 1951-52, Weekes made a bright and breezy start by scoring 70 – a remarkable piece of batting in the face of a tirade of bumpers – in the first Test at Brisbane. But, after a half century in the next game at Sydney, the Barbadian, like his colleagues, fell away in the face of the awesome pace of Ray Lindwall and Keith Miller; while an injury hampered his cause further.

Weekes rehabilitated himself against the Indians in 1953, hitting a splendid 207 in the opening encounter at Port-of-Spain, as he shared in a double century partnership with Bruce Pairaudeau. Weekes followed this up with another hundred, 161 in 334 minutes, and 55 not out in the third match, also in Trinidad. Fully back in the groove, the right-hander collected 86 at Georgetown, sharing in a century partnership with Walcott, and 109 at Kingston, adding 197 with Worrell. For good measure, Weekes thrashed 253 for Barbados against the tourists. The Barbadian headed the batting for the Test series with 716 runs at 102.28 – an aggregate that just overhauled George Headley's previous record for a rubber in the Westindies.

Weekes continued his habit of savaging visiting bowlers when he hit 55 and a rapid 90 not out against England in the first Test at Kingston in 1954, scoring

Everton Weekes during his triple unbeaten century against Cambridge University in 1950

quickly enough to allow Jeff Stollmeyer to declare and give his bowlers sufficient time to win the match.

He fell six short of his hundred in the third match at Georgetown, but made sure in the fourth at Port-of-Spain, as he produced one of the best performances of the series by hitting a splendid 206. He shared in a partnership of 338 for the third wicket with Worrell, a record for any wicket against England.

Weekes joined forces with Walcott against the visiting Australians in 1955, as the pair avenged themselves for their humiliation by the tourists four years earlier. Between them they notched up nine hundreds and numerous fifties, and contrived to draw the match for the home team at Port-of-Spain. In that game Weekes scored 139 – an innings which featured the only six of his Test career – and 87 not out. He shared two third wicket partnerships with Walcott, of 242 and 127, and in the second innings was left just 13 runs short of scoring five centuries in seven consecutive Test innings at Queen's Park Oval. He confirmed his class with a splendid 81 in the third game at Georgetown where, generally, the bowlers had the upper hand, and finished the series with 44 and 56 in the two remaining matches.

Against an England X1 on a goodwill visit to the Caribbean in early 1956, Weekes top-scored with 89 to usher a Westindies X1 to victory at Port-of-Spain, in a foretaste of what he was to serve up on the subsequent trip to New Zealand.

There, he was at his brilliant best and, as one of the few senior members of the party, led by example, stroking his way to five hundreds in his first five matches. Altogether, Weekes hit 940 runs (104.44) including six centuries – four of them in succession – from eight first-class matches. In the first three Tests he got centuries in his only innings: 123 at Dunedin, where he shared in a three figure partnership for the fourth wicket with Collie Smith, 103 at Christchurch and 156 at Wellington, where he shared in century stands with Denis Atkinson and Alfie Binns in better than even time. These performances brought the tourists victory by huge margins and when, in the last match at Auckland, Weekes "failed" – even though he top-scored in Westindies' second innings with 31 – his side collapsed to defeat.

After this magnificent effort, Westindies' premier run machine was expected to be at full throttle against England in 1957. But, apart from a courageous innings at Lord's, where he made 90 on a lively wicket after being hit on his finger early on, he did not play well. He was hindered by ill health and suffered from double vision towards the end of the tour.

Weekes' return to the Caribbean brought an improvement in his health and his play, as he thrashed 197 against Pakistan in front of his home crowd in the first Test at Bridgetown in 1958 and scored fifties in the two games at Port-of-Spain. It was only appropriate that, in his last series, Weekes' brilliant and entertaining career should end on a high note, as he finished the rubber with 455 runs for an average of 65.

A charming man, Weekes was the first of the illustrious three "W"s to retire – a decision he took after a series of unsuccessful operations on a thigh injury which cramped his swashbuckling stlye. He toured the world with several Commonwealth sides and was the national cricket coach of Barbados for many years. He was later awarded an OBE for his outstanding contribution to the game, and will be remembered, above all else, for his relentless pillaging of some of the world's best bowlers.

Today, he is a bridge player of world class standing.

Career details

Born: *26 February 1925*
Role: *Right-hand batsman*
Clubs: *Barbados, Lancashire League*
First-class record: *[1944-64] 12,010 runs (52.90) including 36 centuries*
Tests: *48*
Test debut: *v England 1948*
Test runs: *4,455 (58.61); HS: 207 v India, Port-of-Spain, 1953*
Tours: *India 1948-49; England 1950; Australia 1951-52; New Zealand 1956; England 1957.*

Sir Frank Mortimore Maglinne Worrell

As the first black man to be appointed as captain of Westindies on a long-term basis, Frank Worrell, arguably, was entrusted with the most difficult task in the history of Westindian Test cricket. Worrell, more than any other, knew that he could not afford to fail, but it was the manner in which he achieved his resounding successes, rather than the triumphs themselves, for which he is best loved and remembered.

Worrell's captaincy is held in such high esteem, that it often overshadows the fact that he was one of the most gifted batsmen of his era, and was a member of the magnificent trio of batsmen known as the three "W"s – the other two being Clyde Walcott and Everton Weekes – who dominated the 1950s.

Born at Bank Hall in St. Michael, near Bridgetown, Worrell's talent was obvious from an early age. At Combermere school his confidence was such that he was accused of being conceited by the other players, an accusation which Worrell rejected and resented all his life. Conceited or not, by the age of 12, he was a regular member of the school team, playing as a left-arm spinner who could bat a little.

In his book *Cricket Punch,* Worrell recalled: "I enrolled at Combermere School...which meant first-class cricket, for the schools take part in first-class cricket in Barbados. The school teams are made up of both pupils and masters, and we had on our staff Derek Sealy...but even with a former Test star on your side, it was a bit tough for a 13-year-old boy to be playing in top-grade cricket. Nevertheless, it was great experience, I found myself up against some of the best players in the West Indies, and there is no better way of learning anything than by coming up against the finest exponents."

Worrell was greatly influenced by the batting techniques of George Challenor and was also impressed by his teacher, Sealy. Before long, the youngster's own batting began to blossom and, at the age of 18, Worrell made his debut for Barbados,

...ered as captain,
...ik Worrell was
one of the most
...d batsmen of his
...

217

albeit, primarily as a bowler.

The next season the Barbadian was sent in as nightwatchman in an inter-territorial game against Trinidad. He continued his innings into the next day, and carried his bat for 64 runs and was soon opening the innings regularly. In the following game the slim right-hander hit 188 in five hours, confirming that he was a world class batsman in the making.

Against Trinidad in 1943-44 at Bridgetown, Worrell stroked his way to 308 not out, his career-best score, sharing in a record unbroken fourth wicket partnership of 502 with John Goddard. The Barbadian seemed to have a taste for the Trinidadian bowlers as, in 1945-46, he shared in another unbroken fourth wicket partnership, this time a record 574 runs in less than six hours, with Walcott, his school and Empire colleague, at Port-of-Spain. On this occasion Worrell scored 255 not out, while the partnership itself remains the highest for any Westindian wicket. Even so, Worrell was dismissive of both records, commenting: "The conditions were loaded in our favour, I wasn't all that delighted about it."

Worrell was a detached man, with an air of artistry about his play. Yet, in spite of his success, he was unhappy living in Barbados, where the school-boy taunts of his alleged arrogance never really left him, and he resolved to go and live in Jamaica.

Having cut his teeth in domestic competition, the young man was ready and waiting for the first post-War Test series, against England in 1948. He missed the first match due to illness, but hit 97 in his first Test innings in the second game at Port-of-Spain. In the third match at Georgetown he confirmed his calibre with a stupendous 131 not out – more than twice as many as anyone else on either side – and wrapped up the series with 38 at Kingston to give him a record average for the series of 147.

A graceful and stylish player, Worrell had perfect balance and superb timing, complemented by good judgement and nimble footwork. As a bowler, he could spin the ball although, more often, he bowled fast-medium. His impeccable conduct on and off the field was his trademark, although he was a man of strong principles and refused to tour India in 1948-49, when the Westindies Board of Control refused to

meet his pay demands – a decision he later regretted.

Like other great Westindian players before him, Worrell played league cricket in Lancashire. He enjoyed a long and illustrious career with Radcliffe between 1949-53, setting a record aggregate for the League in 1951 as he scored 1,694 runs at an average of 112.93 – a record which stood for 35 years. Worrell also appeared for Norton in the North Staffordshire League. He adapted well to the Lancashire way of life and read economics at Manchester University.

He visited India with various Commonwealth teams in the early 1950s, which were made up mostly of players from the northern clubs, and enthralled the crowds with his batting which he perfected on the placid wickets of the sub-continent. Indeed, he rated an unbeaten double century he scored at Kanpur as the best innings of his entire career. On the 1950-51 tour he often led the side in the absence of the injured Les Ames, revealing a shrewdness for which he became famous as captain of the Westindies.

Worrell returned to the Test fold for Westindies' triumphant tour of England in 1950. In the avalanche of runs in the second Test at Lord's, the right-hander contented himself with 52 and 45, before opening up with a magnificent 261 in the third game at Trent Bridge. It was his highest Test score and lasted just over five-and-a-half hours, as he shared in seven records, including 283 runs for the fourth wicket with Weekes. Ranked as one of the great innings of Test cricket, *Wisden* described Worrell's performance as being "in scintillating style", while Pelham Warner thought that his partnership with Weekes was the best he had seen in his life. For good measures, Worrell took three wickets for 40 in England's first innings.

The right-hander completed a memorable series by scoring a dogged 138, against a more penetrative bowling attack, at The Oval. He added 172 for the second wicket with Allan Rae, but had to interrupt his innings when he reached his century due to dizziness.

He finished the rubber as the leading batsman with 539 runs at an average of 89.93. Altogether on the tour, Worrell scored 1,775 runs (68.26) with six hundreds and a record stand of 350 with Weekes against Cambridge University. He also took 39 wickets.

Like his colleagues, Worrell found the Australian bowlers more difficult to cope with the following year. Even so, he hit 64 in the second match at Sydney and guided the tourists to their solitary victory in the third game at Adelaide, where, bowling throughout the home side's first innings, he took six for 38.

Worrell underlined his brilliance as a batsman by hitting a rare century on that tour in the fourth game at Melbourne. In a remarkable display of courage, he went on the attack against Keith Miller and Ray Lindwall, despite injuring his right hand early in an innings that lasted nearly four hours. The next highest score was 37 and, afterwards, Worrell revealed that Miller had warned him that he intended to rouse the crowd with his blistering deliveries.

Once again, Worrell was Westindies' leading Test batsman as he finished the series with 337 runs at 33.70 and took 19 wickets at 21.57. Westindies recovered their composure in New Zealand, with Worrell top-scoring twice in the first Test at Christchurch, with 71 and 62 not out. He followed this performance with a century at Auckland, sharing in a partnership of 190 with Walcott.

The campaign in Australia had taken a lot out of Worrell, and he had a quieter time in the home series against India in 1953, although he livened up towards the end with a half century in the fourth match at Georgetown. He also hit an irreproachable double hundred in the final game at Kingston where, incidentally, all three "W" scored centuries for the first time in the same innings. Worrell added 197 with Weekes and 213 with Walcott.

Worrell was made vice-captain when England visited the Caribbean the following year. Once again he began slowly. After missing the first Test, he failed to score in two out of his next three innings. Even so, sandwiched between his two ducks, Worrell hit an unbeaten 76, sharing in a double century stand for the second wicket with John Holt, in the second Test at Bridgetown. While, in the fourth match at Port-of-Spain, he hit 167 and 56 in a masterful display of batting.

Worrell's career seemed to take an irreversible downturn when Australia visited the Caribbean in

1955. After being relieved of the vice-captaincy, he scored just two fifties in the rubber, in the third game at Georgetown and in the fifth at Kingston. But, he returned to the side for the series against England in 1957 and, in spite of his university commitments and some injury problems, Worrell enjoyed a remarkable renaissance topping the tour batting with 1,470 runs at 58.80 and finishing with 39 wickets at 24.33.

The right-hander began the series with a sparkling 81 at Edgbaston – with the help of a runner because of a thigh injury – adding 190 runs for the sixth wicket with Collie Smith. Pressed into service as an opener for the third game at Trent Bridge, Worrell carried his bat for nine-and-a-half hours for 191 runs – a performance which he felt anyone could have emulated on so docile a pitch: perhaps this was Worrell's thinly veiled criticism of his team-mates. Whatever his feelings, having opened the bowling at the start of play, he had to go straight back out for the follow-on after his marathon first innings score, which meant that he was on the field from Thursday morning until Monday afternoon.

In the fourth Test at Headingley Worrell came into his own as a bowler, taking seven for 70 in England's only innings. An accurate left-armer, he bowled as well as anyone during the pace shortage of the early 1950s. In the match against Middlesex on the 1957 tour, on a trying Lord's pitch, he took five for 34 in the county's first innings and scored 66 not out and 61 in low Westindian totals. Indeed, his all-round contribution on the trip prompted *West Indies Cricket Challenge* to comment: "What the West Indian side would have done without Frank Worrell as a batsman and bowler it is hard to conjecture."

After 1957 it became clear that in an increasingly competitive and professional environment, the captaincy and team selection would have to be made on a meritocratic, rather than on a plutocratic, basis, and, when Pakistan visited Westindies in 1958, Worrell was earmarked to lead the side.

In the event, Worrell missed the series because of his studies and, after being included in the tour party to India and Pakistan in 1958-59, he withdrew to continue his courses. Out of the game for two years, Worrell returned for the second part of his cricket career – which proved even more illustrious than the

first – in the opening Test against England at Bridgetown in 1960.

He re-asserted himself with a painstaking 197 not out, lasting 11 hours and 29 minutes, adding 399 in a record fourth wicket partnership with Gary Sobers. Worrell confirmed his standing by taking four wickets for 49 in England's second innings in the fourth game at Georgetown, and finished the series with 61 runs at Port-of-Spain. His performances convinced the selectors that Worrell was the man to lead Westindies in Australia later that year.

His appointment coincided with independence in the region, through the Westindies Federation – the poignancy of which was not lost on Worrell or his team. It was imperative that he succeeded and he more than lived up to the responsibility. An independent man, Worrell was well versed in all areas of the game and had a track record to prove it. Held in the highest esteem by his younger colleagues, he instilled a degree of professionalism in the team that hitherto had been lacking, with a firm, but fair, code of discipline.

In *With the West Indies in Australia 1960-61* Johnny Moyes noted: "(Worrell) alone became the leader and his word was accepted. He had the affection and confidence of his team and gradually they began to improve. They began to play as a team, for Worrell was both realist and idealist and he inculcated these thoughts into his colleagues. They learned to fight as a team. There were no divisions in the side...The spare parts came together to form a machine which could function efficiently under the guidance of the master mechanic."

The tourists lost the series by the narrowest of margins, due, in no small measure, to some questionable umpiring decisions. Even so, Worrell's attacking approach revived the sinking fortunes of the game in Australia and he and his team won the respect of the entire populace, as was shown by the 500,000 people who turned out to greet the visitors on their motorcade send-off from Melbourne at the end of the tour.

In the famous tie in the opening match at Brisbane, Worrell scored 65 in both innings, batting at number five – his new position to allow the younger batting talent to develop. It was appropriate, therefore, that he shared in a partnership of 174 for the fourth wicket with Sobers in the first innings.

In the final moments of the closest Test ever played, Worrell remained impeccably calm imploring his strike bowler, Wes Hall, not to bowl a no-ball, and rallying his fielders. When the match was tied, Worrell said afterwards that he was the only player on the field aware of the result.

Worrell hit 82 in Westindies' win in the third game at Sydney and two fifties in their defeat in the next at Adelaide. The visitors had lost the series, but the moral victory was theirs, even though Australia won the Frank Worrell Trophy – a prize presented by the Australian Board of Control in recognition of Worrell's splendid contribution to the game over recent months, and to be competed for in subsequent rubbers between the two countries.

Although they were beaten, Worrell must have known that victory could not be far away as, at last, Westindies were playing as a team. The Indians were the unfortunate side who ran into Westindies on their upward spiral – and they were crushed 5-0 when they visited the Caribbean in 1962. Worrell hit fifties in the last four matches, being stranded on 98 not out in his last Test innings in front of his adopted home crowd at Kingston. Even so, he headed the batting averages with 88.00 in a series that had given his team the perfect preparation for their trip to England the following year.

Their 3-1 triumph over the "old country" was a suitable epitaph for Worrell, who had led Westindian cricket to its highest peak of excellence yet. Although he was often unfit during that vintage summer, Worrell's magic as captain never waned.

His best innings came in the first Test at Old Trafford, where he declared with his score on 74 to give his bowlers time to dismiss England twice – which they did. In the closely fought second game at Lord's, having played a supportive role in a century stand with Basil Butcher, Worrell ran out Derek Shackleton in England's second innings, in a veterans' race to the wicket. The Westindian skipper must have experienced a sense of *déjà vu* as, once again, with eight runs required off the last over, he found himself urging Hall to keep a tight line and length in the dying moments of a remarkable match.

It was the most exciting Test in another splendid series and, on the initiative of Worrell, led to the instigation of more frequent visits by Westindies to England. *Wisden* declared that "no more popular side have ever toured the old country" while Worrell himself, who retired at the end of that season, put his achievement in its best perspective when he said: "I have had a great run and, as I have satisfied my greatest ambition in the last two years, I have no complaints. My aim was always to see West Indies moulded from a rabble of brilliant island individualists into a real team – and I've done it."

A fine ambassador for Westindian cricket, Worrell is considered one of the best Test captains of all time, winning nine of his 15 matches, losing three and drawing two, as well as being at the helm in the incredible tie against Australia. In 1964 he was knighted for his services to the game.

Away from the sports scene, Worrell was appointed warden of a hall of residence at the University of the Westindies, St. Augustine campus, and became a senator in the Jamaican Parliament. At the same time, he continued to be closely involved in cricket both as an administrator and, occasionally, as a correspondent.

In March 1967 Worrell died of leukaemia. Flags flew at half-mast in Barbados, Jamaica and Radcliffe and a memorial service was held in Westminster Abbey, the first time ever that that honour had been accorded to a sportsman. When his body was taken back to Barbados, to its final resting place overlooking the university campus, it seemed as though the whole population had turned out to pay their final respects.

Richie Benaud, the opposing captain when Worrell took Westindies to Australia, said of him: "He was a great leader of men and one of the finest cricketers on and off the field in the history of the game. It is difficult to realise that the indolent drawl, and feline grace known all over the world are no more. Few men have had a better influence on cricket."

Career details

Born: *1 August 1924*
Died: *13 March 1967*
Role: *Right-hand batsman, left-arm medium-pace bowler*
Clubs: *Barbados, Jamaica, North of England Leagues*
First-class career: *[1941-64] 15,025 runs (54.24) including 39 centuries, and 349 wickets (29.03)*
Tests: *51*
Test debut: *v England 1948*
Test runs: *3,860 (49.48); HS: 261 v England, Trent Bridge, 1950*
Test wickets: *69 (38.73); BB: 7-70 v England, Headingley, 1957*
Tours: *England 1950; Australia and New Zealand 1951-52; England 1957; Australia 1960-61; England 1963.*

Frank Worrell (left) and Everton Weeke in happy mood at Cambridge in 1950 They had good reason: Worrell scored 160 and Weekes 304 agains the University*

Westindian Test Cricketers 1928-88

(excluding featured players)

As Westindian cricket celebrates its Diamond Jubilee of Test match status, we would like to point out that any of the following players could have qualified for inclusion in *100 Great Westindian Test Cricketers: from Challenor to Richards*. Careers are made and broken by the prevailing conditions at the time and the slightest stroke of fortune, good or bad, can shape any international sportsman's future.

Imtiaz Ali (Trinidad)
Inshan Ali (Trinidad)
David Allan (Barbados)
Nyron Asgarali (Trinidad)
Eric Atkinson (Barbados)
Richard Austin (Jamaica)
Leonard Baichan (Guyana)
Arthur Barrett (Jamaica)
Edward Bartlett (Barbados)
Nelson Betancourt (Trinidad)
Alfie Binns (Jamaica)
Lionel Birkett (Barbados, Guyana, Trinidad)
"Bunny" Butler (Trinidad)
Clyde Butts (Guyana)
Robin Bynoe (Barbados)
Jimmy Cameron (Jamaica)
John Cameron (Jamaica, Somerset)
George Carew (Barbados)
Herbert Chang (Jamaica)
Cyril Christiani (Guyana)
Oscar da Costa (Jamaica)
Bryan Davis (Trinidad, Glamorgan)
Frank de Caires (Guyana

Tom Dewdney (Jamaica)
Uton Dowe (Jamaica)
Wilfred Ferguson (Trinidad)
Mike Frederick (Barbados, Jamaica, Derbyshire)
Dickie Fuller (Jamaica)
Hammond Furlonge (Trinidad)
Andy Ganteaume (Trinidad)
Berkeley Gaskin (Guyana)
Glendon Gibbs (Guyana)
George Gladstone (Jamaica)
Alvin Greenidge (Barbados)
Geoff Greenidge (Barbados, Sussex)
Mervyn Grell (Tribidad)
Simpson Guillen (Trinidad, Canterbury, New Zealand)
Ron Headley (Jamaica, Worcestershire, Derbyshire)
Teddy Hoad (Barbados)
Tony Howard (Barbados)
Errol Hunte (Trinidad)
Leslie Hylton (Jamaica)

Tyrell Johnson (Trinidad)
Charles Jones (Guyana)
Raphick Jumadeen (Trinidad)
Lester King (Jamaica, Bengal)
Desmond Lewis (Jamaica)
Ivan Madray (Guyana)
Norman Marshall (Barbados, Trinidad)
Ivor Mendonca (Guyana)
Cyril Merry (Trinidad)
Roy Miller (Jamaica)
George Mudie (Jamaica)
Ranjie Nanan (Trinidad)
James Neblett (Guyana, Barbados)
Jack Noreiga (Trinidad)
Albert Padmore (Barbados)
Clarence Passailaigue (Jamaica)
Thelston Payne (Barbados)
Lance Pierre (Trinidad)
Ken Rickards (Jamaica, Essex)
Alphonso Roberts (Windward Islands, Trinidad)
Edwin St. Hill (Trinidad)
Wilton St. Hill (Trinidad)

Alf Scott (Jamaica)
Tommy Scott (Jamaica)
Ben Sealey (Trinidad)
Frayson Shillingford (Windward Islands)
Irvine Shillingford (Windward Islands)
Sew Shivnarine (Guyana)
Charran Singh (Trinidad)
Milton Small (Barbados)
"Charlie" Stayers (Guyana)
Vic Stollmeyer (Trinidad)
Jaswick Taylor (Trinidad)
John Trim (Guyana)
Vin Valentine (Jamaica)
Leslie Walcott (Barbados)
Ken Weekes (Jamaica)
Tony White (Barbados)
Leslie Wight (Guyana)
Vibart Wight (Guyana)
Archie Wiles (Barbados) (Trinidad)
Elquemedo Willett (Leeward Islands)
Basil Williams (Jamaica)
"Foffie" Williams (Barbados)
Ken Wishart (Guyana)

The Emergence of Cricket in the Caribbean

Barbados

Barbados holds the enviable record of having produced the largest number of distinguished cricketers in relation to its size and population.

The earliest known cricket club in Barbados was St. Ann's, formed in 1806. However, the English colonialists certainly enjoyed the game on the island before that date, insisting that every military establishment should have its own cricket ground.

Before long civilian clubs were set up as well. Two of the best-known were Wanderers and Pickwick, who engaged in intense competition – revealed by the scores from the Barbados Cricket Association's Division One final of 1921. Played over seven successive Saturdays, Wanderers finally overcame Pickwick with totals of 590 and 489 runs as opposed to 436 and 284 by Pickwick!

Similarly the school teams of Lodge, Codrington College and, later on, Harrison College and Combermere School provided the nursery for many of Westindies' finest players. Pelham Warner and George Challenor were products of Harrison College, while Frank Worrell and Wes Hall were graduates of Combermere. For good measure, Clyde Walcott had the benefit of the experience of both establishments.

Barbados hosted the first inter-colonial match in 1865 when they decisively beat Guyana at the Garrison Savannah, with the Bajan captain, F.B. Smith, scoring an unbeaten half century and taking 10 wickets in the match.

In 1891 Barbados staged the first triangular tournament at the Wanderers ground, competing against Trinidad and Guyana: once again the hosts proved the comprehensive victors, much to the delight of a large and enthusiastic crowd, most of whom had taken the afternoon off from work. A biennial tournament was then introduced and in the 12 competitions up until the First World War, Barbados won the trophy seven times establishing themselves as undisputed champions of the region.

England first toured the Westindies in 1895, under the captaincy of R. Slade Lucas, and played their opening match at Kensington Oval. Barbados trounced the visitors by five wickets, with the gifted medium-pacer, Clifford Goodman, taking 14 for 85 for the home side.

Arthur Priestley's English team were defeated even more comprehensively – by an innings and 41 runs – when they visited the island two years later. In 1910 an England side captained by R.A. Bennett also slumped to an innings defeat against Barbados; while A.W.F. Somerset, who led two MCC sides to the Caribbean before 1914, always felt that Barbados were more difficult to overcome than a representative Westindian team. Even so, Barbados were beaten decisively in 1967 when they challenged a Rest of the World side in a game to celebrate their independence. In both innings their batsmen struggled and the Bajans lost by 262 runs.

In the early years, Barbados' dominance was perpetuated by their outstanding captain and gifted batsman, Harold Austin, who played for the island for over 30 years. Towards the end of the 1920s Barbados' overall supremacy began to wane, although there was no end to the remarkable succession of talented individuals who emerged – a trend which has continued to the present day.

George Challenor was Barbados' first batting giant, ably supported by "Tim" Tarilton. Teddy Hoad, one-time captain of the Test side, Harry Ince, and fast bowlers, Herman Griffith and George Francis, were among the other outstanding names from the early days. The three "W"s inspired the Renaissance after the Second World War, whereupon an unrelenting string of stroke-makers, including Conrad Hunte, Seymour Nurse, Gordon Greenidge and Desmond Haynes have successively entertained crowds all over the world. The island has also continued with its rich tradition of pace bowlers: among others, Manny

Martindale, Wes Hall, Charlie Griffith, Sylvester Clarke, Joel Garner and Malcolm Marshall. But, perhaps, Barbados' most famous son is Sir Garfield Sobers, cricket's all-rounder *par excellence.*

Trinidad & Tobago

Like Barbados, Trinidad has a long and rich history of cricketing traditions. It seems that the Trinidad Cricket Club was formed around 1830 and they played Guyana in 1869, before visiting Georgetown for a short tour in 1882. Five years later they easily beat an American touring team. But, despite this progress, their overall development was hampered by their use of matting wickets.

In 1891 Trinidad visited Barbados for the first triangular tournament, and hosted it themselves two years later at Port-of-Spain. But Trinidad were playing at a severe disadvantage because Barbados and Guyana refused to allow them to field their "coloured professionals", a stipulation which lasted until the turn of the century.

Even so, when R. Slade Lucas brought an English team to Trinidad in 1895, the home side played their black professionals, among them fast bowlers, Wood and Cumberbatch, who were largely responsible for the comprehensive defeat inflicted on the visitors. In that match, Trinidad were captained by Aucher Warner, brother of Pelham, who captained the first Westindian side to tour England in 1900. Lebrun Constantine, father of Learie, was included in that first tour party – eventually! The story goes that "Old Cons" couldn't afford the trip to England, but local people rallied round to pay for his voyage and put him on a fast boat to catch the rest of the team who were already under sail. Constantine duly arrived in England to score the first century for Westindies against MCC at Lord's.

At this time Major Bertie Harragin was making a similar impact in Trinidad as Harold Austin had made in Barbados. An astute captain and capable batsman, Harragin was at the forefront of the tremendous advances Trinidad made during the first 10 years of this century, which saw them win the inter-colonial tournament four times.

During these early years, the island produced some outstanding cricketers to rival those in Barbados: André Cipriani, who learnt his cricket in England, was one of the leading batsmen, George John a vibrant fast bowler and Joe Small a versatile all-rounder.

In those days, players made their mark in club cricket and Learie Constantine, one of the finest products of the island's club system, described in *Wisden* how a new black batsman, Wilton St. Hill, became an overnight hero after savaging the bowling of George John during an afternoon match. The relevance of the tale is that, in an environment where membership of a cricket club was based on colour, the success of a young black batsman had far-reaching implications – even though the adulation he received had little bearing on his indifferent international record. Indeed, Trinidad's colour barriers were so institutionalised that much of the island's early cricketing heritage revolved around white families from the Warners to the Grants – including the appointment of the elder Grant, Jackie, who had no experience of captaincy or Test cricket, to lead the Westindies in the 1930s – and later the Stollmeyers.

After the First World War, Learie Constantine, Clifford Roach and Wilton St. Hill safeguarded Trinidad's cricket heritage at the highest level. They were succeeded by such notables as Jeff Stollmeyer and Gerry Gomez, who shared several outstanding partnerships immediately after the Second World War. Later on Sonny Ramadhin, Deryck Murray and Bernard Julien revealed their various gifts to the world and, in recent times, Larry Gomes, Gus Logie and Tony Gray have headed their country's representation in the Test side.

Jamaica

Although Jamaica is the biggest and most populated of the cricket-playing countries in the Caribbean, her geographical isolation hampered her development. Kingston Cricket Club was formed in 1863, but it was a long time before Jamaica took part in the inter-colonial competitions.

Even so, early English touring teams called in on the island and when the Georgetown Cricket Club sponsored the first overseas tour by Westindies, to America and Canada in 1886, the party was captained by a Jamaican, L.R. Fyffe, and included six other Jamaicans. Later on when the United States returned the visit to the Westindies, Jamaica made the highest score against the tourists and also beat R. Slade Lucas' English touring team in 1895.

However, Jamaica's winning ways came to an abrupt end when they visited Guyana and Barbados in 1896 and lost all their matches, and fared similarly poorly against Arthur Priestley's England team later that season. Nevertheless, in 1910-11 Jamaica recorded the first tie against MCC in the Caribbean.

It was not until the 1920s that Jamaica really began to establish herself as a force in the region. Then the talent blossomed forth in the shape of such illustrious figures as John Holt, Frank Martin, Karl Nunes, Ernest Rae and Ivan Barrow. Indeed, in 1921 Nunes and Rae helped Kingston Cricket Club to score 500 runs for seven wickets in one day against St. Catherine Cricket Club, with the other main scorer being George da Costa.

It was during the 1920s and 1930s that many distinguished touring teams from England visited Jamaica, including those captained by Sir Julien Cahn, Lord Tennyson and the Hon. F. S. G. Calthorpe. Jamaica's advance in this period was personified by George Headley, who is rightly regarded as one of the finest batsmen ever produced by Westindies.

The great Headley, who carried the burden of Jamaica's and Westindies' batting for so long that he was nicknamed "Atlas", later gave way to the varied talents of such prodigious players as Frank Worrell (by adoption), Gerry Alexander, Roy Gilchrist, Collie Smith, Allan Rae, Alf Valentine, Jackie Hendriks, Lawrence Rowe, Michael Holding, Jeff Dujon and Courtney Walsh. It is notable that many of the aforementioned players, including all of the wicket-keepers, attended the famous Wolmer's Boys' School in Kingston, which has an enviable record of producing Test cricketers.

Because of her distance from the eastern islands, the practice of picking mostly players within easy reach of the Test grounds for the early matches, in an effort to keep costs down, affected Jamaica the most. Indeed, in the 1930 series against England, Headley was the only Jamaican who travelled to the eastern venues, although seven of his compatriots joined him for the Test at Sabina Park. Five years later pace bowler, Leslie Hylton, went with Headley to play in the Tests on the other islands.

The isolation that affected Jamaica during the early Test days is reflected inside the country itself, where the rural areas are cut off from Kingston. Efforts have been made to integrate cricket on the island and this can be seen in the make-up of the Jamaican team. Even so, although more cricket is played in the country, it continues to be more prestigious to play for clubs in Kingston.

Guyana

Although Guyana is part of the mainland of South America, its way of life remains essentially Westindian and this is reflected in the development of their cricket. It seems that the game was played in Guyana from the early 1830s by the British armed forces, with the early inter-colonial matches being staged at The Parade Ground. British Guiana, as it then was, set the precedent for sending cricket teams overseas by visiting Barbados in 1865 to play the first inter-territorial games, and hosted a return series later the same year.

It was a Guyanese batsman, E. F. Wright, who enjoyed the distinction of scoring the first century in the Caribbean, a feat he achieved against Trinidad at Georgetown in 1882. Four years later Georgetown Cricket Club sponsored the first overseas tour, to America and Canada. This was the first time that Westindies played as a team with players from Barbados, Trinidad, Guyana and Jamaica included in the tour party.

The Guyanese revealed their strength when they won the inter-colonial tournament in 1885-86, but it was more than 30 years before they took the title again. This improvement coincided with the emergence of such gifted players as "Snuffy" Browne, the first black man to be elected to the MCC; Maurice Fernandes, captain of the side when Westindies won their first Test, against England in 1930; the De Caires and Christiani brothers; and Berkeley Gaskin, who made his mark more as an administrator than as a player.

After the progress of the 1930s, Guyana fell away again until Clyde Walcott went there as coach in 1954. He presided over a remarkable upsurge of world-class talent which quickly came to the fore including such prominent figures as Joe Solomon, Basil Butcher, Rohan Kanhai and Lance Gibbs. The first three of these players came from Berbice, an area sufficiently strong to have their own match against the England tourists in 1960.

Their success has been emulated by the cricketing giants who emerged from Guyana to light up the 1970s, including Roy Fredericks, Clive Lloyd and Alvin Kallicharran. One of Guyana's biggest contributions to the regional side in recent years has been their supply of Test captains, embodied by Lloyd who enjoyed unprecedented success. The appointment of Kanhai as captain in 1973 provided the link for Lloyd's remarkable tenure, which was interrupted only briefly when Kallicharran took over the reigns during the World Series crisis.

More recently, Colin Croft and Roger Harper have shone for Guyana in the Test side. They both played for Demerara, one of the leading clubs in Guyana, which also nurtured the talents of the young Gibbs, Fredericks and Lloyd.

Leeward and Windward Islands

Although they played in the Shell Shield initially as the Combined Islands, the Leeward and Windward Islands have competed separately in the tournament since 1982. The various islands have a thriving cricketing culture but, because of their small populations, they were not involved in the early inter-colonial games. At Test level the Leewards have been represented by Antigua and Nevis and the Windwards by Dominica and St. Vincent.

On New Year's day in 1842, the 59th Foot Regiment formed a cricket club in Antigua and 40 years afterwards the Duke of York (later King George V) played cricket on the island. At the end of the 19th century Antigua became the first Caribbean country to field a side made up entirely of black players and, at about the same time, Pelham Warner scored 110 for Lord Hawke's English touring team in the capital, St. John's.

Charles Ollivierre, an outstanding batsman from St. Vincent, was a great success on Westindies' inaugural tour of England in 1900. He averaged over 30 on the trip, including 159 against Leicestershire, and impressed Derbyshire so much that they invited him to play for them in the county championship after the tour. He accepted the offer and set the trend for subsequent Westindians who followed him onto the English circuit.

Grayson Shillingford from Dominica and Mike Findlay from St. Vincent became the first Windward Islanders to play Test cricket, when they appeared against England in 1969. Shillingford's kinsman, Irvine, later continued the trend of choosing players from these islands, while Norbert Phillip and Winston Davis head the list of Windward Islanders who have been selected for the Test team in recent years.

But, of all the islands, Antigua's recent development has been the most exceptional. Largely through the efforts of Andy Roberts and Viv Richards, the island has gained international recognition as a great cricketing force which was reflected in the elevation of the Recreation Ground in St. John's to Test status in 1981.

Danny Livingstone, who enjoyed a distinguished career with Hampshire, was one of the earlier known players born in Antigua. Eldine Baptiste also comes from the island, while it seems that Richie Richardson is determined to follow in the footsteps of his mentor, and Antigua's favourite son and first Test captain, Viv Richards.

Test Match Grounds in the Caribbean

Kensington Oval, Barbados

Home to the local Pickwick Cricket Club, founded in 1882, Kensington Oval enjoys the distinction of being the first ground ever to host a Test match in the Westindies, when play began against England on 11 January 1930.

Enthusiasm for cricket on the island is such that its 10,000 capacity is always stretched well beyond this limit: there is *no* limit to the ingenious methods employed by Bajans to view a Test match! The George Challenor Stand, to the left of the pavilion, is a prominent feature and usually houses the visitors' supporters. The other main enclosures are the three "W"s Stand and the Sir Garfield Sobers Pavilion, opened by the great all-rounder in April 1985.

The ground is known for individual excellence more than close finishes and many of Test cricket's most splendid feats have occurred at Kensington Oval. They include the first Test century for Westindies by Clifford Roach in the inaugural game in 1930, the match in which Derek Sealy, Westindies' youngest ever player, made his debut; and two triple hundreds, by Hanif Mohammad in 1958 and Lawrence Rowe against England in 1974. The ground in Bridgetown was also the scene of the record breaking seventh wicket partnership of 348 runs between local players, Denis Atkinson and Clairmonte Depeiza, against Australia in 1955 – an unlikely achievement which, even today, prompts nostalgic recollections by those who saw it.

In the series against England in 1935 Westindies incurred their only loss at Kensington, on a quagmire of a pitch, where the outcome of the match was determined by who had the best of the wicket. England won the toss and, after both sides had declared once and juggled their respective batting orders, in an attempt to save their best batsmen for an improvement in the pitch, the visitors eventually brought off a fortuitous victory by four wickets. Generally speaking, however, Kensington has happy memories for Westindies who have won 10 of the 23 Tests played there, often by decisive margins.

The crowds at Kensington have bathed in the glory of the cricket on the field, personified by their own seemingly endless conveyor belt of fast bowlers from Manny Martindale to Malcolm Marshall, who excelled on the fast, true Bridgetown wicket, and their depth of master batsmen from George Challenor to Gordon Greenidge; while they are rightly proud of having produced the finest all-rounder the game has known, Sir Garfield Sobers. Their easy-going nature and love of cricket, above all else, means that Kensington Oval has mostly avoided the kind of crowd disturbances that sometimes occur at other venues.

King Dial has become an indispensible part of the Test match scene in Barbados. A gregarious character, who delights in modelling the brightest clothes, he usually makes his entrance during the first over of the day – much to the delight of the crowd – and invariably proceeds to support the opposition vociferously, with a notable soft spot for England! His sporting and vibrant personality, together with his colourful image, encapsulates the mood that engulfs Kensington Oval during a Test.

Queen's Park Oval, Trinidad

Queen's Park Oval is renowned for the splendour of its setting. Situated next to the huge open area known as the Savannah, the Northern Range of mountains provides a dramatic backdrop. As early as 1842 Trinidad Cricket Club was well established and played its first inter-territorial match, against Guyana, 27 years later. Then, in 1896, Queen's Park Cricket Club set up residence at what was then known as the St. Clair Oval. They played on matting made from coconut fibre, before replacing it with a jute matting in 1935. Turf wickets were introduced in the 1950s.

As with the Bridgetown ground, Queen's Park Oval has seen some splendid individual performances. Against England in 1954 all three "W"s made centuries for the second time in a single Test innings and, over 20 years later, against Pakistan in 1977, newcomer, Colin Croft, set a record for Westindies by claiming eight wickets for 29 in the visitors' first innings.

However, Westindies haven't enjoyed the same success at Queen's Park as they have at Kensington. Traditionally a spinner's wicket, conditions at Port-of-Spain have invariably helped touring sides, and also accounts for the large number of high-scoring draws there. The Test arena in Trinidad was the sight of Westindies' first defeat on home soil, when they lost to England in 1930; they were also beaten at Queen's Park by Pakistan in 1958, after the rubber had been settled in their favour. They have lost more Tests at Port-of-Spain than at any other venue in the Caribbean.

The ground has also witnessed two disastrous declarations by Westindies captains. The first, and most famous, came when Gary Sobers declared against England in the fourth match of the 1968 series which lost the home side the match and, as it turned out, the rubber. Then, in 1976, Clive Lloyd miscalculated the depth of India's batting, as the tourists made a record fourth innings score to win the game but not, this time, the series.

Generally speaking, the crowds at Queen's Park Oval have been more volatile than those at Kensington Oval. This can be partially explained by the fact that, apart from Trinidad's Carnival, a Test match is the biggest social gathering on the island. Indeed, because of the huge numbers that come to watch cricket at Queen's Park, and its capacity to hold them, it was financially viable to stage two Tests in a series in Trinidad before the emergence of the Recreation Ground in Antigua as a Test venue. Trinidadians often compare their everyday experiences with the struggles that take place on the field of play and this can sometimes boil over into confrontation. Even so, they know and adore their cricket and tend to be ardently for or against you.

Sabina Park, Jamaica

Sabina Park is one of the smaller Test match arenas but, recently modernized, it is also the best equipped in the region.

Kingston Cricket Club was set up in 1863 and moved to Sabina Park in 1880. Even so, Jamaica was left out of the early years of inter-territorial competition because of her geographical isolation, although most early English touring teams visited the island.

Spectators at the Jamaican Test ground have witnessed many splendid individual performances, often by their own players. Their all-time hero, George Headley, scored an unbeaten 270 there against England in 1935 to secure Westindies' first ever rubber; while the prodigious Lawrence Rowe scored 214 and 100 not out on his Test debut at Sabina Park, against England in 1972.

The sight of Roy Gilchrist and Michael Holding thundering in and overwhelming visiting batsmen also warmed Jamaican hearts. Indeed, at his peak, Holding's pace was so frightening that five Indian batsmen declared themselves "absent hurt" in the tourists' second innings of the match at Kingston in 1976, as the Jamaican exploited a ridge at the northern end of the ground and Westindies romped to victory by 10 wickets.

Sabina Park was the scene of the first Test triple century, 325 by England's Andy Sandham in 1930, and was the foundation of the then highest score ever recorded in Test history: 849. Other landmarks reached at Kingston include the three "W"s each scoring a century in the same innings of a Test for the first time, against India in 1953; and, five years later, the masterful Gary Sobers recorded the highest individual Test score of 365 not out against Pakistan.

Perhaps the biggest disappointment ever seen at Sabina Park came during Headley's final Test appearance, against England in 1954, after public subscription had brought him home. Way past his best, the great man made 16 and 1.

Westindies have a good record at Sabina Park, where there is usually plenty of pace and bounce in the wicket. To date, they have only been defeated three times there, in the mid-1950s, when, unusually, they lacked a quality pace bowler.

Like the Trinidadians, Jamaicans support their local players passionately, but their love of cricket is even stronger. This was best demonstrated when Everton Weekes was drafted into the side as a last minute replacement for the injured Headley against England in 1948. After arriving late from Barbados, Weekes was booed every time he fielded the ball, as the spectators wanted to see the local player, John Holt, replace Headley. But, Weekes scored a splendid hundred, which helped to win the match and the series for Westindies, and saw the Kingston crowd rally to his cause, as he went from being the villain to the hero of the piece.

Even so, their partisan attitude has not always had such happy endings. In the first Test of the series against England in 1954, the dismissal of Holt, LBW for 94, provoked disquiet amongst the crowd.

The Jamaican site has sometimes been the two Test centre for a series and also hosted the hundredth Test in Westindies, when the fifth game in the series against Australia in 1984 was played at Sabina Park.

Bourda Ground, Guyana

The Bourda Ground has been home to Georgetown Cricket Club since 1884. For a long time, the pavilion was a wooden construction and supported by stilts, as most of Georgetown is below sea level.

The venue has won a special place in the hearts of Westindian cricket lovers as the setting for Westindies' first Test victory, against England in 1930. It was in that match that George Headley hit two centuries in each innings and Clifford Roach scored the first double hundred for Westindies. The first post-War victory for Westindies, against England in 1948, was also secured at Bourda.

In 1958 Gary Sobers hit a century in each innings of the Georgetown Test against Pakistan, after his record score at Sabina Park; and, in 1965, local bowler, Lance Gibbs, spun Westindies to success over Australia. He took six for 29 in the tourists' second innings which brought Westindies victory in the match and, as it transpired, the rubber.

Yet, intermingled with these fond memories, there have been troubled times. Bourda did not host a Test against the touring Indians in 1962 and 1976 due to the weather – on the latter occasion this deprived Gibbs of a final Test appearance before his home crowd. Indeed, the poor climate accounts for the large number of draws which have occurred at Georgetown: of the 19 Tests played there so far, 11 matches have been drawn.

The scheduled Test against England in 1981 was cancelled because of the inclusion of Robin Jackman, who had South African connections, in the England side. The Guyanese government has been in the forefront of the campaign to sever sporting links with South Africa and cricket does not come before their political principles.

Bourda was also the scene for a crisis in cricket's own politics: the first major disturbance at a Test match in the Caribbean occurred at Georgetown. The trouble was sparked off by an incident involving the local player, Clifford McWatt, in the third match of the series against England in 1954. He had added 99 runs with John Holt, who was batting with a runner, before the Guyanese was run out attempting to secure the century partnership. This proved too much for the spectators, who showered the outfield with bottles.

Another calamity occurred over 20 years later when, on the eve of the Georgetown Test against Australia in 1978, the World Series Cricketers staged a walk-out and the rift between the Packer players and the Westindies Board of Control became public. A makeshift Westindies team subsequently lost to Australia, though not as decisively as five years earlier against the same opponents, when, after leading on the first innings, the home side collapsed to defeat by 10 wickets.

Despite these problems, there can be no doubting the deep love for the game that exists in Guyana. In his book *Living for Cricket*, Clive Lloyd remarks: "When a Test match is played at Bourda, in the capital of Georgetown, the queues start to form as early as 4am and the ground is filled to capacity long before the first ball is bowled. When the Tests are overseas, radio sets are to be seen everywhere and it's easy to tell whether the West Indies are winning or losing. You have only to look at the expressions on people's faces!"

Recreation Ground, Antigua

To date it has been a lucky ground for Antiguans. Against Australia in 1984, Richards and Richie Richardson set the ground ablaze with a spectacular record partnership of 308 runs for the third wicket, which brought the first Test result on the ground: victory by an innings for Westindies; while the fastest Test hundred ever recorded in terms of balls, from Richards against England in 1986, (his century came up off 56 deliveries) helped the home side to another decisive win. In the four Tests played on the ground so far, 13 centuries have been scored, including three by Richards, and four by other Westindian batsmen in their only innings against India in the fifth match played at the Recreation Ground in 1983.

Although it has only hosted Test matches in modern times, the Antiguan ground has entertained touring English teams since the earliest days. During one of Lord Hawke's visits in the late 1800s, Pelham Warner remarked that Antigua's wicket was "one of the best we played on".

It is too early to assess the nature and character of the ground as a Test arena, and the spectators that come to watch the play, but the Antiguans are some of the most loyal and fervent cricket supporters in the world, and are determined to make the Recreation Ground one of the Caribbean's most attractive venues.

The Recreation Ground in St. John's, the capital of Antigua, is the Caribbean's newest Test venue, hosting its first match against England in March 1981. Its elevation to Test status was in recognition of the progress of the Leeward Islands in recent years, personified by the achievements of Andy Roberts and Viv Richards. It was, therefore, particularly appropriate and, even inevitable, that Richards would celebrate the use of his home ground as a Test arena by scoring a century.